Understanding and Believing

Understanding and Believing

Essays by
JOACHIM WACH

Edited with an Introduction by
JOSEPH M. KITAGAWA

GREENWOOD PRESS, PUBLISHERS
WESTPORT, CONNECTICUT

Library of Congress Cataloging in Publication Data

Wach, Joachim, 1898-1955.
Understanding and believing.

Reprint of the 1st ed. published by Harper & Row, New York, which was issued as no. TB1399 of the Harper torchbooks.
"Bibliography of Joachim Wach (1922-55)": p.
Includes bibliographical references.
CONTENTS: Religion and modern man: The self-understanding of modern man. Stefan George : poet and priest of modern paganism. The problem of death in modern philosophy.--Christianity and world religions: General revelation and the religions of the world. The paradox of the Gospel. Redeemer of man. Seeing and believing. Belief and witness.--Faith and knowledge: The meaning and task of the history of religions. Religious commitment and tolerance. The problem of truth in religion. The Christian professor. The crisis in the university. Hugo of St. Victor on virtues and vices. To a rabbi friend. On felicity. A prayer.
1. Religion--Addresses, essays, lectures. 2. Wach, Joachim, 1898-1955--Bibliography. I. Title.
[BL27.W26 1975] 291'.08 75-31987
ISBN 0-8371-8488-6

Sources and acknowledgments are given in the Introduction, pages xiii–xviii.

The Essay "The Meaning and Task of the History of Religions," translated from the German by Karl W. Luchert, with the help of Alan L. Miller, is reprinted from *The History of Religions: Essays on the Problem of Understanding*, edited by J. M. Kitagawa, 1967, by permission of The University of Chicago Press.

Originally published in 1968 by Harper & Row, Publishers, New York

Reprinted with the permission of Harper & Row, Publishers, Inc.

Reprinted in 1975 by Greenwood Press, a division of Williamhouse-Regency Inc.

Library of Congress Catalog Card Number 75-31987

ISBN 0-8371-8488-6

Printed in the United States of America

Contents

Introduction

Joseph M. Kitagawa

Joachim Wach was known throughout his life as a scholar in the discipline of *Religionswissenschaft*, variously known as History of Religions or Comparative Study of Religions. He was born in 1898 at Chemitz, Saxony. After finishing the Gymnasium in Dresden, and following two years of service in the German army, he studied at the universities of Leipzig, Munich and Berlin. In 1924 he was appointed to the chair of History of Religions at Leipzig, and soon began to publish many important articles and books. His successful scholarly career in Germany, however, came to a sudden end in 1935 under pressure of the Nazi government. He took up residence at Brown University, Providence, Rhode Island. In 1945 he was called by the University of Chicago where he taught until his untimely death in 1955.

Both as a man and as a scholar Wach possessed many enviable qualities. He was endowed with an unusually keen mind, and he had the benefit of affectionate parents and stimulating teachers. He once mentioned the thrilling experience of being taken, when he was eleven years old, to a great Mendelssohn celebration in Leipzig. He was seated next to his grandmother, a daughter of Felix Mendelssohn, in a place of honor, and listened to a performance of the oratorio, *Elijah*. Indeed, from childhood Wach was constantly reminded of the noble heritage to which he was born, especially that of the philosopher, Moses Mendelssohn, and the musician, Felix Mendelssohn Bartholdy. When he started teaching in 1924, the new *Privatdozent* aspired to follow the example of his grandfather, Adolf Wach, the famous jurist who was then on the faculty of law at Leipzig. As a young scholar, impressed by the great German cultural, artistic and scholarly tradition of the nineteenth and early twentieth centuries, Wach was determined to do his share in the rejuvenation of the scholarship of his native land, which had been badly disrupted by the First World War. One can readily understand why he was so greatly saddened by his abrupt dismissal from his chair in 1935, although it was not unexpected. He rarely mentioned this experience, but those who were close to him sensed how deeply his heart was wounded by his treatment by the country of his birth. It is remarkable, however, that Wach found himself so quickly in his adopted land. There he gave wholeheartedly of his time and energy toward the establishment of the discipline of *Religionswissenschaft.* He was convinced that this discipline demanded the cooperation of scholars crossing national, cultural, and religious lines, and that the American universities were destined to serve as leaders in this exciting enterprise.

It is significant to note that during the first half of his scholarly career Wach devoted his major attention to the methodological and theoretical dimensions of religious studies. He firmly believed that *Religionswissenschaft* must be grounded in hermeneutics (the science of understanding and interpretation) which he regarded, following Dilthey, as the necessary link between philosophy and the various branches of human science. Wach's own methodology was based on two related assumptions. The first is the "givenness" of understanding by virtue of the fact that men live on this earth. That is to say, Wach holds understanding to be a primordial phenomenon inasmuch as man is endowed with "eternal human nature" and lives in society and culture. Wach recognized, of course, that understanding is subject to the danger of misunderstanding and lack of understanding as different men attempt to communicate and understand each other by means of gestures, languages, and symbols. Thus, man needs to reflect on the nature of understanding—its limitations, its forms, and its possibilities. Understanding, therefore, is a way of acquiring knowledge, and as such is the basis of epistemological, logical, metaphysical, psychological and ethical inquiries. Furthermore, one cannot underestimate the extent to which understanding is conditioned by history as well as social, cultural and religious factors.

The second assumption of Wach is that man by nature is inclined to religion. He was aware that some men profess and appear to be irreligious or unattuned to religion, but he regarded them as religious illiterates due to lack of training in religion just as some men are unmusical because of lack of training in music. He was further convinced that man possesses the innate capacity to understand religion, which is another way of saying that man can be self-conscious about his own mode of being in this mysterious universe, although degrees and levels of self-consciousness and understanding vary greatly among different individuals for a variety of reasons. At any rate, Wach felt that religion provides one of man's most significant ways for self-understanding and for understanding the history of humanity. Thus he directed what he considered the highest intellectual pursuit, *Verstehen* or the understanding of understanding, toward the nature and structure of religious experience and its theoretical, practical and sociological expressions. He was particularly careful in elucidating the aims, scope and methodological principles of "integral understanding," to use his favorite phrase. For example, Wach was greatly concerned with the question of historical, as well as cultural and religious, "distance" in reference to the adequacy and objectivity of understanding. His problem was, to what extent can one understand ancient Greek art, or a dead religion, and how adequately can a Hindu or a Buddhist understand Judaism, Christianity and Islam? On these questions, Wach was inclined to hold epistemological optimism. He felt that an inquirer who is not a Christian can sometimes understand the essence of Christianity more clearly than a Christian or even a Christian theologian, and conversely, a scholar who is committed to Christian faith can understand other religions better than the adherents of those religions. On the other hand, he did not underestimate the difficulties involved in the attempt to understand one's own religion.

Religion, however, was not only a matter of serious academic and intellectual inquiry to Wach. In this connection, Wach sensed the existence of a paradoxical relationship between "the knowing of a religion" and "the choosing of a religion." While he was confident that the essence of a religion and its structure can be grasped by an inquirer who has acquired scholarly tools and methodologies, he was equally certain that some elements of a religion defy sheer intellectual understanding. To be sure, a poet who has not experienced a love affair can understand love. It is not necessary for one to have fought in a battle to understand a general, and a scholar does not have to become Buddha himself to understand Buddha. And yet, it is so often true in the domain of religion that an uneducated simple believer can, without intellectual comprehension, attain secret communion with his deity, and experience certainty in his innermost self. Furthermore, one's knowledge and appreciation of the doctrinal content and history of a religion, helpful though it may be, does not necessarily or automatically lead to the step of committing oneself to that religious faith. Sometimes the inquirer's heart may be stirred by encountering a great religious personality, or a significant historic event. Such things as these might even stimulate him to develop a deep interest in or sense of longing for the spiritual dimension of life. But the way in which such a sense of "longing" can be transformed into "faith" remains a matter of great mystery. Probably one who has discovered a religious faith is able to give some account of how certain factors and experiences have influenced him to "choose" a particular faith, but he cannot explain the most decisive turning-point of his spiritual life. Faith, to be sure, is not unrelated to knowledge, but it has its own dynamic. Ultimately, faith is "the assurance of things hoped for, the conviction of things not seen" (Heb. 11:1). As a scholar and as a person Joachim Wach aspired to hold within him both "understanding" and "believing" while preserving the integrity of knowledge and faith.

Wach never talked about his own spiritual pilgrimage. We know that he was brought up in the Lutheran tradition, although he was exposed to Catholic, Reformed, and Jewish traditions as well. In his youth, according to his own account, he came under the influence of Stefan George for awhile. Toward the end of the First World War, while serving in the German army on the Russian front, he was compelled to think seriously on the problem of life and death. But thereafter he became preoccupied with intellectual inquiries into various philosophies and religions, Eastern as well as Western, at the expense of his own spiritual or religious pursuit. Fortunately, Wach came to know a young scholar and mystic, Friedrich Heiler, under whom he studied History of Religions. It was Dr. Heiler who encouraged Wach to work on his dissertation, "Grundzüge einer Phänomenologie des Erlösungsgedankens," which was published under the title, *Der Erlösungsgedanke und seine*

Deutung (1922). It was also through his scholarly work in *Religionswissenschaft* that Wach came to know Rudolf Otto, a great historian of religions and a theologian of Marburg, who subsequently exerted a decisive influence on Wach's spiritual as well as scholarly outlook. More significant, perhaps, as far as his own personal aspect is concerned, was his experience in the 1930's. Not only was he personally forced to leave his homeland, but he witnessed the disruption of the once glorious German culture under the demonic regime of the Nazis. Confronted by the emergence of such a colossal power of evil which ruthlessly emasculated and destroyed political, social and educational institutions, Wach came to appreciate the hidden resources of the Christian Church as the most persistent force for the integration and preservation of culture and society.

When Wach settled in the United States in 1935, his initial difficulties in adjusting to the unfamiliar mode of living seemed to be well compensated for by his enthusiasm for the vitality and freedom of American society. He was particularly happy about the fact that Brown University, which initially invited him, is located in Rhode Island, the state of that champion of the principle of liberty, Roger Williams. Wach was a competent and an inspiring teacher. He also gave generously of his time and energy for student activities and the counseling of individual students. Soon he became an active communicant of the Episcopal Church. Teaching as he did in a non-denominational university, he became seriously concerned with the place of religion in American institutions of higher learning. His interest in this problem may be illustrated by a report he prepared about a conference held at Yale on "Religious Ferment on the Campus," which dealt with various matters pertaining to religious activities in the New England colleges. Wach wrote approvingly of the trend toward offering instruction in the field of religion, as an important step toward the integration of educational ideals. Furthermore, he sensed that the period of "historicism" had come to an end and that there was a general desire among youth to receive instruction in the realities of religion and its application to everyday life. Therefore,

> the courses offered in a university curriculum would be incomplete without including at least an orientation in religion as a still vital factor in contemporary civilization. This was considered only a minimum by those whose faculties at present make provision for it.

An increasing interest was noted by the same faculties on the part of student groups in extra- and intra-curricular activities in the field of religion.

Based on these observations, Wach argued in favor of "a full presentation of religious values as such and a complete exposition of the significance of religion as a factor in life and history." He cautioned, however, that organized religious activity on the campus should not interfere with the prerogatives of the various denominational bodies nor with the tradition of religious freedom of individuals. As to the teaching of his own subject, he argued passionately for the significance of Oriental religions not only for those who are interested in religious studies but also for all students in the twentieth century. He went on to say:

> Characteristic of the civilization of the East is the fact that they are altogether less emancipated from the religious background than the West has become since modern times. It is impossible to evaluate rightly historical, sociological and psychological conditions of the Oriental civilizations without a knowledge of the religious presuppositions. The study of religion in the college has for this reason to include—besides the teachings of Christianity—the (1) historical, (2) political, (3) sociological, (4) religious, (5) economical, (6) cultural conditions of the Orient. . . .
>
> Two dangers, however, have to be avoided. The first is a dilettantism which would excel more in quantitative than in intensive work. The second would be the gathering and distribution of an enormous and indigestible amount of material instead of a description and analysis of the important lines of development, types of attitudes, and conditions in the Oriental world. . . . The question of the influence of the East on the West and vice versa, historically traced and systematically studied, is of highest importance for the right understanding and appreciation in the fields of literature and arts in general as well as in the field of religion. A student equipped with such a knowledge is not only able to take advantage of the excellent facilities of the museums and libraries in this country, but to orient himself in the present day's world condition which is destined to increase more interaction among different nations, cultures, and peoples.

It was also during his tenure at Brown that he labored on the publication of his first major work in the English language, *Sociology of Religion* (1944), an attempt "to bridge the gulf which exists between the study of religion and the social sciences." As he states in the Preface: "Personal experience has aided the author in realizing the vital importance and significance of religion as an integrating factor in human society and in understanding its function in the contemporary crisis of civilization in East and West."

Wach's sense of commitment to Christian faith and his concern with the theological implication of *Religionswissenschaft* became more pronounced during the last ten years of his life spent in Chicago. Earlier he had tended to stress the independence of the descriptive task of *Religionswissenschaft* from the normative concerns of theology and philosophy, and he took it for granted that *Religionswissenschaft* was to be taught in the faculty of humanities. Gradually, however, he began to stress the importance of the systematic task, to be sure without minimizing the descriptive task, of *Religionswissenschaft*. Thus, he came to view *Religionswissenschaft* as a link between the normative disciplines and the purely descriptive disciplines. As such, he stressed the importance of not only "bridging the gulf between *Religionswissenschaft* and social sciences," as he stated in the Preface to his *Sociology of Religion*, but also of close cooperation between *Religionswissenschaft* and theology. Ideally, according to Wach in his later years, *Religionswissenschaft* was to be taught both in the faculty of humanities and in the faculty of theology. Parenthetically it might be added that Wach's hope in this respect, despite his effort, has not been fulfilled at the University of Chicago as yet. Be that as it may, Wach labored enthusiastically to establish the discipline of history of religions within the context of the theological curriculum at Chicago, and attempted to clarify the nature of proper cooperation between history of religions and theology. (See his article, "The Place of the History of Religions in the Study of Theology," *Types of Religious Experience—Christian and Non-Christian*, 1951, Chapter I.)

In the present book, we have collected some of Wach's articles and lecture notes which were written during his Chicago days, 1945–55, together with some that were written earlier. In most of these pages, Wach speaks both as a scholar of history of religions and as a committed Christian with profound interest in Christian theology. He felt that just as a student of linguistics has to use not just "language" but particular languages, realizing of course that his own language inevitably colors his understanding of the discipline of linguistics to a certain extent, so a student of *Religionswissenschaft*, to the extent that he is religious, must choose a particular faith for himself because it is impossible for him to direct his religious commitment to "religion" *per se*. The fact that the religious commitment of a student of religion colors and delimits his understanding of religion is unavoidable, but it also enables him to be sensitive to the spiritual dimension of religions, his own as well as others. At the same time, a student of *Religionswissenschaft* who is also a convinced Christian, Jew, Muslim, Hindu, or Buddhist has to shoulder a greater burden of explicating the tension and relation that inevitably exist between his own religious faith and his intellectual inquiry into the nature and structure of religion. He is also in duty bound to manifest in what sense his faith has contributed to his inquiries and in what sense his scholarly discipline has contributed to his faith. Some of the articles included in this volume will indicate how seriously Wach wrestled with these problems.

The present volume is divided into three sections. In the first section, we have selected Wach's three essays which deal with "Religion and Modern Man." Among them, "The Problem of Death in Modern Philosophy" was originally published in 1934 under the title, "Das Problem des Todes in der Philosophie unserer Zeit" (*Philosophie und Geschichte*, No. 49). It was translated by Sister Mary Timothy, R.S.M., of Saint Xavier College, Chicago, and is used by permission of the German publisher, J.C.B. Mohr (Paul Siebeck), Tübingen. In this article, which turned out to be the last important essay Wach wrote before leaving Germany, he deals with the problem of death and its meaning to modern man, a subject which concerned him deeply, by examining the writings of Schopenhauer, Feuerbach, Simmel and Heidegger. Quotations from Heidegger's *Being and Time*, translated by John Macquarrie and Edward Robinson (1962), are used with the permission of Harper and Row.

The essay on "Stefan George: Poet and Priest of Modern Paganism" was found after Wach's death in one of his files, marked for publication. As yet we have not been able to verify whether it has been actually published. If it has been published elsewhere and has escaped our attention, we beg the forgiveness of its publisher. While the author quoted George's poems in German in this article, we have added English verses, translated by Olga Marx and Ernst Morwitz (1949), with the permission of the University of North Carolina Press. Also, we owe gratitude to Miss Nancy E. Auer for clarifying some of the author's expressions. Apparently Wach was enough of a humanist to be fascinated by the aesthetic quality of Stefan George's poetry, even though Wach the Christian could not accept this form of modern paganism. "The Self-Understanding of Modern Man," was translated by Miss Joyce Adams from Wach's essay, "Das Selbstverständnis des modernen Menschen," which appeared in *Universitas: Zeitschrift für Wissenschaft, Kunst und Literatur* (10 Jahrgang, Heft 5, Mai 1955). It is used by permission of the publisher of the journal. In this short article, written shortly before his death, Wach wrote succinctly and appreciatively about the nature of modern man's predicament in his search for freedom. Through it all, however, Wach, the man of faith, affirms: "The creation of genuine culture is only possible for man when communion with the deity, the primary ground of all things, can serve as a source for its creativity."

In the second section, "Christianity and World Religions," we have included some of Wach's articles and notes from his Chicago days dealing with the Christian faith and its relation to other religions as seen from a Christian perspective. Among them "General Revelation and the Religions of the World," was given by Wach as the main address at a meeting of the National Association of Biblical Instructors in December, 1953, at Evanston, Illinois, and was subsequently published in *The Journal of Bible and Religion* (Vol. XXII, No. 2, April, 1954). It is reprinted with the permission of the journal. The other articles—"The Paradox of the Gospel," "Redeemer of Man," "Seeing and Believing," and "Belief and Witness"—are based on Wach's talks at the Bond Chapel of the University of Chicago, addressed to the faculty and students of the Divinity School, under slightly different titles. "Redeemer of Man" was published in *The Divinity School News* of the University of Chicago (Vol. XV, No. 4, November, 1948) and is reprinted here by permission of the University of Chicago Press. Wach gave much to the life of the Divinity School and expected much from its faculty and students.

On one occasion he stated: "In Europe theologians have been challenged by a murderous struggle for existence and have demonstrated that when courage of conviction is strong it is not only respected but also effective. It is because we believe that society, that the world at large, needs spiritual, religious and Christian values in order to survive, not just to perpetuate institutional interests and intellectual interests, that we consider our work in research, teaching and preaching essential." He held that competence in each of the branches of theological learning, such as theology, Biblical study and Church history, is not sufficient. He stressed the importance of a methodological consciousness of the interrelationships between these fields based on awareness of the theological principles which constitute these fields and serve to define the nature of their subject matters and to determine their function in the whole of theology. He was never more serious than when he asserted that mature understanding of Christian faith is not attainable in today's world unless some sympathetic knowledge of other religions is interwoven into one's understanding of the Gospel. In Wach's view, the relationship between *Religionswissenschaft* and theology must be two-way. While a historian of religions must be open to the criticisms and contributions of theologians, he has in his turn a great deal to contribute to the work of theologians. For example, the study of the Old and New Testaments must presuppose some familiarity with the religious ethos of ancient Semitic, Greco-Roman and Near Eastern religions. The history of Christianity, especially in its earlier phase, is intrinsically related to the development of Gnosticism, Manichaeism and Islam. Modern society cannot be understood if the influence of the non-Christian world on the last two centuries is not taken into consideration. Discrimination and judgment on moral and social issues in contemporary life is vastly aided by a comparison of standards as well as practices in West and East. The psychological nature of man has been analyzed by Eastern sages in a way which modern psychology cannot overlook. Concerning spiritual culture and growth much can be learned from Eastern sources. As far as community and its functions are concerned, a comparison with the rise, growth, integration and disintegration of religious groupings and religious institutions outside the Christian fold is indispensable. Furthermore, religion in its relation to culture ought to be studied on a comparative basis. Basically, what Wach had in mind was not simply adding indiscriminately a variety of facts and data of other religions to

Christian theology. He sensed that the new generation in both Europe and America no longer finds meaning in the traditional religious heritage. In this situation, theology as it has been known has become irrelevant because it has been by-passed by the cultural and religious revolution that is taking place in the traditionally Christian, as well as the non-Christian, parts of the world. Thus Wach advocated a basic re-orientation of Christian theology. By the same token he, as a historian of religions and a committed Christian, hoped to play a significant role by reexamining the religious sources made available by the discipline of *Religionswissenschaft.*

In the third section, "Faith and Knowledge," we have collected several of Wach's papers written for a variety of occasions. "The Meaning and Task of the History of Religions (Religionswissenschaft)" was originally published in *Zeitschrift für Missionskunde und Religionswissenschaft*, L (1935), No. 5 under the title, "Sinn und aufgabe der Religionswissenschaft." It has been translated by Mr. Karl W. Luckert with the help of Mr. Alan L. Miller, and was included in *The History of Religions: Essays on the Problem of Understanding*, edited by J. M. Kitagawa (Volume I of *Essays in Divinity* under the general editorship of Jerald C. Brauer), The University of Chicago Press, 1967. This article has been reprinted here with the permission of the University of Chicago Press. "Religious Commitment and Tolerance" and "The Problem of Truth in Religion" are selected from among the lectures given in India in 1952 when he served as Barrows Lecturer. "The Christian Professor" was written in 1947 for the University Commission of the World Student Christian Federation (WSCF), of which Wach served as chairman. The manuscript was sent to the editor by Dr. A. John Coleman of the University of Toronto, who was then secretary of the University Commission. "The Crisis in the University" was written as a review article and appeared in *The Student World* (Vol. XLII, No. 4, Fourth Quarter, 1949). It is used here by permission of the WSCF. "Hugo of St. Victor on Virtues and Vices" is Wach's own translation and was published in the *Anglican Theological Review* (Vol. XXXI, No. 1, January, 1949); it is reprinted here by permission of the publisher. "To a Rabbi Friend" was based on a speech by Wach given at an occasion in honor of a rabbi, a graduate of Brown University, when Wach was at

Providence. "On Felicity" was given in 1953 at the ordination service of one of Wach's former students. Last of all, we have included "A Prayer," given by Wach at the opening of a conference on "The Meaning of History" sponsored by the University Commission of the WSCF in 1949.

A collection of essays such as this is bound to be uneven. It is difficult to bring out all the facets of a man, especially when his life touches upon as many areas of learning and work as Wach's did. It is hoped, however, that this small volume will convey something of Wach's attitude toward faith and knowledge. To him, faith needed knowledge to grow, while knowledge had to be inspired by faith. His life was thus motivated by the double-edged objectives of "understanding and believing." In the long run, Wach will be remembered not only by the learned books he wrote and by his dedication to teaching but also by the noble character reflected in his simple and contagious faith.

The publication of this book would not have been possible without the encouragement of Dean Jerald C. Brauer, Professors Mircea Eliade and Charles H. Long of the Divinity School of the University of Chicago. The editorial work has been greatly aided by Dr. Charles S. J. White of the University of Pennsylvania, Dr. Robert S. Ellwood, Jr. of University of Southern California, and Mr. Alan L. Miller of the University of Chicago. The manuscript was typed by Miss Gloria Valentine, who is now Mrs. Donald Hugh Smith. It is our modest hope that this book will bring some consolation to the members of the Wach family, especially Frau Susanne Heigl-Wach and Pfarrer Hugo Wach and his wife, Elizabeth. They must know, as Wach's friends and former students do, that ". . . he died, but through his faith he is still speaking" (Heb. 11:4).

JOSEPH M. KITAGAWA

Swift Hall
The University of Chicago

I

Religion and Modern Man

1.

The Self-Understanding of Modern Man

Man is surely regarded by many as being completely different today than he was yesterday or the day before yesterday. Those maturing in any one year seem to differ greatly in their outlook and interests from those of the preceding year, and still more greatly from those of a previous generation. Often, nineteenth-century man seems as remote from us today as Enlightenment, Baroque or Renaissance man. And we are aware of almost no common ground with the men of the Middle Ages, the early Christian era, or classical Antiquity.

Did Spengler not make it clear twenty-five years ago that there are no channels of understanding between different eras and cultures? Modern man hears from all sides not only that he possesses no means of communication with the past but also that today an unbridgeable gap has opened even between individuals. It is thus no wonder that he seems to himself alienated and abandoned. The hoplessness characteristic of Existentialism arises from a feeling of complete isolation which is powerfully expressed in contemporary art and philosophy, for example, in the works of Kafka, Heidegger, and Sartre.

A complex interaction has produced this consciousness of alienation in modern man. Perhaps we should refer more cautiously only to a great number of individuals in a particular part of the world as being dominated by this feeling. Precisely the intellectuals, who in the nineteenth century provided Europe with optimistic and energetic leadership, are today in many parts of the world the most discouraged. Various economic, sociological, political, and philosophical factors have contributed to this feeling of alienation. Thus, the malaise is not limited to particular social groups, such as the so-called proletariat or the so-called middle class, or to particular nations with their individual histories, or to particular age groups. Whereas in the nineteenth century, groups—the nobility, the bourgeoisie, the working class—could feel a solidarity based upon a division into social classes and professions, this is possible today only in small measure. Interpersonal relationships are determined more and more by economic competition, the struggle for existence in which the individual is involved, rather than by a sense of group unity. It is alarming that the individual's intense feeling of alienation, which even in the fairly recent past would have been considered distinctly pathological, is today so widespread that it represents one form, at least, of the self-understanding of modern man.

Whoever does not find in himself or in some of those closest to him such an inability to communicate is confronted with evidence of it in contemporary art, in painting and sculpture, in poetry and music, and even in ballet. It often forms the only common ground between the modern artist and his public. We have already referred to philosophical or scientific orientation as a factor contributing to this situation. Three figures will serve as illustrations for this point. Darwin represents the theory of the struggle for existence and the desirability of those traits which equip a creature for this struggle. Nietzsche stands for both the diagnosis of modern decadence and the ideology of power as privilege. Finally, Freud represents the analysis, free from illusion, of the individual concerned solely with the gratification of his drives. In every case, modern man's consciousness of alienation was intensified as a result of these ideas. Surrounded by enemies from within and without, cut off from aid and comfort, he seems thrown back more and more upon his own resources.

In this situation, three attitudes become possible. Spokesmen for each can be found in contemporary literature. The most radical consequence is the urge to end as hopeless an existence of complete isolation, a second possibility is the search for self-forgetfulness through either refined or coarse pleasures, and the third is the "heroic" posture corresponding to the Stoicism of antiquity, that is, enduring one's fate without faith, hope, or love.

We have tried to characterize a particular form of self-awareness in modern man, namely that of existence in complete lack of communication, in radical individuation. Here the past, the group, one's fellowmen have nothing more to say. Whether without or through some fault of his own, man finds in his isolation that paths to the broadening of his horizon are closed off. The second half of the nineteenth century had historicized European man to such an extent that Nietzsche found it necessary in his famous work on the use and abuse of history to call attention to the threat to life which a preponderance of tradition represents. This was the era of mixing of styles in architecture and interior decoration, the age of historicism. It ended with the First World War.

Today we suffer not from too much but in many cases from too little historical consciousness. The names of the great German historians such as Ranke, Droysen, Mommsen, Dilthey, and Troeltsch have lost much of their force in their own country. Everywhere, the bond with the past has been weakened. Yet what a source of strength it could provide for the individual, for a people and a culture! Especially when it does not serve narcissistic purposes, but is interpreted as a warning and an example. Dilthey was right in saying, "Man does not arrive at self-understanding through brooding about himself, out of which arises only the great Nietzschean misery of hyper-subjectivity. Man achieves awareness of his own possibilities for good and evil only through his understanding of historical reality."

We have mentioned the group as another possibility of transcending the magic circle of the individual ego. In the past, sociology, as the study of groups, played a considerably less important role in Germany than in France or America, probably because the most important form of human social organization, the state, served as the subject of political science and similar fields, all of which had been developed previously. The smaller communal circles such as the family, the vocational group, and the religious congregation were regarded as insignificant in comparison to the state. To be sure, Otto von Gierke, the great legal historian, had made evident to his countrymen in a monumental work the significance of such circles to the German peoples in ancient times and into the Middle Ages. But the national state limited significantly the freedom and autonomy of smaller groups. True democracy cannot arise where the individual is confronted by the state as the epitome of communalization. The twentieth-century disintegration of the family is for bourgeoisie as for proletariat one of the most significant factors in the process of isolation undergone by the individual in modern times. There are indications that the nadir of this trend has been passed and that a reintegration is beginning. Sociology, as pioneered in Germany by such men as Lorenz von Stein, Rob Mohl, Gustav Schmoller, Werner Sombart, and Max Weber, taught us to distinguish between groups centered around living and those formed with a particular end in view. While the medieval guild belongs to the first category, modern vocational organizations, which usually have a purely political or utilitarian character, are examples of the second. It is obvious that an organization formed solely for some specific end offers little to a member seeking release from his alienation. On the other hand, although its obligatory nature may be felt as constriction, a group centered around living does provide the individual with security, encouragement, human proximity, and an opportunity for communication.

To be sure, modern man has understandably been made distrustful and sceptical by his disappointments with compulsory or pseudo-groups, especially those of a political nature. He prefers honest isolation to a false, artificial, or forced communalization. So-called Existentialism, especially in the literary form given it by Camus, Sartre, and Bataille, has expressed this position ambiguously. Only genuine community is worthy of our consideration, but does it still exist? Modern man differs even from his immediate predecessors as greatly in his position vis-a-vis the group as he differs from them in his relationship to the past.

The same holds true specifically in his relationship to his fellow-men. To the gap perceived objectively there corresponds a subjective awareness of isolation. Even in the shrewd philosophical analyses of Dilthey or Scheler, the view of "thou" as a problem is joined with the positive conviction that a true understanding is conceivable, that the gap separating one self from another can be bridged either through direct intuition or indirectly through verbal expression. This is doubted today by Heidegger and even Jaspers.

Here again artists, especially poets, speak out more directly than the philosophers: "Again and again, however well we know the landscape of love . . . again and again we go out two together under the old trees, make our couch once more among the flowers, face to face with the sky" (Rilke: Leishmann's translation).

Constantly aware that the continuity, dignity, value, and claim to justice of his own personality are questionable, without knowledge of the past, threatened in the present, and lacking hope for the future, how can such a self reveal itself to, trust in, join with, a "thou"? And yet Friedrich Schlegel was right in saying that "no one knows himself insofar as he is only himself and not another at the same time."

The amazing rise of the study of mental and emotional disturbances—the popularity of psychoanalysis, analytical psychology, and psychosomatic medicine—bears witness to the threat hanging over interpersonal relationships. From these therapeutic disciplines is awaited the cure of those symptoms which arise with alienation, anxiety, and hopelessness, and which prevent the individual from finding the way to the "thou." Friendship, marriage, all personal ties between human beings are affected by this crisis.

In all that has been said up to now we have ignored one—and probably the most important—dimension in man's self-understanding. The autobiographical evidence of the past as a whole bears witness to man's awareness of a relationship to the supernatural, infinite, and divine which has existed throughout his conscious history. This relationship might be interrupted, disturbed, and obscured by many other considerations. It might be questioned at its very foundations. Yet it has been restored again and again. Ranke meant this in saying that all that man does or does not do depends on the religious concept in which he dwells. One may well ask here, "Are there no religions without God?" The answer is—no. The essence of religious experience—and in this it is distinguished from every other kind of experience—is the awareness of a supreme absolute power which we call God. Where this awareness is lacking, where man feels himself to be confronted by, for example, impersonal fate or speculates about the nature of the absolute, one cannot speak of religion in the true sense.

Throughout all the millennia of which we have historical knowledge, the deity has been experienced, feared, and sought as a vast source of power. The deity might provide inspiration, aid, and growth in strength; it could be slandered or misinterpreted in despicable misuse. Because he always filled out the contours in his picture of the deity, man has often assumed falsely that peoples of various ages and lands had invented their gods. Yet they are actually the expression of his understanding at a given point of the divine nature. Man has felt himself in every age to be in touch with the divine existentially—to use a fashionable word—that is, in terms of experience and emotion. This contact is only secondarily a matter of conscious thought, of expression in specific acts of veneration and service which thus become the occasion for the association of like-minded individuals.

Nowhere and never has man been regarded as "man" in the complete sense of the word where this dimension has been lacking. Only in very recent times has it been possible to exclude from human self-understanding this knowledge of the divine confrontation, this relationship otherwise necessary to the concept of humanity.

During the First World War, a book appeared which at that time attracted much attention but today is no longer read as much as it deserves to be: *Das Heilige* by Rudolf Otto. The author, one of the leading experts on both Christianity and the non-Christian religions, demonstrates that the fundamental experience which we call religious, far from being an illusion, represents a perception which provides its own evidence. To be sure, we find marked individual differences between the religions of the world and, within many of them, further varying and contradictory interpretations of the nature of the absolute.

That man is no less aware of the divine than of his own existence—this truth established so effectively by Augustine and later brought into confusion by Descartes—is a conviction which extends over the whole earth. In his feelings, thoughts and wishes, in both quiet meditation and in the experience of the Other in the conflict of desire with obligation, in a thousand different situations, man becomes aware of this relationship. The perception may be followed by the most varied reactions, ranging from fanatical conviction to nagging doubt, from obedience to rebellion. While a minority in the higher cultures interprets the ground of being as impersonal, the overwhelming majority of all men has experienced it in every era as a "thou." Many utterances have been carried over to this "thou" from the "thou" known empirically through experience with one's fellowmen. This has often occurred in a thoughtless and frivolous manner, often in naive unconcern with the misunderstanding which might arise from it.

We are acquainted with the so-called anthropomorphisms in the religions of the world, with those stories of the gods which sound blasphemous yet are often intended as quite otherwise. To be sure, such utterances have no place in the highest forms of reverence for the divine. Nevertheless, the danger of uncertainty and scepticism grows with reservations towards any positive utterances concerning the ground of being. Especially where, as so often in the modern world, only one form of utterance—that limited to sense perception—is regarded as legitimate. And yet there can be no doubt that we perceive a phenomenon diversely if the phenomenon in itself has many levels and many forms. We can speak of certain entities only in terms of myth or symbol; perhaps we cannot speak of them at all, but can only turn towards them in position and gesture.

Here again, because he has unlearned and forgotten so much, how much modern man has to learn! And still the dimension which is involved in his self-understanding is of the utmost importance. For thus man in the Occident and Orient may become aware in the future of the self in all its possibilities and connections and thus correct the hopelessly foreshortened and even mutilated self-image which is so widespread today. Moreover, the individual, cut off from all contact with his fellowmen and with the very sources of existence, has thus lost his creative powers.

The creation of genuine culture is only possible for man when communion with the deity, the primary ground of all things, can serve as a source for his creativity. And here the meaning of a paradox is opened to us. The enemies of religion have so often maintained that man is only truly free, only really himself, when he has completely freed himself of all ties to the divine. This was the gospel of the eighteenth-, nineteenth-, and twentieth-century atheists. In reality, the result was an impoverishment of the power to create culture, a power of which we have only gradually become fully aware. No man finds his true creative freedom until he acknowledges his dependency and understands himself as a "child of God." The servant of God, as the poet and novelist Carl Hauptmann once said, is the highest of the liberated.

Thus anchored, we are free to do justice not only to the world of the senses surrounding us, but also to the world of values which demand our recognition. Nature appears to the man lacking faith and love only as the scene of exploitation or as a neutral backdrop before which the drama of his fate unrolls. Nature can also be regarded with reverence and a feeling of responsibility when it admits as a transparent medium the light of divine creativity. The poet Jean Paul once asked, "How can one think of the great and the small at the same time?" And he answered, "If one thinks first of the great. When one looks into the sun, dust and gnats become most readily visible. After all," he adds, "God is the sun for all of us. The world of values, patiently awaiting discovery and recognition, is ready to give of its riches. Truth and beauty, justice and goodness, dignity and wisdom become visible again and begin to determine our actions. Not until his eyes are opened again to these things does man begin to understand himself as that which he was meant to be."

We close with an anecdote from the literature of the Mohammedans. A man who was beside himself said to God, "O God, open a door for me at last." Rabia, who happened to be sitting there, said, "O fool, is this gate then closed?"

2.

Stefan George (1868-1933) Poet and Priest of Modern Paganism

At the end of 1933 a German poet died whose work and personality undoubtedly deserve the often misused epithet "great": Stefan George. Poet, prophet, and legislator, Stefan George reminds us of the great men of Antiquity, and his personality as well as his work reminds us continually of the Antiquity of Empedocles and Plato.

I very vividly remember how, when I was attending the Gymnasium, a book from George fell into my hands for the first time. Albert Verwey, George's friend and companion in the titanic struggle to attain a new practical culture, had made George known in the Netherlands even before anyone had noticed him in Germany. My first acquaintance with George ended in astonishment. The total lack of any punctuation and of capitalization as well as the obscure language made me immediately aware of the fact that here was a man who was not easily approached. And yet, the exquisite power and richness of his choice of words strangely captivated me. Today also, George is a man, a prophet, who is not easily understood—even for someone who reads German fluently and who has a wide background in poetry. It would, indeed, be contrary to George's nature if his books could be easily understood. Yet, he who reads him persistently or, to be even more precise, he who listens to him with all the power within him, shall succeed in understanding even more fully George's "hymnal" mind. The structure of his powerful poems will then become more and more transparent.

The Word. George must first of all be characterized as a man of the word, of language. This is not to say that he was a so-called "word artist." Rather, he is one of those very few, even among the greatest of poets, who does not use words superfluously. He does not talk—he "speaks." From his earliest youth on he regarded the "word" as sacred, having no peace of mind unless he had found the word which would not just be a sign but be instead the body of the soul of things:

> Des sehers wort ist wenigen gemeinsam:
> Schon als die ersten Kühnen wünsche kamen
> In einem seltnen reiche ernst und einsam
> Erfand er für die dinge eigne namen—
> (*Das Jahr der Seele.*)

> The word of seers is not for common sharing:
> In curious kingdoms, earnest and alone,
> When first his wishes roused him with their daring
> He summoned things with names that were his own.[1]

The young poet, who was unknown in his own country and only appreciated by the French, the Belgians, the Dutch, and the Poles, started alone the great endeavor of purifying the language—salvaging the "word." This labor was not only directed against carelessness, against "verbiage," but also against the kind of conceptualization which attempts to exhaust the meaning of things by abstraction. George does not carry on this continuous fight theoretically or polemically, but simply by not saying anything which "isn't." Thus, his fight for purifying the language is neither an aesthetic movement nor a reaction, under romantic influence, to the dominant naturalism of his time. No, he has a deeper background; for language is, according to Gundolf, the last recourse of God in man. The struggle for a pure and clear language is essentially a struggle against barbarianism, against a culture without spirit, a culture without God. Hence already in this respect the

[1]The English translations of George's poetry cited in this text have all been drawn from Olga Marx and Ernst Morwitz, *The Works of Stefan George* (Chapel Hill, N.C.: The University of North Carolina, 1949). All page references, unless otherwise specified, are references to that volume. We shall henceforth quote only by the name of the original collection and the Marx and Morwitz page reference. The first passage quoted is from *The Year of the Soul*, p. 94.

poet's religious nature comes to the foreground, since George's words are more like the incantation of a magician, not the words of a "word artist." George's word is creative; it does not speak *about* things but it "*is*" the things themselves. To put it another way George speaks exorcistic words.

The Figure. By means of his exorcistic words George forms figures. He is not the one who confesses but the one who forms. He does not belong to types like Augustine and Goethe but to Homer, Pindar, Dante, and Shakespeare. We sense the breath of Antiquity. It is all pure Hellenic air, accentuating clearly and purely the beautiful lines of the divine and the human figures (shapes). In George we do not deal with reflection nor with the expression of feeling but something is always set before us to see. Whether the theme is Antiquity (*Die Bücher der Hirten—und Preisgedichte*) or the Middle Ages (*Der Sagen und Sänge*) or the East (*Der hängenden Gärten*), we are always spellbound by the power and clarity expressed in the forms. The Latin spirit which was so close to George, which he admired in his youth in the hymns of the Church, and which he discovered later on in Antiquity and in his French friends, is already strangely and strongly apparent in these early works. It is not just the words which are original; George possesses such a high degree of poetic gifts that the very image of which he speaks has the freshness and power of that which has been created. No wonder that Pindar inevitably comes to our minds.

Distance. The bearer of this word, the creator of these forms, must go his own way. He cannot let himself be guided by the masses for he would no longer understand nor see the original word and the pure image. George revolts against nineteenth-century culture. This revolt contains a high degree of self-consciousness expressing prophetic calling. In self-imposed isolation he refrains from publicity and publications. Never before has the word of Horatius been so true as in the case of Stefan George:

> Odi profanum vulgus et arceo.
> Favete linguis: carmina non prius
> Audita musarum sacerdos
> Virginibus puerisque canto.

Or in the poet's own words:

> Zu meinen träumen floh ich vor dem volke,
> Mis heissen händen tastend nach der weite

Und sprach allein und rein mit stern und wolke
von meinem ersten jügendlichen streite.
(*Das Jahr der Seele.*)

I locked myself in dreams and shunned the crowd,
With frantic hands I groped for wider space,
Alone and pure avowed to star and cloud
The first encounter with my young dismays.[2]

As a pagan puritan he fights against abstractionism. His words as well as his gestures are as strong and as hard as his own sharply accentuated face: he is the ruler at a distance, a great despiser but also a great lover. Above all, however, he is the conscious bearer of the dignity of beauty.

Prophecy of Life. We have already called attention to *Das Jahr der Seele.* It is worth noting how the poet in this work, which is the most human and the warmest of all his poetry, refrains from any poetic psychology, and how he avoids even more stringently the common fault of expressing uncontrollably the cry of his soul. I quote one of the most beautiful poems:

Komm in den totgesagten park und schau:
Der schimmer ferner lächelnder gestade,
Der reinen wolken unverhofftes blau
Erhellt die weither und die bunten pfade.

Dort nimm das tiefe gelb, das weiche grau
Von birken und von buchs, der wind ist lau,
Die späten rosen welkten noch nicht ganz,
Erlese küsse sie und flicht den kranz.

Vergiss auch diese letzten astern nicht,
Den purper un die ranken wilder reben
Und auch was übrig blieb von grünem leben
Verwinde leicht im herbstlichen gesicht.

Come to the park they say is dead, and you
Will see the glint of smiling shores beyond,
Pure clouds with rifts of unexpected blue
Diffuse a light on patterned path and pond.

Take the grey tinge of boxwood and the charm
Of burning-yellow birch. The wind is warm.
Late roses still have traces of their hue,
So kiss, and gather them, and wreathe them too.

[2]*The Year of the Soul,* p. 93.

Do not forget the asters—last of all—
And not the scarlet on the twists of vine,
And what is left of living green, combine
To shape a weightless image of the fall.[3]

Is this the painting of an autumn landscape as experienced by an aging soul? Or is it the confession of an aging soul expressed in the colors of autumn flowers? It is neither of these, for the external and the internal are completely at one with one another. Instead, it is a new reality rising before us in word and in form; the same movement in the soul as well as in nature is revealed to us through the word of George. We are far removed from all pathos and from the brokenness of the modern man. Instead, the poem is before us like a Greek vase, just like others of his poems appear as Greek temples. He who is looking for a Weltanschauung must look elsewhere for the poet does not "view" the world—such conceit is far from him. Instead, the world itself is revealed in and through his word.

Is it then pure "literature"? Yes and no. Yes, if we mean by it that the poem does not pretend to be anything else but a poem. No, if one associates it with the French concept "littérature," i.e., playing flirtation with beauty. George knows, however, that the powerful word itself discloses life; he also knows that Beauty needs its priests. Once George was characterized as a French aesthete and a priest in one and the same figure. But these two are not distinct, for Beauty is the divinity of life and life is the body of Beauty. We sense it in the poem which follows. The tone becomes more priestly and at the same time more prophetic:

Ich forschte bleichen eifers nach dem horte
Nach strofen drinnen tiefste kümmerniss
Und dinge rollten dumpf und ungewiss—
Da trat ein nackter engel durch die pforte:

Entgegen trug er dem versenkten sinn
Der reichsten blumen last und nicht geringer
Als mandelblüten waren seine finger
Und rosen rosen waren un sein kinn.

Auf seinem haupte keine krone ragte
Und seine stimme fast der meinen glich:
Das schone leben sendet mich an dich
Als botem: während er dies lächelnd sagte.

[3]*The Year of the Soul,* p. 81.

Entfielen ihm die lilien und mimosen—
Und als ich sie zu heben mich gebückt
Da kniet auch er, ich badete beglückt
Mein ganzes antlitz in den frischen rosen.
(*Der Teppich des Lebens*, "Vorspiel.")

When pale with zeal, I searched for hidden store,
For strophes weighed with grief, and things that flow
In drowsy and uncertain round, I saw
A naked angel standing in the door.

He brought the spirit which was buried in
Itself a wealth of precious blooms, his hand
Was like the flowering almond, and a band
Of roses, roses clustered at his chin.

He did not wear a heavy crown and when
He spoke his voice was almost like my own:
"Dispatched to you by radiant life, I come,
An envoy!" So he said, and smiled, and then

He dropped his sheaves of lilies and mimosas,
But when I stooped to gather them, he too
Was kneeling. In delight I bathed my brow,
And cheeks, and mouth in newly-opened roses.[4]

The religious thrust becomes already stronger. Experience takes the form of encounter, of an "I-Thou" relationship; life sends its angel to its prophet. Poet and angel are, however, to be distinguished: "He spoke his voice was almost like my own." The tone of the poet becomes ever more solemn. His experience becomes a struggle with life, in order to obtain the blessing of Beauty:

Gib mir den grossen feierlichen hauch
Gib jene glut mir wieder die verjünge
Mit denen einst der kindheit flugelschwünge
Sich hoben zu dem frühsten opferrauch.

Ich aber bog den arm an seinen knieen
Und aller wachen sehnsucht stimmen schrieen:
Ich lasse nicht, du segnetest mich denn.
(*Der Teppich des Lebens*, "Vorspiel.")

"Give me the solemn breath that never failed,
Give me the fire again that makes us young,
On which the wings of childhood rose among
The fumes our earliest offerings exhaled."

[4]*The Tapestry of Life*, p. 118.

> But then against his knee I bent my arm,
> And all the tongues of waking longing stormed:
> "I will not let you go unless you bless!"[5]

Self-consciousness is more and more replaced by the realization that he is called to obedience to a Power:

> Nun hält ein guter geist die rechte wage.
> Nun tu ich alles was der engel will.
> (*Der Teppich des Lebens*, "Vorspiel.")

> But now a blessed spirit holds the scales
> Now I am governed by the angel's will.[6]

Guided by the angel of life the poet now perceives the multiple threads of the tapestry of life as a transparent whole. The Church of his Rhineland as well as the Hellas of his eternal love have taught him to see. Now the images of life stand before him as if hewed from pure marble. Has there ever been a purer, more sober, and more powerful myth about the entrance of man into the world than the following poem?

> Aus dunklen fichten flog ins blau der aar
> Und drunten aus der lichtung trat ein paar
> Von wolfen, schlürften an der flachen flut
> Bewachten starr und trieben ihre brut.
>
> Drauf huschte aus der glatten nadeln streu
> Die schar der hinde trank und kehrte scheu
> Zur waldnacht, eines blieb nur das im ried
> Sein end erwartend still den rudel mied.
>
> Hier litt das fette gras noch nie die schur
> Doch lagen stämme, starker arme spur,
> Denn drunten dehnte der gefurchte bruch
> Wo in der scholle zeugenden geruch
>
> Und in der weissen sonnen scharfem glühn
> Des ackers froh des segens neuer mühn
> Erzvater grub erzmutter molk
> Das schicksal nährend für ein ganzes volk.
> (*Der Teppich des Lebens*.)

> From brooding pines an eagle upward swept
> Into the blue, and toward the clearing stepped

[5]*The Tapestry of Life*, p. 118.
[6]*The Tapestry of Life*, p. 119.

Two wolves. They lapped the shallow pool and swung
To stark attention, marshalling their young.

And then across the glossy needles whipped
A flock of hinds, and drank, and shyly slipped
Back to the dusk of woods, but one remained
Alone among the reeds to wait his end.

Here the lush grass had never felt the blade,
But hands had been at work, for stems were laid
And further on a plough had ridged the sod
Where in the fertile odour of the clod

And happy in the white and stinging sun
With fields and gains their novel toil had won,
Arch-father delved, arch-mother milked,
Shaping the fate of all this human ilk.[7]

The visionary power to which this image witnesses, portraying the transition of nature into culture, is experienced by the poet as a gift, a mystical gift:

Sie ist nach willen nicht: ist nicht für jede
Gewohnte stunde: ist kein schatz der gilde
Sie wird den vielen nie und nie durch rede
Sie wird den seltnen selten in gebilde.
(*Der Teppich des Lebens.*)

It is not at your beck, is not for each
Accustomed day, and not what guilds could share,
And never for the many, nor through speech
It comes incarnate rarely to the rare.[8]

Life is sacred and he who robs its sacredness had better beware, for he is the outcast who approaches life's feast "(well) adorned and yet unhallowed."[9]

Prophecy of the God. We know that George had a difficult time after he had written his *Der Teppich des Lebens.* Would he be able to remain at the height he had attained? Melancholy runs through his *Lieder von Traum und Tod.* To be sure, there is no trace of romantic Weltschmerz in this poem. Nevertheless, there is the echo of a life apprehended as "fame and glow, pain and bliss, death and dream."[10] But new life approaches when a new

[7]*The Tapestry of Life*, pp. 130–31.
[8]*The Tapestry of Life*, p. 130.
[9]"Wohl geschmückt doch nicht geheiligt." *The Tapestry of Life*, p. 136.
[10]"Glanz und ruhm rausch und qual traum und tod." *Songs of Dream and Death*, p. 154.

vision breaks through: God incarnate. This incarnation must, however, not be interpreted in terms of George's Mother Church. What is meant is indeed incarnation, but not the one and the "once for all" incarnation confessed by the Church. What happened in Christ can happen today. Yes, indeed, it does happen and it has happened. The tone of the following poem is still and tender:

> Und der heut eifernde posaune bläst
> Und flüssig feuer schleudert weiss dass morgen
> Leicht alle schönheit kraft und grösse steigt
> Aus eines knaben stillem flötenlied.
> (*Der siebente Ring.*)

> And he who blows fanfares today and hurls
> A jet of fluid fire, knows: Tomorrow
> The sun of grandeur, force, and grace may spring
> From the untroubled fluting of a boy.[11]

Even more strongly than at first George's total spirit comes to stand over against the life of modern times, i.e., over against positivistic science, naturalistic or impressionistic art as well as over against the modern spirit which knows of no gods because it cannot see them. It is exactly at this point that George parts company with Verwey, Goethe, and Nietzsche. He replies to Dante that it is easy to create hell but that it takes far more to proclaim love. The latter is far more necessary:

> Ich nahm aus meinem herd ein scheit und blies—
> So ward die hölle, doch des vollen feuers
> Bedurft ich zur bestrahlung höchster liebe
> Und zur verkündigung von sonn und stern.
> (*Der siebente Ring.*)

> I took an ember from my hearth and blew,
> And hell was fashioned, but I needed torrents
> Of blaze to light the highest love to glory
> And to exalt the sun and all the stars.[12]

Among the circle of pupils, hierarchically structured, a small group had formed itself which, in wild enthusiasm for the then little-known Bachofen, had discovered the force of the life of passion. George broke with these *Kosmiker* who glorified the earth over and above the creative spirit, and glorified the passions of the

[11]*The Seventh Ring*, p. 156.
[12]*The Seventh Ring*, p. 157.

flesh over and above the nobility of the soul. A total breach was only a matter of time. Rejecting bodily passions, he served as ever before the creative, formative spirit. And yet, he knew that the spirit is no spirit without the body. He knew that the body, like the spirit, belongs to the very essence of man. Thus, he rejected spiritualism as well as naturalism. Only he who knows of the body and also of spiritual perception, putting both at the service of the god, may be called a sage:

> Drei sind der wisser stufen. Nur der wahn
> Meint dass er die durchspringt: geburt und leib.
> Die andre gleichen zwangs ist schaun und fassen.
> Die letzte kennt nur wen der gott beschlief.
> (*Der Stern des Bundes.*)

> Three rungs for those who know—and none but fools
> Try to dispense with that of birth and flesh.
> The other, just as strong, is grasp and vision,
> But only he the god knew, knows the last.[13]

The great Mother of Antiquity is not an "idea" such as an abstract idealism regards her, but neither is she a ruler in her own right. The spirit must tame her and must force her to do a great work:

> Dass sie ihr werk willfährig wieder treibt:
> Den leib vergottet und den gott verleibt.
> (*Der siebente Ring.*)

> Submissively she plies her work afresh:
> Turns flesh to god, embodies god in flesh.[14]

Once again we sense how close George is to Antiquity when he at last finds the divine body, the incarnate god, in the shape of a beautiful youth from a suburb of München called Maximin. His physical and spiritual beauty accompanied George for a short time only for, as the poet expresses it mystically, "according to an earlier made agreement he had to leave the earth soon." Only when one reads the sober words, glowing with inner passion, with which George describes his encounter and his life with Maximin as well as his departure, can we get an impression of this pagan incarnation-faith. A new faith in a savior bursts into the open and is accompanied with all the ancient symbols:

[13] *The Star of the Covenant*, p. 270.
[14] *The Seventh Ring*, p. 178.

Dem bist du kind, dem freund.
Ich seh in dir den Gott
Dem schauernd ich erkannt
Dem meine andacht gilt.

Nun wird es wieder lenz—
Du weihst den weg die luft
Und uns auf die du schaust—
So stammle dir mein dank.
(*Der siebente Ring.*)

To some you are a child,
To some a friend, to me
The god whom I divined
And tremblingly adore.

. . . .

Now spring is here again,
You bless the air, the path,
And us on whom you gaze...
So take my faltered thanks.[15]

And in a poem to his contemporaries, which reminds one of the ancient Egyptian and Hellenistic throne-hymns, he writes:

Ihr hattet augen trüb durch ferne träume
Und sorgtet nicht mehr um das heilge lehn.
Ihr fühltet endes-hauch durch alle räume—
Nun hebt das haupt! denn euch ist heil geschehn.

In eurem schleppenden und kalten jahre
Brach mun ein frühling neuer wunder aus.
Mit blumiger hand, mit schimmer um die haare
Erschien ein gott und trat zu euch ins haus.

Vereint euch froh da ihr nicht mehr beklommen
Vor lang verwichner pract erröten müsst:
Auch ihr habt eines gottes ruf vernommen
Und eines gottes mund hat euch geküsst.

Nun klagt nicht mehr—denn auch ihr wart erkoren—
Dass eure tage unerfüllt entschwebt—
Preist eure stadt die einen gott geboren!
Preist eure zeit in der ein gott gelebt!
(*Der siebente Ring.*)

Your eyes were dim with distant dreams, you failed
To guard and tend the holy fief and knew

[15]*The Seventh Ring*, p. 194.

That everywhere the glow of life had paled.
Now lift your head, for joy has come to you!

New miracles of spring have put to flight
The year you suffered slow and icy gloom,
With hands like April buds, with licks of light,
A god appeared and stepped into your room.

Unite in happiness, no more alloyed
With cravings for an age of vanished bliss,
You too have heard the summons of a god,
It was a god who granted you his kiss.

You also were elect, so do not mourn
For all the days which unfulfillment sheathed.
Praise to your city where a god was born,
Praise to your time in which a god has breathed![16]

Body and soul have found and have penetrated each other in a visible divinity. The priest, in mystical rapture, feels himself in the midst of bounteous light:

Ich bin ein funke nur vom heiligen feuer
Ich bin ein dröhnen nur der heiligen stimme.
(*Der siebente Ring.*)

(I am) a flicker of the holy fire,
(I am) an echo of the holy tongue.[17]

Legislation. "Poets are the hierophants of an unapprehended inspiration, the mirrors of the gigantic shadows which futurity casts upon the present, the words which express what they understood not; the trumpets which sing to battle and feel not what they inspire, the influence which is moved not, but moves. Poets are the unacknowledged legislators of the world."[18] I need not add to this. The true poet is always prophet and seer and legislator of his time. This is the reason why George parted company with his French friends for he saw them as lacking the faith in the power of the word. After all, even the best of French poetry suffers from being too much "littérature." It must not be thought, however, as if George, now that he has found his gods, makes his appearance as a religious and political teacher. No, he remains a poet who

[16]*The Seventh Ring*, pp. 197–98.
[17]*The Seventh Ring*, p. 204.
[18]Percy Bysshe Shelley, *A Defence of Poetry* (Boston: Ginn and Company, 1891), p. 46.

is concerned only with saying and doing things. Yet, he moves closer and closer to the realization that he is a man who proclaims his god, a prophet speaking to his age. He is aware of the fact that he stands with his message in the midst of a time of fulfillment—Kairos—in the midst of a country, Germany, which awaits its rebirth.

> Aus einer ewe pfeilgeradem willen
> Fuhr ich zum reigen reiss ich in den ring.
> (*Der Stern des Bundes.*)
>
> I curve an age that tends to arrow-straightness,
> I lead the round and wrest into the ring.[19]

We live at a turning point in time and the "Lord of Turning" must rule our life. The Middle Ages, "which your time indicts as wild and savage,"[20] sought to encounter God. Our time only knows of idols. But, in despair and barbarism the new god is born, whom the poet proclaims:

> Ich sprach den spruch, der zirkel ist gezogen—
> Eh mich das dunkel überholt entrückt
> Mich hohe schau: bald geht mit leichten sohlen
> Durch teure flur greifbar in glanz der Gott.
> (*Das neue Reich.*)
>
> I spoke the magic and I drew the circle.
> Before I drown in night a vision sweeps
> Me upward: Soon the god will set his weightless
> Foot on my cherished land—the flame made flesh.[21]

The question has been asked whether George, whose last book of poetry was called *Das neue Reich*, is to be understood as having been the forerunner of the "Third Reich."[22] Indeed, his poetry contains much of what was the driving force behind the national-socialistic state. Nevertheless, the struggle of the poet is not the same as that of the soldiers and the statesmen. All this is clearly discernible in his war-poems, which are among the most beautiful ever written. In these poems George suffers and bleeds together

[19] *The Star of the Covenant*, p. 251.

[20] "Die ihr die wilden dunklen zeiten nennt." *The Star of the Covenant*, p. 253.

[21] *The Kingdom Come*, p. 285.

[22] See J. Gaudefroy-Domombynes, "Stefan George, annonciateur du noveau Reich," *Mercure de France*, CXLIV (January, 1934), 31.

with his people rooted in the German soil. Yet, the fight fought outside, killing his dearest pupils, is not the real fight.[23] The enemy is elsewhere, and yet present here and now:

> Zu jubeln ziemt nicht: kein triumf wird sein,
> Nur viele untergänge ohne würde—
>
> Am streit wie ihr ihn fühlt nehm ich nicht teil.
> (*Das neue Reich.*)
>
> You shall not cheer. No rise will mark the end,
> But only downfalls, many and inglorious—
>
> The struggle, as you wage it, is not mine.[24]

His total passion is spent for the rebirth of his people:

> Ihm wuchs schon heran
> Gestählt im banne der verruchten jahre
> Ein jung geschlecht das wieder mensch und ding
> Mit echten maassen misst, das schön und ernst
> Froh seiner einzigkeit, vor Fremden stolz,
> Sich gleich entfernt von klippen dreisten dünkels
> Wie seichtem sumpf erlogner brüderei
> Das von sich spie was mürb und feig und lau
> Das aus geweihtem träumen tun und dulden
> Den einzigen der hilft den Mann gebiert.
> (*Das neue Reich.*)
>
> A younger generation rises toward him,
> The youths who, steeled by times of galling pressure,
> Again have honest standards for the probe
> Of men and things who—fair and grave and proud—
> In alien worlds accept themselves for what
> They are, avoid the rocks of brazen boasting
> And the morass of would-be brotherhood,
> Spat out the lifeless, stale, and base, and from
> Their consecrated dreams, and deeds, and sorrows
> Begot the only one who can restore.[25]

If we apply this poem to the reality of the "Third Reich," then, there is indeed much fulfilled prophecy. Nevertheless, at the core there is in George much more criticism, for George's "Reich" is

[23] See Freidrich Wolters, *Stefan George und die Blätter für die Kunst* (Berlin, 1930), p. 441.
[24] *The Kingdom Come*, pp. 291, 290.
[25] *The Kingdom Come*, p. 296.

in final analysis not of this world. The fight of the poet does not concern the breakdown of France, but the downfall of this rotting, godless culture (*Brand des Tempels*). His pupils glorify Caesar, Frederick II, Napoleon, but the rebirth is not gained with weapons. All this is expressed in the "Hymn to Death," which reminds us of Tyrtaeus:

> Wenn einst dies geschlecht sich gereinigt von schande
> Von nacken geschlendert die fessel des fröners
> Nur spürt im geweide den hunger nach ehre:
> Dann wird auf der walstatt voll endloser gräber
> Aufzucken der blutschein—dann jagen auf wolken
> Lautdröhnende heere dann braust durchs gefilde
> Der schrecklichste schrecken der dritte der stürme:
> Der toten zurückkunft!
>
> Wenn je dieses volk sich aus feigen erschlaffen
> Sein selber erinnert der kür und der sende:
> Wird sich ihm eröffnen die göttliche deutung
> Unsagbaren grauens—dann heben sich hände
> Und munder ertönen zum preise der würde
> Dann flattert im frühwind mit wahrhaftem zeichen
> Die königsstandarte und grüsst sich verneigend
> Die Hehren, die Helden!
>
> (*Das neue Reich.*)

> When these generations are purged of dishonour
> And hurl from their shoulders the shackles of bondage
> And feed in their vitals the hunger for virtue,
> The flashes of blood will illumine the millions
> Of graves of the fallen, then thundering armies
> Will ride over clouds and the terror of terrors,
> The third of the tempests will sweep through the country:
> The dead turning homeward.
>
> When men of this nation no longer are cowards
> Or weaklings, but feel their vocation and mission,
> Their hearts will decipher the message of heaven,
> In dread beyond measure. Their hands will be lifted,
> Their lips will be turned to the homage of honour,
> The flag of the king, the legitimate symbol
> Will fly through the dawn and be lowered in praise of
> The hallowed, the heroes![26]

Christianity and Paganism. The question which remains is

[26]*The Kingdom Come*, p. 333.

whether the process of man becoming man, which the poet proclaims, is the process of man's deification? In other words, is it the poet himself who produced the god? George answers it in *Der Stern des Budnes:* "Discard reflection! Spirit pray!"[27]

It hardly needs any argument to say that the new religion proclaimed by George is pagan. Undoubtedly, Roman Catholic Christianity has had a great influence upon George. Gundolf remarks that it is this influence which differentiates him from Goethe.[28] The worship and the word of the Christian Church continue in his work, and the relationship between experience and worship has seldom been so precisely expressed as in the next poem:

> Wer schauen dürfte bis hinab zum grund
> Trägt ein gefeiter heim zu aller wohl
> Den zauber als Begehung und als Bild.
> (*Der Stern des Bundes.*)

> Who was allowed to see the depths becomes
> Immune, and for the common good transmits
> The spell as rite and image.[29]

Nevertheless, it is a pagan worship. The divine figures of Antiquity reappear in George's work. Instead of being the Roman Catholic Rhinelander, he is the Greek for whom all that is is divine. Yet, George gives us three things, which we as Christians need to be concerned with: (1) the realization of existence, (2) the attempt to renew culture, (3) the victory over an areligious positivism by a stark, deep religious paganism.

1) George never speaks about a situation—he stands in the midst of it. He does not speak about the gods—he addresses them. This is relevant for our time which, in philosophy and theology, has relinquished the attitude that man is sovereign, controlling the world with his analytical intellect or conquering it with his feeling. We are more modest today, once again concerned with man as he is placed in concrete situations. After having run around the world during the past century with concepts and feelings, we are once again placed in the unique situation of going right across the world. George is in this respect not only a guide, he is the prophet who calls us, the poet who puts us in the midst of life itself. For George existence and incarnation are corollaries. This also concerns

[27]"Schweig gedanke, Seele bete!" *The Star of the Covenant*, p. 265.
[28]Friedrich Gundolf, *George* (Berlin, 1920), p. 38.
[29]*The Star of the Covenant*, p. 275.

the Christian. The answer of the poet to a scientist, that he who does not stand at the center never achieves anything (*"wer nicht in der Mitte steht gelangt niemals hin"*) has great depth. Existence is only there where the god is present. God is only present when man truly "is." The question as to whether the pagan belief in incarnations, such as we know them from India and from Antiquity, is a roadblock to the Christian Incarnation-faith may be a difficult question to answer. Nevertheless, it is of the greatest importance that the image of the Incarnation, having become totally foreign to modern naturalistic and idealistic thought, is once again experienced and understood. George calls us to kneel down before a god who "is." And all this in a time which attempts to cover up its inner hollowness with false decorations of Weltanschauungen. The call to kneel down is also the cause of the hymnal character of George's poetry. It means a great deal in our time to know once again what hymns are. If we read the ancient Latin ecclesiastical hymns we are struck by their directness, their pointedness. While our hymns meditate about or speak of God, they *address* him. George's poetry has in common with them their pointedness as well as their awareness of concrete reality.

2) This renewed consciousness of existence gives rise to a renewed culture: to liberate man from pure concrete fact, objectiveness. George's powerful words are directed against a culture which knew how to obey neither passion nor spirit. Wolters relates the story that Max Weber once charged George with being unable to live without technology, without financial and economic institutions, i.e., without Silverberg & Cie. The poet replied that only he who carried a part of Silverberg & Cie. within himself could not live without them: "If telephones and railroads were to stop today, Mr. Silverberg and Cie. could no longer exist—but I and my people would."[30] George is great in his struggle for a new culture from within. One will look in vain for any refined aestheticism, like Hofmannstal's, or for any sultry mysticism, like Rilke's. No, George's words sound strong and hard. His protest is directed against the omnipotent instinct, against prostituting the spirit. This protest is not polemical, but his words are spoken with the peace of a priest who knows that, whatever may happen outside, he must speak his words.

3) The most important thing for us Christians, however, is that

[30]Wolters, *op. cit.*, p. 476.

in George, once again, a powerful religious paganism is addressing us. Instead of a godless positivism or a godless mechanized culture, we are standing face to face with genuine non-Christian religiosity. We Christians are, so to speak, waiting for that, because genuine Christianity is born at the point where the Powers of this world are known and served. Negation is not an enemy with which Christianity can live and fight. Only demonic affirmation can bring the Church new struggle and new hope. Yes, indeed, one may say that what was wrong with Christianity in the past centuries was that it had no opposition. Enlightenment and Positivism, Idealism and Humanism are not directed against Christianity; they fought against other enemies and each of them thought that they kept the essence of Christianity—each in their own way. But if the signs of our time do not lead us astray, we may say that the Church can expect new opposition: servants of foreign gods. We can only be grateful for this for we have nothing to expect from a mixture of Christian values with others. Jahweh can only be served by those who know of Baal. To kneel down before the appearance in the flesh of our Lord Jesus Christ can only be done by him who knows the flesh himself.

It is meaningless to polemicize with George. One can treat the greatness or the relativity of his incarnation-experience ironically, as a Roman Catholic theologian did: "Observe—there is again coming into existence out of primeval times the Civis Romanus of the last pagan era. In his monstrous unconditionedness, with impunity, he is able to make his young friend a god and his horse a consul."[31] We perhaps do better to say with George's friend, the passionate Roman Catholic Ludwig Derleth: "I have read your book. I should like to say, there are no new gods."[32] George the pagan can teach us a great deal. He can teach us how overpowering the expectation of the Coming Lord can be. Although we shall seek the fulfillment of this expectation in the "*einmaligkeit*" of Jesus Christ, nevertheless we can understand him when he says:

> Von welchen wundern lacht die morgen-erde
> Als wär ihr erster tag? Erstauntes singen
> Von neuerwachten welten trägt der wind
> Verandert sieht der alten berge form

[31] *Ibid.*, p. 506.
[32] *Ibid.*, p. 352.

Und wie im kindheit-garden schaukeln blüten—
Der strom besprengt die ufer und es schlang
Sein zitternd silber allen staub der jahre
Die schöpfung schauert wie im stand der gnade.
Kein gänger kommt des weges dessen haupt
Nicht eine ungewusste hoheit schmücke.
Ein breites licht ist übers land ergossen—
Heil allen die in seinen strahlen gehn!
(*Der Stern des Bundes.*)

What light has touched the morning earth with wonder
As on the first of dawns? The wind is sated
With the astounded song of wakened worlds.
The timeless mountains seem to change their shape,
And flowers nod as in the days of childhood.
The river laps against the shore and drowns
The dust of ages with a wash of silver.
Is this a state of grace? Creation trembles,
And everyone who walks the road is ringed
With majesty which he is unaware of.
Across the land a wealth of sun is flooded,
And all who move within its beams are blessed.[33]

[33]*The Star of the Covenant*, p. 268.

3.

The Problem of Death in Modern Philosophy

Historical periods with monolithic or closed culture systems—taking the word "culture" in Nietzsche's sense to mean the unity of style pervading all external manifestations of life—give a harmonious, unified response to the great questions of existence. Our present time, however, no longer draws its life from the depths of a unity that enables it to apprehend and to experience the realities of nature, time, and love in a homogeneous, a priori frame of reference in which all practical and theoretical attitudes toward existential phenomena are regulated by a compulsory standard or norm. In the culture of the West a plurality of such norms vie for preeminence. This pluralism arises primarily from the fact that the historical forces that originally helped shape the modern world are still at work today in varying degrees of intensity and in varying combinations. One need mention only antiquity and Christianity as two examples of supranational cultural forces which have become an integral part of our *national* heritage. It is not just that they influence the thinking and acting of modern European man in individual and more or less critical instances. But the whole standard of values, the basic orientation toward life implicit in the exterior forms of classical antiquity and Christianity, are at work in the a priori principles which at least co-determine the thinking and behavior of individuals and of groups in the present in which *we* live.

Because the gap created by diverse philosophical outlooks, value systems, and ultimate objectives among modern men of the West (such differences having existed of course to a more or less marked degree in *all* times) can no longer be bridged by the unifying power of cultural forces that rest upon common historical hypotheses, diverging and even conflicting principles and attitudes have arisen in present-day man. Again and again (since the great movement of the present day toward integration is still in its initial stages) we perceive this rupture in modern man's relationship to the ultimate problems of life.

Practical conduct in life and reflection do not always directly correspond with one another. Reflection is governed by its own set of laws which can at times lead it far afield from what actually takes place in the world of deeds and actions. In the philosophical process it creates a tradition which consistently subjects to a thorough re-examination the problematic questions of existence which tend to solve in a caustic way matters of practical judgment and behavior. In this connection it would be well to remember that, as Wilhelm Dilthey has shown, in all cultural milieux which have developed a philosophy, this philosophy has originated in theology. Philosophy of religion therefore was originally philosophy derived *from* religion. Religious norms are the primary ones; philosophy explicates and—later on—criticizes them. So it becomes understandable that it is not only in its formulation of questions that philosophy adopts and implements the thematic structures of theology; even in its substantive content and its conception of value the philosophical mode of thought is indebted to religious norms.

Three times in the course of the history of ideas in the West—and each time in a somewhat more radical way—a process of emancipation occurred which had as its formal and material object a more or less marked autonomy of philosophical reflection. This is first seen in the evolution of Greco-Roman culture. We are not interested here in asking to what extent philosophical speculation in that period appeared as a function of the emancipation from the views and value systems of the hereditary religion that had already occurred in practical life. We are not questioning the extent to which philosophy anticipated and influenced this emancipation, nor the extent to which a reciprocal process was going on.

It suffices to say that in the philosophical thought of late Antiquity—prescinding for the moment from the influence of foreign modes of thought and experience—we can perceive a philosophical stance that diverges sharply in many respects from the pristine religion on questions about the ultimate meaning of existence. The philosophic position of the Middle Ages, which springs from the new religious impulse generated by Christianity, undergoes a similar development. Here too, in spite of a formal correspondence, philosophic views, values, and ends were liberating themselves from the norms of religious dogma. To the extent that the movements for renewal, among them Humanism, the Renaissance and the Reformation, signified the onset of a new religious spirit there develops with the beginning of the modern period a new style of philosophizing, which despite the growing nationalism of European peoples exhibits common characteristics in the various countries of the West. Looking at this new epoch of philosophic endeavor we are struck by the reluctance of modern thinkers to deal with central problems of existence, with questions of life and death. This reticence corresponds to the distance maintained by the new philosophy of the nineteenth century, particularly in its last phase, from any of the attempted solutions derived from the norms of faith.

In the following sections we shall concern ourselves with various conceptions of death. Even in cases where there has been no reflection about the end of life, we can still speak of man's *relationship* to death, for in every time and place, even on the most primitive cultural levels, we encounter an awareness, however vague and indefinite, of the inevitable approach of death. The forms this relationship assumes may vary from aversion and indifference to a positive affinity for death, an affinity that can be stoic, heroic, or Dionysian.

Not until one has reflected on death does anything like a *problem of death* emerge. Some of the various formulations of this problem and their solutions will be discussed in this essay. In general, an individual's speculation about death will not only take place within a more general schematic framework but it will be colored by the presuppositions of this larger view. The individual thinker's way of looking at death will appear merely as a variant form of a basic conception derived from religion. The history of ideas in both the East and West reveals a succession of such basic conceptions. The classical and Christian conceptions and interpretations of death exhibit such an a priori which is then modified (within each system) depending on the historical period or the geographical region

(High Middle Ages, Baroque, etc.). We need not be concerned here about the unusually broad systematic question of whether a relevant way of thinking about death which would correspond to a purely natural orientation is even possible. We will start with the situation described above, namely, that in the past one hundred years the diversifications in Weltanschauungen have grown progressively stronger. Here, the general schemata mentioned earlier appear to be less clear and less determinative; the posing of a problem therefore and its solution become more individual and less representative, more personal and less binding. In almost direct contrast to the philosophies of other periods, the death-philosophy of modern thinkers tends to express highly individual attitudes toward reality. Such attitudes, however, are perhaps partially determined even now by the conceptual framework of older traditions, by the categories and forms, moods and basic tenets, for example, of antiquity or Christianity.

Despite the fact that they proceed from totally different starting points we find a common element in the various approaches to death which will be considered in this essay, for all attempt to point up a *meaning* in the primarily biological phenomena of dying and death. This perception of significance outweighs the popular tendency to conceive of death as an external entity approaching either as enemy in the form of the Fates who sever the thread of life or as a friend in the manner of the legendary German figure, *Freund Hein.*

The popular view is replaced by the interpretation of death as something so intrinsic and proper to life—to each individual life—that life can be fully comprehended in its true nature and really lived only when it is conceived and fashioned in the light of its relationship to death. That is, in the philosophical systems to be considered here death no longer appears as the inexorable interruption of life at some unknown future moment which we prefer to remain veiled, nor as an evil which one flees from. Neither does it appear as the gateway to a new, changed, but essentially continuous life. Instead, death becomes life's goal.

The life of one who lives in the knowledge of death, in the awareness of what death really is and how it functions in existence, will be lived differently from the life of one whose knowledge and understanding of himself does not include the awareness of such a life-death relationship. Modern thinkers agree, in spite of different interpretations of the essential nature of man, that the premonition of death is the first and most effective reminder to man of his true self and his destiny.

SCHOPENHAUER

> Motto: Death is the real inspiring genius or the MUSAGET of philosophy, which is why Socrates also defined it as *thanatos melete*. Moreover, without death there would scarcely be any philosophy.
> (Schopenhauer, *Werke*, II, p. 542.)

The existential fact that provides the starting point for Schopenhauer's philosophy of death is the fear of death which he sees dominating all living things. "Everything that is born comes into the world with this fear." As much as the philosophers may prove that such fears are groundless since death is not an evil, the horrors of death do not decrease. Animals, too, know fear of death, although according to Schopenhauer such knowledge cannot be proper to them. Man who possesses the certitude that death is coming suffers the greatest torment. Where does this fear come from? According to Schopenhauer, it is based on the identification of the human individual with his finite phenomenal appearance. He shrinks back in dread from death as the end of this finite presence, an end which he falsely regards—as will be shown—as final destruction. But what is there in man then, that gives rise to this "*fuga mortis*"? Is it perhaps the mind, the intellect, or the understanding? Schopenhauer takes pains to prove that this cannot be the case. It might be true if the intellect were able to convince us of the value of the life that is threatened by death. But, Schopenhauer contends, the intellect constantly points out the contrary—that we live in a world of finitude, suffering, and death. The loss of something that has no value in itself cannot be grounds for complaint.

Schopenhauer mentions further considerations to clinch the argument that our reflective faculty cannot be responsible for the fear of death. For doesn't reflection show us that the thought of non-existence in some future time need not frighten us? In the past, before we were born, weren't we also non-existent? Still further, this same intelligence will and must tell us that death need not be something frightful for it actually doesn't *exist* at all (or at best only for a moment); as soon as it sets in, consciousness, to which existence with all its gains and losses is linked, expires. "From this standpoint, Epicurus contemplated death," Schopenhauer says approvingly, "and he quite rightly said of it '*ho thanatos meden pros emas*' (death is no concern of ours), explaining that when *we* are, death is not; and when *death* is, we are not." If man were merely a knowing creature, death would be for him, not only a matter of indifference, but even something he might welcome. The basis of fear is not however the *thought* of the end of a life that "no one considers as particularly worthy of regret." Something else causes us to fear, and to recoil from the annihilation of the organism. That something cannot be traced back to the intellect. Here we are touching on something elemental, something more central than the intellect of man. What this is we find in Schopenhauer's anthropological writings, which parallel the basic principles of his metaphysics. As we know, his metaphysical system is dominated by the idea that the principle of all things is the will which switches on a light in the intellect. This light—a consciousness—then illumines the darkness of blind impulse. "Basically we are far more at one with the world than we ordinarily think; its innermost being is our will; its external phenomena are our ideas."

The will, whose anthropological form is the body, that is, the total organism, corresponds to the cosmic will. It is in the will that the passionate resistance of the creature to the apparent threat of destruction originates. Fear of death is rooted in the will. The imminence of its apparent annihilation—repugnant to the will's primitive essence of blind urgency—fills the will with loathing. We therefore maintain that the necessary separation of the knowing and willing faculties of man enables us to perceive more readily that the source of mortal fear is to be found in the will and only in the will. Anthropologically as well as cosmologically, the intellect is secondary. According to Schopenhauer, the human intellect depends on the somatic life of the organism; but this latter is dependent on the will. The human body appears as a kind of intermediary member between the will and the intellect. The great reluctance of the will to separate itself from its natural partner, the intellect, is understandable; for without the intellect as its guardian and guide, it is blind and helpless.

This source of man's fear of death leads directly to the realm of metaphysics. But it is nevertheless true that this anxiety which, as has been shown, is rooted in the depth of man's metaphysical nature is founded on a false idea, an illusion. The will to life always desires life; it desires, by reason of its very being, continuance in life. Actually, it *cannot* really be destroyed at all, but the erroneous notion that it is even threatened arises from a misunderstanding regarding the identity of our true and therefore indestructible nature with the Weltgrunde, the will.

To believe that death means the complete dissolution of the person is just as false as to assume that the cessation of life in one area is synonymous with the annihilation of the life principle. Birth and dissolution do not touch upon the roots of things—one of Schopenhauer's deepest convictions which he repeats in ever-new variations. These are mere semblance, and hence only relative. The language of nature is a valid one for this world of appearances, where we speak of the existence or non-existence of the individual creature, where death and life are opposites. But this language is only a "*patois du pays*," one to be taken with a grain of salt, or to speak more accurately, one which is determined by our intellect.

The tendency of the intellect to schematize binds our acts of cognition to time, place, and causality—thus creating the false impression that existence is limited to that of the now-dying individual. Thus, Schopenhauer can say, "Whenever an individual person experiences mortal anguish, one witnesses a peculiar, even absurd spectacle. The lord of the worlds is frightened at the prospect of perishing, of sinking into the abyss of eternal nothingness; while in reality everything is filled with his being and there is no place where he does not exist. For he is not sustained by, but rather sustains, existence." Inasmuch as the intellect is rooted in the somatic life of the organism—or better, inasmuch as the organic body is identical with the will presenting itself spatially to the intellect—the consciousness that is proper to the life of the subject—finite, coming into being at birth and ending at death—can be likened to a lantern which is extinguished after it has served its purpose. But this pertains only to the temporal phenomenon of will, that is, the individual and therefore the intellect; it does not pertain to the will itself. In ever changing modes and conditions nature presents itself to the intellect imprisoned in the principle of individuation (*principium individuationis*)—a point of view, however, which is valid only when the thinking process is determined by the principle of causality. In all change something remains the same. The nature-force as well as matter remains untouched by change, by the beginnings and endings of existence. "In spite of time, death and corruption, our integrity still remains." Thus, in Schopenhauer's opinion, everything that wills existence is actually in existence, permanently and without end. The notion that the reflecting "I" (ego, self) as subjective consciousness will one day perish need in no way cause terror or regret; for the "I" that really matters—Schopenhauer speaks of an equivocation in the use of this pronoun—cannot die. Schopenhauer expresses this idea in terms which, as we shall see, the Hegelian, Feuerbach, his polar opposite, could also have used. "The time when I shall no longer be, will come, *objectively* speaking; subjectively, however, it can never come." In this sense he agrees with a statement of Spinoza, "*sentimus experimurque nos aeternos esse*." Inasmuch as Schopenhauer's metaphysics recognizes a middle ground—that of ideas—between the *in se* of the will and the phenomenal world,[1] we can expect that his philosophy of death will also take this into consideration. This he does by pointing to the role of the species, which he sees as the objectification of will —the idea existing in time.

In each particular thing he sees "the eternity of the idea" (idea being expressly equated here with species) stamped on the finiteness of individual beings. The innermost essence of a living creature represents not so much the individual, but the species. The will to life is immediately rooted in the species, which is its direct objectification. In the will we find the element of permanence, the primordial principle. Since in the most profound and best part of ourselves, we feel ourselves to be eternal, the loss of our individuality need not distress us. Individuality can be lost because it represents a union which, when it comes to an end, is irretrievable. Nevertheless we can be certain that we have within us the possibility of innumerable individualities. With this Schopenhauer wants to console those who cling to their own "selfness"—to their right to speak of themselves as an "I". Their deeper real selves, he says, are assured of an eternal present. Thus, according to Schopenhauer, a person who dies for his country with the conviction that his true self will

[1]This middle ground of ideas is discussed in the third book of Schopenhauer's major work (*Die Welt als Wille und Vorstellung*).

live on in his countrymen can look upon death as a flicker of the eye which does not interrupt the act of seeing. "My person, which is but a very small part of my real being, perishes; but I know that death can put an end to nothing more than what was brought forth at birth."

Schopenhauer believes that death's terrors stem primarily from our belief that our self (Ich) disappears at death while the world remains. But, he maintains, the exact opposite is true in reality. The world of external phenomena disappears, but the innermost core of the self perdures, that center that bears within itself and then brings forth the subject in whose ideas (Vorstellung) alone the world has existence." What sleep is to the concrete singular individual, death is to the will as the true reality, the "*Ding an sich*."

When Schopenhauer calls death the guiding muse of philosophy which "qualifies and elevates" the philosophical sense of wonderment, he does so because death, while not the only force involved, is nevertheless the most portentous and most impressive phenomenon capable of awakening man to his *true* nature and of guiding him to it. Death is of such grave ethical and pedagogical import that Schopenhauer can refer to it as the "real outcome and therefore the purpose of life." By disposing us for the perception of identity death helps us to realize what Schopenhauer believes is the only meaning and goal of all that happens, namely, the will's conversion, the will's mortification, and the will's dissolution. Existence, for this way of thinking, means aberration and guilt—a guilt that constantly perpetuates and renews itself and to which every man contributes, especially the man of evil who absolutizes his individuality. The threat of death therefore is looked upon as *punishment*. Death is "the great moment of redress, of rectification," but it also offers the possibility for atonement. It is our glorious opportunity "*nicht mehr Ich zu sein*," that is, to exist no longer as an I, a separate ego; it represents, in other words, the possibility for the deeper self to find the freedom which could not be realized under the dominance of the principle of individuality. One should look for this opportunity, according to Schopenhauer, not *im operari*, in acting, but *im esse*, in being. The apprehension of its truest, most proper potentiality by the real "I" is identical with the great phenomenon which lies at the heart of Schopenhauer's metaphysics of the cosmos —the phenomenon of the will's conversion.

The thought of self-actualization, self-development, and self-perfection is practically foreign to an ethical system like Schopenhauer's. Death, therefore, can have no positive significance regarding the form and content of individual existence as such. The crucial question put by death is not directed to the individual personality, but to the will. The will decides in freedom whether it wishes or does not wish to continue to be. For this reason Schopenhauer calls the hour of death a *crisis* in the truest sense of the word—a last judgment.

The thought of redemption dominates Schopenhauer's philosophy of death as well as his ethics. Death for him is redemptive in a three-fold sense. The knowledge of death and the understanding of its real nature and significance leads to the critical moment of insight which is also judgment; this represents a temporary liberation. The onset of death perfects the work of deliverance for the singular individual existence, and in so doing prepares for the existence which is final and absolute.

FEUERBACH

In time, O Man, earth's grandeur crumbles
into dust.
Why vest therein the fullness of your
trust?
—(Angelus Silesius)

While Schopenhauer is one of the most widely-read philosophers, this is not the case with Ludwig Feuerbach. To study his thought, one must have recourse to his two well-known major works, *The Essence of Christianity* and the *Essence of Religion.* Not as well known, but scarcely less interesting are his *Thoughts on Death and Immortality* which, as Feuerbach himself later said when lecturing on the essence of religion, already contain *in abstracto* what the later works present *in concreto.* Anyone interested in Schopenhauer's ideas on the problem of death will find them in concentrated form in the major treatise mentioned above, but he will also come across references to and further developments of the question in almost all of his less important writings. With Feuerbach this is not the case. It would be almost impossible to lift out of the two basic works mentioned his philosophy of death. Thus we are justified in turning to his earlier writings on this point.

We cannot go into Feuerbach's philosophical development here;

one of the newer and more comprehensive research projects attempts to throw more light on it than had been done in the past. Nevertheless we must realize that the Feuerbach who speaks in these writings is still very much under the influence of Hegel, his earlier master—a fact strikingly evident in the style of his thought and expression in his early essays. Admittedly there might be a certain satisfaction in contrasting the ideas of Schopenhauer, the self-styled polar opposite of Hegel, with the ideas of one of Hegel's adherents on the same subject.[2] This, however, is not the real reason for our linking them together. We feel rather that it would be instructive to familiarize ourselves with an approach to the problem of death which arises from a life-consciousness that is not only very different from that expressed in Schopenhauer's philosophy, but even to all appearances radically opposed to it. If we may be allowed a catchword to clarify the matter—Schopenhauer's total and abysmal *pessimism* incessantly strove to demonstrate by empirical as well as speculative methods the transitoriness, worthlessness, and nothingness of existence. It also prompted him to begin his philosophical discussion on death with the statement that death is a matter of serious concern. Implied in this statement is the further notion, of course, that life too is something other than an amusing diversion. In Feuerbach we find a completely different attitude—an unconditional, frenetic affirmation of life and delight in this world. What form then does a philosophy of death take that is based on such assumptions?

Any view of death that really corresponds to its true nature presupposes, according to Feuerbach, the right understanding of the relationship between *life and death*. It is false to assume that life on this earth is but a prelude to an eternal life hereafter, entered through death as through a door, and appearing as the source of all values[3] which by implication are then denied to earthly existence.

All thoughts of a life beyond (which may well result from wishful thinking, Feuerbach conjectures) are fantastic, arbitrary aberrations. In connection with this we have to realize that our understanding of death's true nature, which can be gravely distorted by such

[2]Schopenhauer once said of Feuerbach, "He is a Hegelian. That is all there is to say."

[3]From his earliest writings to his last Schopenhauer waged a passionate, life-long war against this belief.

notions, needs renewal through fresh reinterpretations and new applications. "Only when man realizes again that death is a phenomenon that cuts off completely and forever the life of the individual, only then will he take courage to begin life anew and to make what is absolutely true and essential, what is truly infinite, the theme and the substance of his human activities." This statement of Feuerbach can be understood in all of its ramifications only when the positive meaning of death is made clear. One thing must be borne in mind: for Feuerbach there is no "life" after death unless it be in a completely different mode than the current doctrine of immortality assumes. Death therefore takes on a finality, which makes us confront with renewed seriousness the question about its nature and meaning.

Death, Feuerbach maintains, is grounded in a manifold principle: an "undetermined," infinite ground, which is God; a "determined," finite, physical, and intermediate ground which is represented by time, space, and life; and finally a "determined infinite" ground which is consciousness or spirit. In the following section we will attempt to prepare for the understanding of the profound, arresting ideas which Feuerbach expresses in this speculative, abstract form.

"Whatever is the ground and principle of your life," says Feuerbach, "is also the ground and principle of your death." The ultimate, metaphysical ground of my life and therefore of my death is God. As the infinite being he encompasses within himself the affirmation as well as the negation of the finite. We are able to comprehend him only by abstraction, by negating the finite. The de facto situation corresponds to this hypothesis—the infinite actually *is* the real, true, nullification of the finite. The mutability, changeableness, finiteness of things are grounded in the real *being* (*Sein*) of the infinite. Thus Feuerbach can say that every thing, even the most finite of all, would be infinite, unchangeable, and permanent, if he infinite did not exist. "Only in and through the infinite does the finite exist as finite; and in its finiteness death, its nullification, is contained. Thus we must realize that everything that exists has its limits and boundaries; nothingness alone is limitless. "There is only one weapon against encroaching nothingness, and this weapon is the boundary, the limit; this is the only mainstay of an object, the bulwark of its being." The limits or the *form* of a phenomenon are not its external shape, but rather its configuration, its mode of existence, the focal point of its nature which determines and contains everything in itself. Therefore, each thing is what it is, not by reason of its matter but because of its form or limits.

Applied to man (Feuerbach illustrates his thesis in detail for every stage of organic life) this means that with reference to the matter that compose them, all men are equal. "The element in which you exist and out of which you are fashioned is the will or freedom." But the manner of willing qualifies the universal element of will which Feuerbach sees as the essence of man.[4] The *one* will by being *your* individual will becomes a "specified, limited, distinct will." With it the character comes into being. Feuerbach expressly identifies the essence of man with his character—the measure and the precise mode of his willing.

We have seen that as the finite is bounded by the infinite so too life has limits beyond which it cannot pass. We should not even try to conceive of any other mode of existence for it. "Each distinct individual," as Feuerbach clearly states, "is nothing other than his body, nothing without his determined body." "The end of the body's earthly existence is the end of the self." All sublimation or abstraction which conceives of an existence beyond death in any type of watered-down or glorified form falls under the same criticism pronounced earlier on prevailing notions of immortality.

Feuerbach's views on anthropology further confirm such impressions, for here he asserts that the relation of the human soul to the body is the same as that of fire to the matter it consumes. Fire cannot exist without matter to act upon; so too the soul, which Feuerbach regards as "life in its purest form, sheer activity, and holy, transcendental fire," must die when the body, its spatial correlative and object, is consumed. For when the soul has thus consumed the body, nothing more remains upon which it can exercise its activity. The name we give to this final extinction of life is death.

The discussion would not be complete—and here we come to an explication of the third principle of death, that which is determined and infinite—if we did not consider the nature of man and the human soul in relation to the phenomenon of death. The human soul is not oriented and directed exclusively toward the body (except as the seat of sensation) but the soul can separate from the body to become an object through and in itself—as spirit. Spirit, according to Feuerbach, represents the extreme frontier of

[4]In this Feuerbach approaches remarkably close to the thought of Schopenhauer—at any rate he is at this time still under the influence of the Idealists.

everything physical. In being universal it differs from the determined singular personality, the *distinct* individuality. What the unity of will was for Schopenhauer becomes in Feuerbach's system of thought the unity of *spirit.* "As a conscious being, you are one with Consciousness; as a thinking being you are one with Thought in which all things are unified and united. You are annihilated spiritually; you are dissolved into the spirit." Thus we see the significance of such a statement as the following, "Reason is the real death of the individual." For it is in the intelligence or the reason that the physical reaches its limits. With this the third principle of death becomes evident; the true and deepest self actualizes itself, establishing itself in the face of all that is not proper to it. That is, it manifests itself as spirit. The external realization of this negation is death.

Feuerbach then develops these thoughts along other lines, exploring their epistemological, metaphysical, and ethical implications; and we are again reminded of Schopenhauer when he speaks of the separation of existence from essence—a distinction that persists through his whole life.

Man differs from all other living creatures by reason of his ability to become an object present to himself. In his awareness of universal being, of spirit, man becomes aware of himself. As a person, man is spirit in limitation. "As light is refracted in colors only by passing through definite physical matter, so too is consciousness refracted by the encounter with the object, the individuals, and is changed into the separate colors of individual persons." The essence of the universal spirit, which is identical in all persons, is at the same time the abstract principle of the individual personality.

In epistemological terms this means that in the "I," the thing that knows (the subject), and the thing that is known (the object) must be distinguished.

> Because you are able to distinguish yourself from your being, because you can objectify yourself (place yourself outside yourself), you will also die; for the inner activity of objectification, the interior capacity for distinguishing and dividing, must also exist as an object in nature.

Death is nothing more than "the separation of your existence as object to yourself from your existence as subject knowing itself." "Anything that exists only as object is dead." The power to distinguish presupposes freedom; it is an expression of freedom. Where there is no spirit, no freedom, no inner nature, there is also, according to Feuerbach, no death. "You will die because you are a free, conscious, thinking being." Consciousness, the power to separate, to distinguish, is the condition for death—the phenomenon that renders death possible. Death is possible for plants and animals only because "spirit is already breaking forth in them, freedom is already taking root in them." A stone is not in itself the principle of its own activity; a plant, however, Feuerbach says, is the principle identical with its changes. Inasmuch as the changes are not merely external, but rather the inner life-impulse of a phenomenon representing the totality of its living being, it follows that only that which is itself the principle of its own change can have a *history*. Such a creature that has a history is man. The more a spirit of independence takes the place of dependence on others, parents for example, the more he *becomes* man. "To come into existence means to individualize oneself." Not until the ground of his being is *within himself*, does his real life (and we might add, the possibility of death) begin.

Another way of saying the same thing is that the more man becomes spirit, the more freedom he has. Thus in this sense it is valid to say that thinking represents the outermost limits of the life of the being that thinks. Insofar as the most profound thought (that concerned with the infinite being) represents the perfection of thinking, Feuerbach, true to Hegel, considers as the highest life only that which is found in religion, science, and art. *This* is the life which surpasses all material, transitory existence, which is, as we shall see, the only form of "life" above death.

Feuerbach's development of his ideas on death then takes a metaphysical turn. It has already been said that it is the infinite alone which delimits the finite. Contained within this finiteness is its nullification—death. Therefore, a being in which nothing of the infinite dwells, cannot die. Death means nothing more, according to Feuerbach, than that the burden of infinity breaks the vessel of finite being which contains it. A modern poet, who was thoroughly familiar with the thought of death, expressed a similar idea in the lines,

> Be, at the same time, know the terms of negation
> the infinite basis of your fervent vibration,
> that you may completely complete it this one time.
> (Rilke, *Sonnets to Orpheus*, II, 13.)

Insofar as God is not only the God who affirms but also the God who negates the existence of the individual creature, he is both the principle of life for this being, and the principle of his death. We must seek the limits of personal existence in him. This is not intelligible if besides thinking of God as nature, personality and spirit, one does not also comprehend him as that which he (according to Feuerbach's seemingly paradoxical thesis) can only be as suprapersonal spirit, that is, as love.

Feuerbach maintains that love, which witnesses to the fact that our being must have others to whom it can relate, is only the tangible sign of a bond deeper than itself, of a *true unity*. One can love only insofar as he is more than person, that is, by reason of his essence, through which he is one with the other. Here we hear echoes of the monotheism of Spinoza, Schelling, Schleiermacher, and also of the young Hegel. "Just as the person who has experienced love has experienced everything, so too he who has known love, has knowledge of everything—Know love and you know God and his consequence, death." Love means overcoming existence-for-oneself in the surrender to the being of the other "Man loves, he *must* love." And the truth and value of the love is to be measured by the magnitude of the thing loved. "The more you surrender of yourself, the greater your love," Feuerbach teaches, and again, "The moral, the specifically human nature of man consists in his giving up his merely natural autonomous being, in laying a foundation for his existence—in existing through another, in finding the ground of one's own being in the being of another." The *moral* man will be disposed to surrender his being only for the sake of a higher value, never for the sake of a lower. His innermost self, says Feuerbach, will be his other self—the infinite object in which he loses himself.

Here at the deepest point the identity between self-surrender, love, God, and death becomes clear. "The will which, in the realm of morality, thought, and religion, impels you to surrender yourself, the will which even in passion unites a man with others—it is that same will which drives death out of nature."

> With the same will, and only in the will, with which you will truth and love, you also induce death; it is one and the same will which causes death in nature, the death of the self, virtue, love, and thought.

We are moving here in the confines of metaphysics and ethics.

Feuerbach turns the problem in an ethical direction when he culminates this train of thought with the theory of freedom mentioned above. The self-seeking egotistic will of man takes leave of itself in the universal spirit-will. Feuerbach recognizes in this a kind of pre-established harmony in that the "counterpole of spirit" (*das Andere des Geistes*), that is, nature, enters into such an interior and intimate union with the true will of man that any negation within will be accompanied by a like negation in external nature. "The free act of man," Feuerbach maintains, "must exist simultaneously in nature as necessity; the spiritual dissolution of the self must be paralleled by a simultaneous natural, corporeal end." Thus death, as a free act, becomes the ultimate proof of *love*. "Love alone can solve the riddle of immortality." Love, by virtue of the true knowledge it gives of oneself and others, causes us to realize the nothingness of being-for-oneself and the identity between the real "I" and the beloved object. Because of love the whole of life is henceforth constituted, in a negative way, in the denial of the false self and, in a positive way, in the contemplation of the beloved. And finally the finiteness acknowledged through love, the finiteness signifying the nothingness of the naked self emerges—to stand alone in death. "For death is the revelation of your lonely and forsaken being-for-yourself." "Only once will you exist as pure ego, only once will you exist exclusively unto yourself. This moment is the moment that nullifies existence—the moment of death." Wherever this is recognized, death loses its terrors. "The thinking person, the man of deeper insight, overcomes death; for he recognizes death for what it is, a process bound up with moral freedom. He sees himself in death; he acknowledges in it his own will, the act of his own love and freedom." The image of death as the grim reaper no longer finds any place in his thought.

Penetrating more deeply into this subject, Feuerbach then shows that death does not begin with natural dissolution, but rather culminates and ends there. In the natural death-process, an "exhaling," a breathing-forth of the interior hidden death takes place. In external, physical death, Feuerbach continues, the death that is immured within is disengaged, unfettered, and set free. Similar notions can be found in Rilke's *Malte Laurids Brigge*. In the works of this poet death does not come to man from the outside; it disengages itself rather from his own inner being, where it has long been dwelling and lying in wait. Death does not appear alone, without a mediator; it is, according to Feuerbach, the "mediated negation." The mediator of death is life itself, for every stage in life is at the same time the death of an earlier stage. "Death does not break in upon us violently or unexpectedly; it is ushered in and introduced after the stage has been set." This profound interpretation is intended to replace the crude and primitive portrayal of death as the man with the scythe.

> Does death emerge from the charnel-house? Does it rise up out of the earth or break in like a thief in the night? Is death perhaps a skeleton or a human figure with its own existence? Absolutely not. It is but the external appearance of the act of inner dissolution and separation; it is the verification of your love, the public proclamation of a truth which your whole life has witnessed to in secret—that outside of the beloved object or without it, you are nothing.

In the face of death's terrors Schopenhauer, who like Feuerbach looked upon death as the absolute end of the individual, took comfort in the thought of the indestructible continuity of the metaphysical part of man's being. The will endures, even if the intellect dies. Ludwig Feuerbach agrees that death means separation, the severence of the immortal from the transitory. But what does he consider the permanent, imperishable, element to be?

Inasmuch as the existence of man has as its essential purpose the deepening of his finite personality into a true, more profound spiritual self—in this sense an uninterrupted process of anamnesis and spiritualization—we found it intimately involved and implicated in the existence of others. As it grew and developed we saw it liberate itself from these others and then surrender itself anew in love and the fulfillment of its destiny.

> Just as when you lay in the womb of your mother, you were bodily developed and enclosed by her, so too your very self lies in the maternal womb of the consciousness of others by which you were embraced and comprehended before you comprehended yourself. Your knowledge of yourself in this life always remains closely interwoven with the knowledge others have of you.

Again Feuerbach touches on Schopenhauer, who sees a similar correspondence between pre- and post-existence. We die, but others still remain. "Your essence survives, humanity survives, unaffected and undiminished by your death." "Man is eternal, spirit is eternal, consciousness is imperishable and unending." Thus for Feuerbach death is nothing other than the process through which our consciousness which is, as it were, a charge entrusted to us during life, is once more given back to others. "Just as at your beginning you existed only in the consciousness of others, so too at the end you will exist only in their consciousness." "You yourself and all that is in you will perish; but by perishing you become an object of memory, of spirit." Isn't it true that even in life, where the past is concerned, a man exists for the most part only as a person *remembered*? So one day he will fully become "ideal being," a pure object of the intelligence, a something "communicable and communicated"—a name. As long as something exists *realiter*, it remains an object of blind passion; only when it exists in the past can it become an object of knowledge.

Since all philosophical theories about death contain implicit attitudes toward the problem of time,[5] Feuerbach addresses himself also to this phenomenon. "Acheron," he writes, "is really the stream of time which carries the living over into the shadow-realm of spirit. Time alone constitutes the bridge spanning existence and essence; time alone brings the world to consciousness and reason."

Feuerbach sees consciousness as the sun of humanity in which we find the great secret of unity.[6] "As the ear of corn ripens in the sun, so too do you mature and ripen into the fullness of a person, warmed by the sunlight of the consciousness of mankind, eternally perfect yet ever incomplete, eternally developing, creating within itself. In death you sink back into eternal sleep, into the unconscious peace of nothingness, exhausted by the heat from the sun of consciousness, which drains and consumes the individual."

Life, speaking metaphysically and ethically, is continual communication. It comes to an end when its purpose is fulfilled. You go on living only as long as you have something to communicate. When you have communicated all you have, if nothing more is left than the last dry husk of your personality, then you surrender yourself. This act of surrender is death. Death is the last word that

[5]In this connection see Heidegger, *Being and Time*, which is discussed in the last section of this essay.

[6]In spite of his enthusiastic bias toward life, Feuerbach is still enough of an idealist not to play life off against spirit. He takes spirit, rather, to be the meaning of life.

you speak, the word in which you utter yourself completely. By the "word" of death you breathe your being into others. It is the last act of communication.

Like Schopenhauer, Feuerbach strives continually to make us see that death terminates our empirical existence with absolute finality. In the face of this, any attempt to cling to this existence with false ideas of immortality (the afterlife conceived as a mere prolongation of this existence, for example) has met with failure. Feuerbach emphatically underscores the No that death speaks over the person. Death, he stresses, *is* an evil for which there is no curative herb growing—not even, as he bitingly adds, on the dung-heap of theology. Death, truly the "purest form of desolation," is "life's most horrible void."

But Feuerbach's understanding of individuality differs from that of Schopenhauer for whom individuation means error, failure, and sin. Feuerbach is very much aware of the irretrievable element which, in the death of any man, is gone forever. "It is true that new beings constantly take over the places of those who have died. But this being that now is and that one day will be no longer, this unique being, will never return again; it is lost to us eternally. The place occupied by this being will remain forever empty. This being, therefore, is unique, something that happens only once. A man is precisely this kind of certain, definite individual, who exists only now, only this once."[7]

Individuality is not as strongly accented in Feuerbach's thought, however, as it will be in the death-philosophy of the thinker to be considered next. Feuerbach—at least in that phase of his development that is of interest here—is, like Schopenhauer, too much the metaphysician to attach the importance that Simmel does to the finite, phenomenal aspect of things.

For Feuerbach, the disciple of Hegel, life in its finiteness is mediated by spirit, just as for Schopenhauer, it is mediated by will. But contrary to Schopenhauer, and even in direct opposition to him, Feuerbach does not allow the fleeting quality, the brevity of existence and therefore of the individual being to detract from its worth. Length, he maintains, is not the determining factor; the content of life and the manner in which it is actualized—that is what de-

[7]Such a passage could also have been written by Schopenhauer, but with him it would have had quite a different ring.

termines and decides. Life triumphs over death. It is the real Feuerbach who speaks in the rapturous hymn to life which terminates his reflections on death:

> Every entity, the substance of every being, is both non-temporal and supratemporal; every limit in time is a boundary, a negation of time itself; every moment of fulfillment is eternity, infinity. Eternity is nothing other than the fulfillment and final destiny of time, the dynamic, efficacious negation of time in time. Eternity is strength, energy, victory, act. It is act, however, only when in time it stands above time, only when in time it negates or denies time.
>
> Every moment of life is existence fulfilled, infinitely significant in its own right, brought forth by itself, resting in itself, an unqualified affirmation of itself. Every moment is a draught which drains the cup of infinity to the very dregs, which then like the magic cup of Oberon refills itself out of its own plenitude.
>
> Fools say that life is but empty sound, that it is consumed like smoke, that it vanishes like the wind. No, life is music, every moment a melody or a soulful, fully-rounded tone. Musical tones too pass away, but each tone, as tone, has significance. Before this innermost meaning and soul of the tone, evanescence disappears as something vain and unimportant.

A half-century after Feuerbach and under the influence of Nietzsche in particular the new Life-Philosophy takes up the thread of the argument again, basing it however on totally different assumptions. In the following section we will consider one of the turn-of-the-century thinkers whose thought is closely related to the Life-Philosophy tradition.

SIMMEL

> It is astonishing how few of the pains of men have passed into their philosophy. (Simmel, *Fragments and Essays*, p. 17.)

Not long after the war, Heinrich Rickert, one of the leading transcendentalist thinkers in Germany, attempted in a controversial essay to characterize "Life Philosophy," and in the list of important thinkers who propound similar views of this philosophy, he included Georg Simmel. In no other adherent of the tradition do we encounter such a serious, vital attempt to understand and to come to terms with the problem of death. Simmel considers as inappropriate any conception of death which sees it as an overpowering force threatening life from the outside, or as a separate entity, either friendly or inimical, which we must one day confront, or as a necessity, which though actual is not intrinsically related to life. He emphatically dismisses such images of death as the final snipping of the thread of Fate or as a skeleton—images which may be intelligible within the framework of an earlier tradition, but which have been superseded by deeper insights into the relationship and interconnection of life and death. As long as death is thought of as a force above life and independent of life,[8] it will preserve its gruesome and dreadful character; and it will consequently evoke such responses as heroic rebellion, lyrical submission, or indifference.

Primitive peoples, Simmel maintains, frequently show no concern at all about death; for them it is just a fact of existence. As in the non-human organic world, death is merely a phenomenon peculiar to the genus. "Man" dies, it is true, but the individual man does not die. "Wherever individuals are not distinct, the mortality of the individual is swallowed up in the immortality of the species." Here we encounter a crucial point in Simmel's thought. The increasing degree of individualization (Simmel sometimes uses the uncommon expression "*Individualistik*" for this notion), which we see evolving in the history of mankind, means "according to our universal scheme of values" "progress and a higher level of development." Simmel is furthermore fully convinced that the capacity for death is in direct proportion to the extent to which life is individualized. Since we can distinguish between *Sterbenkönnen*, that is, the "ability to do the act of dying" and *Getötetwerden*, the passive acceptance of death as a "being-killed," figuratively speaking, then we can use the expression *sterben*, "to die" only to refer to the end of a highly individualized phenomenon. The capacity for dying, as Simmel remarks in an allusion to Goethe's idea of immortality, is the "seal of higher existence." Since the onset of the modern period, individuality has been valued as a great and irreplaceable good—a development that has resulted in a new and deeper conception of death.

As biological research on the structure of organisms shows, the

[8]For this reason death is often symbolized as a human figure, external to its victim.

chance of recurrence diminishes as we move from the simple structures of the lower organisms to those of greater complexity. Simmel says, "It was not until the condensation of cells into a unity that produced an individual Gestalt or form that death came to be. He develops this idea further by proving that the *truly* individual being, by reason of his personal a priori, compenetrates to a far greater degree than does the less highly individualized being, the cosmic matter common to all life. Thus this higher individual would seem to be more a "*causa sui* than an *effectus mundi*." Hence infinitely more is lost at the death of such a one than at the death of an ordinary creature. The conjunction of matter and form—categories which play a crucial role in Simmel's thought—takes on a unique character. The closer the union between them, the more devastating its operations. "Metaphorically speaking, a form is said to be individual, when after selecting a single, unique piece of matter it fashions together with it a reality. Once this reality is destroyed, the form or Gestaltung is incapable of further realization." That is why death is so much more radical, the more highly individualized a being is. Only the individuality truly dies.

Precisely here, in the case of a highly individualized life, we feel the strong pull of the tension between life and death. Our awareness of the irretrievable nature, the uniqueness of this very life which we see threatened with annihilation heightens the tension. Now the relation of man to death is determined, as Simmel shows, by the fusion of knowing and not-knowing—knowing that the arrival of death is inevitable, but not knowing the time of its coming. This standing-on-the-boundaries regarding the time of death coupled with the knowledge that death is certain to come[9] characterizes our human situation.

To the extent that we take the two dimensions (knowing and not-knowing) into account in our behavior, we allow our life to be determined and formed by its last end. We plan nothing which would not be consonant with the length of human life, but we get along, as we can and must, without knowing the exact "hour."

Reflection however gains from this situation a critical insight—the recognition of the immanence of death in life, of death as the fashioner of life. Simmel's realization of this truth does not become the basis for demonstrating the questionable nature of existence

[9]Feuerbach proposed a similar idea.

as in Schopenhauer; nor does it become the stimulus, as with Feuerbach, of a Dionysian affirmation of life. Simmel is not much concerned about interpreting and evaluating the matter or content of life; he seeks rather to reveal the formal metaphysical dimension of the problem, to disclose the structural laws operating in all life. From this perception of structure follows a corresponding attitude toward death.

Simmel's thesis that death is a formative agent of life is borne out empirically in the biological adaptation of all living beings. In such a process existence appears as a union of two moments—the conquest of life and the flight from death. This dual tendency points clearly to the formative character of the end. Simmel compares us to men on a ship, who are walking in a direction opposite to that in which the ship itself is going. "While they walk south, the deck on which they walk and they with it are borne to the north." To realize that from the outset death is intrinsically conjoined with life and that as a "*charakter indelebilis*" is one of the a priori determinants of life—that is our task. It is not only at the hour of death that death sets a limit for life; but in every moment of life, whether we are waxing or waning, on the sunny heights of life or in the shadows of its low places we are such as will one day die. Death as a "formal" element colors all of life's contents; the form and quality of each living moment would be different if there were no death. Even inchoate budding life already exists as part of a total framework which is oriented toward death.

One is reminded here of a line from Jean Paul, "The moment we begin to live, Fate launches the arrow of death from eternity's heights—it goes on flying as long as we continue to breathe. And when it finally strikes us, we cease to be." Simmel, moreover, agrees with Feuerbach that it is as false to imagine that we die only at the moment of our actual death as it is to think that we are born only at the moment of our birth. The fact is that we are being continually reborn, so to speak, into something new. Of course we do get the impression when we watch some men die, that their death and the form it takes seems arbitrary or accidental. These are the men whose lives reveal no inner form in any deep sense, so that it seems irrelevant whether their lives are of longer or shorter duration. As Simmel remarked, "They do not have within themselves the capacity to 'do' the act of death."

One of Simmel's favorite ideas, which he developed in an admittedly Hegelian passage, is that life by its very nature demands death (antitheses) as the "other" toward which the entity develops and without which it would not have its specific meaning and form. These polarities, however, merge in a synthesis, that is, in something higher and beyond life and death, which cannot be touched by this opposition. For his metaphysics of life, which culminates with the idea that life's transcendence is really immanent, Simmel depends on Schopenhauer's teaching on the will to life. Here the one aspect, the inexhaustible continuity of life, never depleting itself in any one pattern or form, is clearly recognized. Simmel of course would supplement the notion that life as an "absolute concept" is always *Mehr-Leben* (more-life) with the further notion that it is also *Mehr-als-Leben* (more-than-life). In the sphere of epistemology, experience shows that consciousness existing as self-consciousness means that the I-as-knowing becomes the object, the I-as-known.[10] In the ethical sphere, the individual will's ability to speak as something greater than itself, that is, as universal will, the capacity of the archetypal phenomenon of life to raise itself above itself, to become the *Sich-uber-sich-selbst-Erheben*, shows that this "self-intensification and self-abandonment" is precisely the mode of its unity, of its "abiding within itself." Even the individual personality in which life assumes tangible form and in which it reaches its zenith can never be its final Gestalt; in it and through it life presses on eternally. According to Simmel, that *Mehr* ("something more") does not belong *per accidens* to life which, as far as its quantity goes, is constant. Life, rather, by definition is "movement, which in every stage and at every moment draws being into itself in order to transform it into itself." "Never leaving its own center, it reaches out toward the absolute, as it moves in this direction it becomes "more-life." But it also extends itself into the reaches of nothingness; and just as it exists as sustaining and increasing life in *one* act, so too it exists as sustaining and declining life in *one* act, *as* act."[11] The phenomenon of death does not disprove the fact that life points to something beyond itself. Simmel sees death as a tangible demonstration of this fact.

[10]Simmel's ideas here correspond to those of Feuerbach, though no direct connection between them has been evinced.

[11]Those familiar with the philosophy of Heidegger will be reminded here of his thought.

Life, as we have seen, is not only *Mehr-Leben*, but also *Mehr-als-Leben*, that is, creative life. Simmel believes that the characteristic mark of life "on the level of spirit" is the generation of autonomous, meaningful content—a process analogous to the begetting of new beings on the physiological level, who are distinct and independent of their creator. Here he takes exception to Schopenhauer's subjectivistic notion of a "created" world expressed in the formula that the world is my idea, created by me. Simmel wants us to recognize the "otherness" (*Anders-Sein*) of these creative movements of life as counter-poles of life itself. He sees precisely in this "something more," which life creates and then assimilates again, the formula and condition of the life that is lived.

Simmel's penetrating analysis of the "shift to idea" cannot be treated here, other than to say it is an attempt to throw light on the phenomenon that the forms or functions which life generates for itself out of its own inner dynamic eventually become autonomous, existing in their own right so that life in turn serves them. But we would like to pursue the thought that the life-death antithesis is spanned by a higher unity—life in the absolute sense which, as Simmel says, both underlies and transcends the fixing of limits and conditions by life and death. With this we can perceive the direction to be taken to find the answer to the question: which life ends with death, which life continues?

In both Schopenhauer and Feuerbach we found a distinction in the "I" which made it possible to distinguish the inner enduring core of the self from its phenomenological changing aspects. Simmel refers to the analogous continuity of the "I" which exists independently of what the consciousness contains, and which is confirmed or extended with every new experience. We become aware of such a continuity when we find values persisting independent of life, and when as a consequence we can distinguish mentally between life and its phenomenal content. Our awareness is further heightened by the experience of death.

A crucial question for the understanding of Simmel's approach to the problem of death refers to the mode of existence of this "I," which neither exists in reality nor is identical with an unreal idea, a merely prescribed value. It is a question here of the essence and the value, the rhythm [of change] and the real intrinsic meaning, all of which are proper to our existence as "this particular piece of world." It pertains to "what we actually are from the very outset and to what we have not yet but can become."

During our lifetime we go on trying to separate our "I" more and more fully from the contingencies to which it seems bound. But in life we only succeed in approaching this ideal. These abstract notions of the philosopher are paralleled once again by the imagery of the poet:

> I live my life in circles that grow wide
> And endlessly unroll;
> I may not reach the last, but on I glide
> Strong pinioned toward my goal.
> (Rilke, *Book of Hours.*)

For Simmel who, like Feuerbach, wished to exclude from the discussion all substantive ideas, this alone can be the meaning of immortality—that the "I" exists, not by reason of anything extrinsic to it, but only by reason of its intrinsic self. Death then would be the borderland where all particular content falls away.

Simmel calls attention to the two kinds of ideas on reincarnation which are found among primitive peoples. These views represent polar extremes between which we can locate a more subtle conception of an enduring "I." On the one hand we find the belief that the person is fully incarnate at the moment of birth and that he grows in knowledge by a process of anamnesis, that is, by remembering or recognizing ideas which have always been part of him; and on the other hand we have the Buddhist view that denies the existence of any personality to that aggregate of thinking and acting which it considers the "I" to be.

In contrast to this substance-oriented mode of thought, Simmel takes a dynamic approach to the problem. He sees the human soul moving from birth to death through epochs and phases which differ greatly from one another in content. Amidst the flux, however, something remains the same—a fundamental and primary relation between life as such and its multiplicity of experiences. This "a priori formal principle of action and suffering" constitutes the individuality, which is not to be identified with the substantive content inextricably bound up with life. From this ontological principle (which is not to be confused with the individual reality whose form it is) could be derived speculatively a lofty theory of metempsychosis, namely, that this form or principle then passes over into other beings totally different in content from those it has previously informed. One could then conceive of a chain of such highly individualized existences characterized by the same substantial form and succeeding one another in time, which would really be one and the same being. It is of no little interest that Simmel, like the two earlier thinkers mentioned, feels that the theory of post-existence must be paralleled by a corresponding theory of pre-existence. We might believe then, according to him, that a man could have acted differently, that he could have become something else, without losing his identity. As in the thought of Schopenhauer and Feuerbach, the idea of individuality is closely linked to the idea of freedom. The transcendental "I" shines through the empirical "I." The empirical "I" passes away, but the transcendental "I" abides.

We cannot resist including a few illustrations from Simmel's aesthetic essays which clarify his theories on death. Two powerful expressions of creative genius, Rembrandt's portraits and Shakespeare's dramas, serve to illustrate a particularly crucial point in Simmel's thought, namely, the close connection between individuality and death. The great masterpieces of *classical* art, Simmel says, were not at all concerned about portraying the individuality of the subject; they sought rather to reveal the inner laws governing the external form that embodies the idea—in short, the type. In contrast to the classical ideal, Rembrandt captures life in its fullness, in all of its individualization. According to the *principle of immanence* death is an integral part of life's totality. Simmel points out the intrinsic relation between the conception of death and the artistic conception of man in general when he says, "In many Italian portraits one gets the impression that death will overtake these men in the form of a dagger thrust; with Rembrandt's figures one senses that death will flow into life as a further unfolding and developing of life's integral wholeness." Contrasting the portraiture of Rembrandt with that of Rubens he notes that behind the elemental exuberant life in Rubens' paintings one senses an implicit abstraction—that this is life without death. Rembrandt, on the other hand, imbues his figures with a life which at the height of its dynamism also encompasses death. "The sense of death's presence in the greatest of Rembrandt's portraits corresponds to the measure to which they have as their object the absolute individuality of the person."

It is the same with Shakespeare's heroes. Here too death seems to dwell within the lives and actions of the main characters. Its actual occurrence has merely symbolic value; for it is of no real consequence whether these persons meet death through poison or the dagger. Their dying is tragic in the true sense because it arises out of the very law and meaning of their lives; death indeed vanquishes the will-to-life, but at the same time it fulfills life's innermost commitment. This verifies once more the truth found in Rembrandt's portraits with their mysterious glimmering of death out of the shadows, namely, that a profound connection exists between life, individuality, and death.

In summary, then, we see that in Schopenhauer's metaphysic of will, death is viewed as a universal fate, not as a free act and not in reference to the individual being that dies. It is rendered powerless by the indication of its metaphysical significance. Feuerbach's metaphysic of spirit views death as the individual's free act of love in which he witnesses to his true self. Death for him has a universal dimension in that it serves as the harbinger of the liberation of man's true essence; it has further a particular individual dimension inasmuch as every man dies in his own unique way. Simmel emphasizes above all the immanent character of death and its profound connection with the individuality of the person. Unlike his predecessors, Simmel does not accent so completely existence after death or in death, that is, the enduring will or spirit, whose liberation for Schopenhauer and Feuerbach appears to be the ethical function of death.

By defining death in an oblique and formal way as the existence of an essential principle which endures through the succession of changing individual beings, Simmel portrays death not so much as the transition from the non-real to the real, but as the terminus and the goal of entities whose unique, irreplaceable value is in no way lessened by a comparison with the primary metaphysical reality, the stream of life.

HEIDEGGER

> Before I pass over to universal history—
> of which I must always say: "God knows
> whether it is any concern of yours"—it

> seems to me that I had better think about this, lest existence mock me, because I had become so pompously learned that I had forgotten to understand what will some day happen to me as to every human being . . .
>
> (Kierkegaard, *Concluding Unscientific Postscript*, p. 243.)

It is not difficult to discover a connecting link between Simmel's thought and that of Heidegger. In a critical passage on Being-towards-death which occurs in his main work, *Being and Time*, Martin Heidegger refers explicitly to Simmel's philosophy of death. He takes issue with Simmel for failing to differentiate clearly between the biological-ontical and the existential-ontological aspects of the problem. Though we are aware of the great difficulty involved, we will nevertheless attempt in the following section to isolate a single point of crucial importance from the rigidly delimited, close-knit texture of the Heideggerian pattern of thought, namely, the problem of death. Heidegger's propensity for coining his own words often makes it difficult to paraphrase their meaning with any great precision—a fact that is reason enough for letting Heidegger speak for himself whenever possible. Neither a satisfactory outline of his philosophical system nor an analysis of the influences which helped shape it can be given here. In the following discussion we will try to indicate the field of vision against which we will then delineate Heidegger's position on the phenomenon of death.

Heidegger inquires first about the way in which death presents itself to us. Our knowledge of death comes primarily from our experiencing the death of others. More precisely, we do not in any genuine sense experience death, but we are merely present at it. In this given condition our knowledge about death, as objective knowledge, involves no responsibility on our part; it belongs in Heidegger's terminology to the sphere of the neuter *das Man*, or the "they."[12] This is the sphere in which the self, the form which *Dasein* sometimes takes, is present not as an authentic personal self but as an inauthentic being with others. Death here is spoken of in an inauthentic sense—using expressions such as "a case of

[12]*Das Man* refers to the German impersonal pronoun denoting an indefinite subject of action. *Das Man* could be rendered in English as "people" or "the public," but these terms fail to convey the sheer impersonality of the pronoun.

death" (*ein Todesfall*), or "Someone or other dies" (*Man stirbt*). In this way one lulls one's fears about dying with the thought that after all one who fortunately is still living is not the "someone" who dies in the expression *Man stirbt*. One is reminded here of similar expressions for the same phenomenon used by Kierkegaard, whose major philosophical work demands growth toward subjectivity. Heidegger drastically contrasts the physiognomy of death in the depersonalized sphere of the general, the public, with its mien in the sphere of concrete, individual being.[13] Inasmuch as one suppresses one's "courage unto death," hiding from himself his most authentic "Being towards death," one betrays the fact that he is not relating here to his *own* death, but is rather taking refuge from it through flight. But even the preoccupation with death, the brooding and pondering over it, will give no access to what is essentially "unknowable."[14] There is no such thing as substituting for another in death. "No one can deliver the other from his own death." "We are all called to die," Luther said, "and no man can die for the other."

The act of dying reveals that death is constituted, as Heidegger like Kierkegaard before him puts it, by *Jemeinigkeit* (that is, the fact that it is my *own* death and no one else's that I must die) and *Existenz* (that is, the unique, personal, conscious being of man as possibility). Heidegger expressly distinguishes between the terms *verenden*, used to express the perishing of anything alive, for example, an animal; *ableben* (to live out one's life) meaning to suffer death passively without assuming any existential relationship to it; and *sterben*, in which one's being *is* truly "towards death." Thus it will not be by observing others die that one comes to understand what death is, but only by one's own individual openness toward it. Like Simmel, Heidegger speaks of the fusion of certainty and uncertainty in man's attitude toward death—certainty regarding death's future imminence and uncertainty regarding the time of its coming. A crucial element in the uncertainty, moreover, is the fact that this "when" can be any moment at all.

All *Dasein*, insofar as it is "Being in the world," is inconclusive

[13]*Existieren* is a term used by Heidegger to express man's peculiar way of "being there"—individual, unique, personal, in contrast to the existence of a stone, for example.

[14]*Unerfahrbar*, means incapable of being known without personal experience.

and implies something still to be settled. To experience it as an "existing whole" is impossible, for it would then no longer be "Being in the world." As long as it is, it displays a lack of totality, a non-wholeness; it still has to become something which it not yet is.

The "ending" in which *Dasein* (as long as it is "there") terminates does not have the sense of stopping, as the rain stops; nor does it mean a disappearing, as bread disappears when it has been used up. The "end" of *Dasein* implied in the word "death" is rather a "Being towards the end of this entity." This means that *Dasein*, which is already "not yet," stands from the very outset in a relation to death.

Death is something impending, something that stands before us. But death is unique; it is not impending in the same way as other phenomena, for example, a trip, the arrival of someone, or a storm. Death is distinctive in that it is a "possibility of being" which *Dasein* itself has to assume. It is, Heidegger continues, the "possibility which is one's own, which is non-relational, and which is not to be gone beyond."[15] In death there is no representing one another, no communicating, no experiencing in advance. "Being towards death" is not concerned primarily with knowledge, but with an inner state of mind. Objectively, such a state of mind is anxiety. Neither for Heidegger, nor for Kierkegaard in whose thought it is a key concept, does anxiety mean fear; nor does it refer to any arbitrary mood of weakness. It is used rather to designate *Dasein's* basic state of mind, that is, *Dasein's* consciousness that it exists as being thrown towards its end.

Anxiety has a distinctive *telos*. It reveals to man his "Being towards his own potentiality for Being." That is, it shows his freedom to be free to choose and to comprehend himself. Anxiety is a basic state of mind of *Dasein*, because above and beyond that which is disclosed in other possibilities of *Dasein*, something discloses itself here in a special way in that here the individual sees himself lead to himself. "This individualization brings *Dasein* back from fallenness—from Being fallen in the world—and reveals to it that authenticity and inauthenticity are possibilities of existence."

[15]*Being and Time*, tr. John Macquarrie and Edward Robinson, New York, 1962, p. 294. Heidegger is again indebted to Kierkegaard here, whose ideas he then develops further.

Heidegger's philosophy sees the essential character of "Being in the world" as care. Just as anxiety is not to be confused with fear, so too the concept of *cura*, which Heidegger impressively traces in the history of ideas, is to be distinguished from all practical worry. Care is an objective character of *Dasein*. In the phenomenological language of Heidegger, to say that *Dasein* is care means to say it is "Ahead of itself," as "Being alongside." Thus *Dasein*, insofar as it is Being towards one's own potentiality for Being, is said to be present at hand, yet already always "beyond itself" and already always "ahead of itself." As "Being in the world," it essentially includes one's fallenness in the world and also one's "Being alongside." It means "concern" and "solicitude."

Heidegger speaks of "existence," "facticity" and "fallenness" as the three constitutive elements of this Being. But, as we have seen, "Being ahead of itself," that is, the relation in which Being becomes open to its own potentiality, includes the possibility of being free for authentic existential possibilities.[16] To a great extent *Dasein* comports itself "unwillingly" towards these possibilities, that is, it would let them, in the fallenness in the world, pass. It is inauthentic and remains self in the sense of the "they self" (*Manselbst*). But *Dasein* need not shift itself permanently to the inauthentic way of being. Inasmuch as the existential structure called projection[17] belongs to the constitutive state of Being, it can comport itself also in a positive way: it can become essential in its authentic existence. In Heidegger's formulation, "*Dasein* discloses itself to itself in its ownmost and as its ownmost potentiality for Being."

Dasein, which has lost itself in the public "they" (*das Man*) is called back to its authentic self by the voice of conscience as the "summons to its own guiltiness." In Heidegger's language, the term "Being-guilty" refers to the "lagging behind its distinctive goal of being,"[18] or better, its "notness" which through "projection" is already proper to it as such. Therefore the call of conscience can be described as a "calling back in which conscience calls forth."[19] "It calls *Dasein* forth into the possibility of taking over, in existing, even that thrown entity, which it is; it calls *Dasein* back to its

[16] *Being and Time*, p. 237.
[17] *Ibid.*, p. 185.
[18] *Ibid.*, p. 330.
[19] *Ibid.*, p. 333.

thrownness so as to understand this thrownness as the null basis which it has to take up into existence."

What this turn of phrase—so reminiscent of Schelling and Kierkegaard—is trying to express is that conscience-anxiety is to be considered as a proof that *Dasein* in understanding the summons of conscience is brought before the uncanniness of its self. This self-projection upon one's own guiltiness Heidegger calls resoluteness. It is openness toward one's own potentiality of Being. For this reason resoluteness does not isolate *Dasein* from its world, but "pushes" it into concerned and solicitous Being—into Being for Others and with Others. Thus *Dasein*, when it is resolute, can become the conscience of others. *Dasein* is indeed delivered over, thrown, to its own potentiality for Being its Self as its authentic destiny; but it is also thrown out upon a world and exists factically with others.

We have seen that Heidegger's philosophy conceives of *Dasein* as care. Inasmuch as it is placed or "thrown" into the world, *Dasein* —which is "between the two apparent ends, birth and death"—is at any given time delivered over to death. It is "Being towards death." That is, the flight from death that characterizes the life of the "they" (*das Man*) is only an inauthentic "Being towards death." The authentic "Being towards death" cannot consist, as said before, in thinking about one's death. Such a way of disposing of death would be detrimental to its potentiality. What is demanded rather is anticipation or "running ahead" into this uttermost possibility. It is, so to speak, being at home with it, which corresponds to resoluteness. Thus the uttermost potentiality for Being is taken upon itself by *Dasein*.

Resoluteness appears as understanding the end of Being, as "running ahead into death." Heidegger, in characterizing resoluteness further, says, "It conceals within itself the authentic Being towards death as the possible existential modality of its own authenticity." Resoluteness is not a way of escape, Heidegger says, taken in order to overcome death; it is, on the contrary, the understanding which, hearing the call of conscience, frees for death the possibility of acquiring power over *Dasein's* existence.[20] Such a position need not lead one to flee from the world into seclusion, but rather will bring the *Dasein* of man "without illusion into the resoluteness of taking

[20] *Ibid.*, p. 357.

action." The author of *Being and Time* formulates his ideas in another way: the sober anxiety which we feel in the face of the possibility mentioned above is coupled with an unshakable joy.

We have seen that the potentiality of the end is non-relational[21] insofar as it *lays claim* to individual *Dasein* as individual; no togetherness is possible here. It is furthermore not to be gone beyond, that is, it is the last among all possibilities which are determined by the end, and thus is to be understood as finite, and in the face of it all static fixation in existence already attained collapses. It is certain, but indefinite. Inasmuch as the state of mind which constantly holds itself open to this threat has made itself known as anxiety, "Being towards death" is essentially anxiety. In this state of mind, according to Heidegger, *Dasein* finds itself face to face with "the nothing of the possible impossibility of existence."[22] The preservation of this tension characterizes the attitude of freedom, freedom towards death. In the following crucial sentence Heidegger summarizes his conception of death:

> Anticipation reveals to *Dasein* its lostness in the they-self, and brings it face to face with the possibility of being itself, primarily unsupported by concernful solicitude, but of being itself, rather, in an impassioned freedom towards death—a freedom which has been released from the illusions of the "they," and which is factical, certain of itself, and anxious.[23]

Expressed in another way, it means that *Dasein* does not have an end at which it merely ceases to be, but that it exists finitely, that is, in a relation to the end. Heidegger once expressed this by saying that *Dasein* constantly "walks under the eyes of death."

We have seen previously that Schopenhauer's teachings on death concentrated on the exposition and interpretation of its metaphysical significance. He is not concerned about the patterning of *Dasein* according to our knowledge of identity which, as it were, anticipates death—a process crucial to Heidegger's system. That which "happens" is basically a matter of indifference to that which is essential. Feuerbach's reflections on the essence and meaning of death lead

[21]That is, *Dasein* in death is cut off from all relations with others.
[22]*Ibid.*, p. 310.
[23]*Ibid.*, p. 311.

to the imperative of the authentication of being, which even at that time he interpreted as a spiritualization of being. From this, he maintains, there must follow in and through all of life the confirmation of the highest love. Simmel's death philosophy sees the life process as a natural occurrence, which rises to the heights of irretrievable individuality and which enjoys its uniqueness, so to speak, in the awareness of its end. Heidegger's concept of anticipation and of freedom towards death does not seek to overcome life. We have already seen how he repudiates all fleeing from the world. "Only Being free *for* death gives *Dasein* its goal and pushes existence into its finitude." By grasping its own distinctive possibility *Dasein* is led into the "simplicity" of its fate.[24] Heidegger defines fate as *Dasein's* primordial historizing which lies in authentic resoluteness and in which *Dasein* "hands itself down to itself, free for death, in a possibility which it has inherited." Death is universal—"and yet has chosen"—death is its own. This interpretation could in a special sense take Angelus Silesius' words as its own:

> I say, because it's death alone that makes me free.
> Death must of all good things most perfect be.

Dasein is being in temporality. Life, then, should spring from the depths of the tension between its last end and the finite demands of life.

> If *Dasein*, by anticipation, allows death to become powerful in itself, then it understands itself as free for death in its own superior power, the power of its finite freedom. For in this freedom which "is" only in its having opted to make such a choice, it takes over the powerlessness of abandonment to itself and comes to a clear vision that has been disclosed.[25]

In Schopenhauer's treatise it is life as a whole that is confronted with death. In Feuerbach's system man as spiritual being faces death; in Simmel's thought it is "the" individual which the philosopher confronts with death. Heidegger sets the concrete self in a relation to death and wants to preserve it in this relation. As in none of the other systems discussed, we find in Heidegger's philosophy an explication of the problem of death from the standpoint of the existential Being becoming its Self. Feuerbach who,

[24] *Ibid.*, p. 435.
[25] *Ibid.*, p. 436.

unlike Schopenhauer, assigns a positive value to the person, conceives of the self in the Hegelian sense, in a static-objective way. Heidegger, on the other hand, following the existence doctrine of Kierkegaard, Hegel's great critic and opponent, finds like his mentor the essence of the Self and its deepest and most authentic life in the subjective relation and statement.

The initial force of Christianity, taken up by Augustine and characteristically changed and renewed by Luther and then Descartes, repeats itself again, but with important modifications. For the Christian thinkers mentioned above, with whom Kierkegaard directly aligns himself, it was the Being of man towards God, for whom the self knows itself to be created, that determined how the great questions of existence were to be answered. Heidegger's methodically grounded analysis of *Dasein* passes over this relationship completely. The vista opened in his writings offers no justification, as the death-philosophy of Schopenhauer still did, for considering God and death together.

II

Christianity and World Religions

4.

General Revelation and the Religions of the World

"At the heart of the theological issue today lies the problem of revelation."
(L. S. Thornton,
Revelation and the Modern World, p. 129.)

We shall proceed in this discussion upon a topic central to the field of the history of religions and of the comparative study of religions, on the assumption that we are all familiar, in broad outline, with recent developments in the study of religion which have tended to concentrate our attention on the problems of the nature of general revelation and its relation to special revelation. Such developments have taken place both in the last twenty-five or thirty years in *theology* and in the field of the *history of religions*.[1] The best general statement on the problem in theology, it seems to me, has been given by Alan Richardson in his *Christian Apologetics* (1947). He has shown that, instead of contrasting natural (non-Christian) and revealed knowledge of God as had been done previously, the theology of liberalism eschewed the notion of revelation while neo-orthodox theology has been inclined to acknowledge only *one* special revelation.[2] The famous controversies between Barth and Brunner, and between Hocking and Kraemer, illustrate this

[1]For the development of Protestant theology in that period, cf. D. D. Williams, *What Present Day Theologians Are Thinking* (1952) and for the History of Religions, J. Wach, *Types of Religious Experience* (1951), Chap. I, "The Place of the History of Religions in the Study of Theology."
[2]Alan Richardson, *Christian Apologetics* (1947), Chap. V.

phase of theological discussion.[3] Meanwhile, a highly important attempt at a constructive statement concerning the nature of general and of special revelation had been made by William Temple in his great work *Nature, Man and God* and in a briefer article in *Revelation*, edited by John Baillie.[4] Here, you will remember, in Lecture XII of his book, entitled "Revelation and its Modes," Temple rejects an all too sharp distinction between the different works of God, "so as to regard some of these as constituting His self-revelation and the others as offering no such revelation." Here the famous passage occurs which may serve as a motto for our discussion:

> "We affirm then, that unless all existence is a medium of Revelation, no particular revelation is possible. . . . If there is no ultimate Reality which is the ground of all else, then there is no God to be revealed. . . . Either all occurrences are in some degree revelations of God or else there is no such revelation at all. . . . Only if God is revealed in the rising of the sun in the sky can he be revealed in the rising of a son of man from the dead, only if he is revealed in the history of the Syrians and Philistines can he be revealed in the history of Israel."[5] Theologians like John Baillie, H. R. Niebuhr, Alan Richardson, and Leonard Thornton are in agreement with this philosophy.

Not only in theology but also in the history of religions the concept of general revelation has been stressed by those who have helped to overcome the era of historicism. We shall name here especially Nathan Söderblom, Rudolf Otto and G. van der Leeuw.[6] Though all three men are theologians, the better part of their life work was dedicated to the history of religions, and that is why we feel that we are justified in claiming them for our field. Just a half-century ago, in 1903, very shortly after Troeltsch's *Die Absolutheit des Christentums* (1900), Soederblom published his booklet, *The Nature of Revelation*. "A revelation of God," he says there, "is present wherever a real religion is found. When God is known,

[3]Cf. esp. *Natural Theology*, ed. J. Baillie, 1946; *The Authority of the Faith* (Madras Series), 1939; W. E. Hocking, *Living Religions and a World Faith*, 1940.

[4]William Temple, *Nature, Man and God*, 1934, repr. 1949; *Revelation*, ed. John Baillie (1937).

[5]*Nature, Man and God*, p. 306.

[6]For a brief survey cf. G. Menching, *Geschichte des Religionswissenschaft*, 1948, pp. 74ff.

it may be imperfectly and through a distorting medium, there he has in some degree allowed himself to become known, yes, made himself known."[7] He does expressly reject the two theories proffered to explain "the existence of religious faith and truth outside the Biblical revelation through the interference of demons or the activity of man's reason." "No religion is a product of culture, all religion depends on revelation," says Soederblom with special reference to Troeltsch's thesis. And in a passage very similar to Temple's previously quoted statement, he refers to the elevated and powerful elements found in the "Babylonian and Assyrian expressions of piety" and claims that in "this age of world missions, it is high time that the church acquainted itself with the thought of the general revelation of God." Yet, "in Israel a new content of revelation comes in through new revealers,"[8] and in Jesus Christ we see the "fulfillment of revelation"—Soederblom uses this term which is so objectionable to Dr. Kraemer—"the fullness of the Godhead bodily." "So Christianity," he says, "may be called revealed religion in a special sense," a "unique species of revelation."[9]

Rudolf Otto, who may have been influenced by Soederblom's use of the term "the Holy," has, as the first among modern historians of religions, given real content to the notion of general revelation by his analysis of religious experience as a communion with the holy, and his demonstration of the ubiquity of the "*sensus numinis*."[10] It is well-known that he indicates the relationship between special and general revelation, as he sees it, by the sharp contrast into which he places "the Son" as over against other charismatic men of God. But it has to be admitted that this powerful expression of a religious conviction by the author of *The Idea of the Holy* is not matched by an articulate statement of the methodological aspect of the problem.

A similar criticism, it seems, has to be levelled against the great modern historian of religions to whom we owe *Religion In Essence and Manifestation*, Gerardus van der Leeuw.[11] And yet we feel that

[7]N. Söderblom, The Nature of Revelation (1933). Cf. also *Natürliche Religion und Religionsgeschichte* (1913), esp. V and VI.

[8]*Op. cit.*, p. 52.

[9]*Op. cit.*, pp. 52, 36, 68.

[10]Cf. Robert F. Davidson, *R. Otto's Interpretation of Religion* (1947); and J. Wach, *Types*, Chap. X, "R. Otto and the Idea of the Holy."

[11]G. van der Leeuw, *Religion in Essence and Manifestation* (1933, 1938); cf. *Pro Regno, Pro Sanctario* (1950).

he is as much concerned with illumining the fact of general revelation as with pointing up the meaning and significance of the special revelation in Christ. It is characteristic that in his magnum opus he treats revelation in the section on "The World." When man will enter into contact with the world, he needs, according to van der Leeuw, revelation in order to be able to "follow God."[12] Yet the Dutch scholar expressly rejects the distinction between general revelation which everyone could have and a special one which "was accessible only to one of a particular faith" ("*die einzig dem in bestimmer Weise Gläubigen geschenkt ware*").[13] Rightly he stresses that revelation is never general in the sense that it would not be addressed to someone in particular; *all* revelation is, he says, particular in that it is given to *me* ("*insofern sie immer mir ursprünglich gegeben ist*"—agreeing here with Christian existentialism). *Qua* phenomenologists—in the peculiar sense in which van der Leeuw uses this term—we have to regard as revelation "whatever offers itself as such." We can distinguish, though, between a genuine and a non-genuine revelatory experience ("*Offenbarungserlebnis*"). G. van der Leeuw, who has contributed the article on "revelation" in RGG,[14] believes that the historian of religions has to regard as revelation all that which claims to be such. I think it would be fair to say that the Dutch scholar assumes general revelation though he denies that the "*Elementargedanke*" or the notion of a religious a priori could do justice to the content of actual revelation. He wants to distinguish between *intuition* as it occurs in the arts and the sciences, and *revelation*; he assumes grades and gives a detailed account of the media of revelation at various stages of the development of religion. Revelation, according to van der Leeuw, may be experienced first in mana (that is: "powerful objects"); then in the Word; then in an inner voice; then in mediators and, finally in the incarnation of the Logos—a development toward the more personal modes.

With these teachings we have arrived at a juncture where it becomes evident that the *separatism* which characterizes much of the work in history of religions and in theology is in the process of being overcome. The *historian of religions* is ready to admit that

[12]*Op. cit.*, p. 844.
[13]*Op. cit.*, 85, 1.
[14]*Religion in Geschichte und Gegenwart* IV, pp. 654ff.

he needs to transcend the purely empirical approach which since the end of the nineteenth century has limited him to description and cataloguing, and quite a few of the *theologians* are ready to see that they have to take note of and include in their constructive work the new material which the historians of religions have put at their disposal. The viewpoint from which this interpretation is to be undertaken, will for the Christian theologian be Christian principles. For the Jewish theologian it will be the Torah, and for the Mohammedan, the Islamic faith. It goes without saying that the great achievements of the preceding era in critical methods and historical research should be safeguarded, but that is not the same thing as treating them as aims in themselves. The last fifty years have witnessed a resurgence of a normative interest, the desire for an *articulation of our own faith*, an articulation which takes cognizance of the widening of the horizon which has taken place in the nineteenth century and which, above all, is firmly rooted in the tradition of our Christian faith. I am convinced that we have a great potential treasure-house in the writings of the Christian Fathers who were at their time facing the same basic problems in apologetics as we have to cope with. In his very stimulating lectures on *Revelation and the Modern Mind*,[15] L. S. Thornton has illustrated from the writings of Irenaeus how singularly illuminating the concept of primordial revelation is for the interpretation of non-Christian religions in the light of general revelation. And the same Father has been quoted amply by Jean Danielou in his *Salvation of the Nations*.[16]

It remains for us to summarize now briefly the statement of one eminent modern thinker who has recently devoted an important work to our problem. I have in mind Paul Tillich's statement in the first volume of his *Systematic Theology*. There seems to be some ambiguity in the rather detailed section which deals with the "Reality of Revelation." He says that "there is no revelation in general,"[17] but what he means is that revelation is always had in a concrete situation, that there is, as he puts it, no "*Offenbarung überhaupt*." He definitely thinks of revelation in a pluralistic sense as he recognizes various fields and *media* which may become revela-

[15]*Revelation and the Modern Mind* (1950).
[16]Jean Danielou, *The Salvation of the Nations* (1949).
[17]Paul Tillich, *Systematic Theology* (1951), p. 111.

tory (nature, history, groups, individuals, the word—the latter not a medium in addition to other mediums but "a necessary element in all forms of revelation").[18] So Tillich stipulates on the history of religions a three-fold *preparation* for what he call the *final revelation*, namely conservation, criticism, and anticipation.[19] The second, the critical preparation, can be divided again into a mystical, a rational and a prophetic type. Though Tillich mentions only the history of Israel, the New Testament, and Church history in which this process takes place,[20] we are, I think, not wrong in assuming that the history of religions generally shows us examples of such preparation. Tillich sees the center of the history of revelation dividing the whole process into preparing for and receiving of revelation. The bearer of the receiving revelation is the Christian Church.[21] Religions and cultures outside it and ("even more") nations and churches within it, are in the stage of "preparation." But the Christian Church is based on the final revelation and is, as Tillich says, "supposed to receive it in a continuous process of reception, interpretation, and actualization."[22] Definitely then, Tillich rejects both contentions that there is only *one* revelation (that in Jesus Christ), and that there are such everywhere and that none of them is ultimate.[23] "The history of revelation is a necessary correlate of final revelation." A distinction is made rightly by Tillich between universal and general revelation, the former meaning "a special event with an all-embracing claim" while he identifies, as we saw, general revelation with "revelation in general." Because of the intimacy of the unity with the Father and because of the totality of his sacrifice, Jesus Christ is the universally valid, final revelation.

Thus, we have found some agreement between some theologians and historians of religions as to *the fact of general revelation* or revelation outside of Christianity. From here on, then, we will not be further concerned in this lecture with the argument of those who deny this fact, in the traditional black and white fashion or otherwise with or without an acquaintance with non-Christian religions. We shall rather discuss *the nature of general revelation*, and further, the form which it takes in other religions.

[18]*Op. cit.*, p. 124.
[19]*Op. cit.*, p. 139.
[20]*Op. cit.*, p. 143.
[21]*Op. cit.*, p. 144.
[22]*Op. cit.*, p. 144.
[23]*Op. cit.*, p. 138.

We agree with Rudolf Otto that the *sensus numinis* is universal. All men possess potentially a sense of the Divine. How can we account for that theologically? Some have pointed to the Holy Spirit who comes into the world to enlighten every man. Thus, according to L. S. Thornton,[24] "as all religion presupposes revelation, so all genuine response to revelation is made under the influence of God's spirit." Therefore J. Danielou is right when he says: "The task of the missionary is rather one of *redirecting* the *religious sense* so that it may attain its true object. He is not faced with a *religious vacuum* which he must fill, as it were, from zero."[25] Important implications for the theory and practice of missions follow, but this is not the place to develop them.

We cannot agree with a definition which the Indian theologian Dr. Moses suggests in his thesis on *Religious Truth and the Relation Between Religions*[26] when, following A. Richardson, he calls general revelation "revelation in the world of nature, in the conscience and reason of man," and "special revelation" revelation in the events of history and in prophetic individuals. We rather hold that genuine religious experience is the apprehension of the *revelatum wherever it occurs*, that is, within whatever ethnic, cultural, social or religious context. That would mean that there could be revelation in Judaism, Islam, Hinduism, and Buddhism and many other religious communities besides Christianity. This may sound like an indorsement of the *relativism* of some representative of the Religionsgeschichtliche Schule past and present who refuse to go beyond the acknowledgment of general revelation. Over against this view we agree with its critics who claim that this is not enough and insist that there is particular revelation. We part ways with them when they insist that there can only be *one* particular revelation. There are Christians but also Jews, Mohammedans, Hindus, and Buddhists who do so insist. Actually, every instance of general revelation is a particular one as we have previously implied. It is arrogance to subsume all non-Christian expression of religious experience under the heading of "human self-enfolding."[27] Does this recognition of a plurality of particular revelation reduce God's revelation in Jesus Christ to *one* other *among many?* No, its unique-

[24]Thornton, *Revelation*, p. 18.
[25]Danielou, *Salvation*, p. 20.
[26]D. G. Moses, *Religious Truth and the Relation between Religions* (1950), p. 60.
[27]H. Kraemer, *The Christian Message*, p. 103.

ness is not only not obscured, but actually rendered more credible by lesser revelations. I will not respect and love my friend less because I know other people whom I respect, but more so. Canon Richardson has rightly said that we do not need to denigrate other religions because we are Christians. We agree with Dr. Kraemer when he answers the question: "Who owns revelation?" Neither Christians, nor Jews, nor non-Christians can pretend or boast to be in possession of it: "Revelation," he says, is *es ipso* an act of divine condescension. The real Christian contention is not: "We have the revelation and not you," but pointing gratefully and humbly to Christ: "It has pleased God to reveal himself fully and decisively in Christ; repent, believe, adore."[28] This is exactly right. It is also true that the special revelation in Christ "contradicts and upsets all human religious aspiration,"[29] that the Cross is in a sense "antagonistic to all human aspirations," that is, Christian and non-Christian aspirations. Many faiths, *one* Cross!

The problem of general revelation is not identical with that of the so-called points of contact, which is really a question of missionary approach, nor with that of spontaneity and receptivity, divine and humane. As all revelation must be acknowledged to depend on divine *grace* for its reception, as well as its occurrence, there is no difference between general and special revelation in this point. J. Danielou errs when he says,[30] "In other religions grace is not present." As Rudolf Otto has shown, in his study of *Christianity and the Indian Religion of Grace*, there is a tremendously strong awareness of divine grace in theistic Hinduism. The same is true of Mahayana Buddhism, as L. de la Vallée-Poussin has proved. There are two other aspects which have to be considered in a discussion of general revelation: In which sense are we to speak of it if we wish to conceive of general revelation as "*preparation*," and what about the problem of *truth*? There is good reason to refer to the religion of ancient Israel as preparatory. "It appears," says H. R. Niebuhr,[31] "that we have religious knowledge apart from revelation in our history since we can speak about God with members of non-Christian communites, not only with Jews whose memories we

[28]*Op. cit.*, p. 119.
[29]*Op. cit.*, p. 122.
[30]*Salvation*, p. 8.
[31]H. R. Niebuhr, *The Meaning of Revelation* (1941), p. 176.

largely have made our own but with Mohammedans and Hindus, using words which appear to have some common meaning." Among most Christian scholars there will be agreement that the apprehensions of the Hebrew faith are preparatory for the Gospel in a sense in which no other particular revelation is. This is recognized in the Old Messianic scheme of promise and fulfillment ("*Weissagung und Erfüllung*") and in the the conception of a "*Heilsgeschichte*." I might remind you in this connection of Will Herberg's interesting address on "Judaism and Christianity: Their Unity and Difference."[32] In his *Salvation of the Nations*, J. Danielou has enumerated three points which mark the advance of the Hebrew over other "revelation," namely the understanding that God, as the living God, intervenes directly in the life of the people, the understanding of and stress upon the fundamental unity of God, and, finally the understanding that God reveals himself as the God of holiness.[33]

We do not share Wilhelm Herrmann's scepticism. In *The Communion of the Christian with God*, he doubts that we could understand even the religious life of a pious Israelite because the facts which he interpreted as revelation do not have this power for us anymore.[34] Recent attempts to dissolve the close relationship between the two Testaments have only renewed our conviction of their indissoluble unity which we have to uphold also against distinguished non-Western Christian theologians.

We still remain within the *chronological* order when we attribute a modicum of preparatory character to the religions of ancient Iran, Greece and Rome, including the so-called mystery cults, and perhaps those of Egypt and the ancient Near East. This is not only to claim historical connections, a pursuit with which the scholars of the Religionsgeschichtliche Schule were preeminently engaged, but rather to recognize, *phenomenologically* speaking, a type of religious experience which, because it was characterized by a strong sense of the awesome mystery of the nature of ultimate Reality, may be called *preparatory*, notwithstanding profound differences. Now what shall we say with regard to religions which,

[32]JBL, XXI, 1953, pp. 67ff.

[33]*Salvation*, p. 24f.

[34]W. Herrmann, *The Communion of the Christian with God* (transl. 1895), p. 49.

antedating Christianity, show no historical or causal relations or none which could be documented? That would include the so-called primitive religions, lower and higher; those of the middle type, dead and alive, such as the religions of the Aztecs, Teutons, Japanese, and finally world religions such as Hinduism, Buddhism, Confucianism. (Islam, dependent upon Christianity, and the faiths derived from it are in a special category.) Here only a *phenomenological* approach can help.

The first, and most important of all questions, to ask—and here we have an unexpected ally in Karl Barth—is: how is Ultimate Reality, how is *God apprehended?*[35] As Christians we know of the supreme manifestation of God in Christ Jesus that is and must remain our standard, but that cannot mean that the apprehensions of the Divine which occur in these religions is to be seen as nothing and treated on a par with the claims of cults of *finite* values such as blood, soil, class, etc., as Barth suggests. It is not that we wish to play up the intimations which we find in an analysis of the religious experience of these religious communities to compete with the claim that the Christian kerygma has upon us, but rather to illumine the latter in the light of these experiences and their expression. And it is not necessary that we examine the non-Christian expressions of the experience of God, by viewing them under categories borrowed from Christian dogmatics and the Christian doctrine of God. We should also seriously consider what implications these non-Christian apprehensions have for thought, life and conduct in those communities. But there is more to general revelation even than that. There is no doubt in my mind that it is significant if in some religions, e.g., in primitive religions a very incisive *preparation* has to precede any attempt to enter into contact with the supreme reality—vigils, fasting, purifications, meditations. It is also significant that some religions seem to stress heavily what R. Otto has designated as the *mysterium tremendum*: the religions of Melanesia, of Western and equatorial Africa, of the Mayas, Aztecs, Assyrians, Japanese, and Islam and the Lamaistic form of Buddhism. In others, especially the so-called mystical, the aspect of the *mysterium fascinosum* prevails. Let us consider one more important instance where it is justified to speak of preparation for the Gospel in non-Christian religions. F. Thomas Ohm, the outstanding German Catho-

[35]K. Barth, *Die Kirchliche Dogmatik* (1932), I.

lic missionary expert, has gathered in a large volume the evidence for the many expressions for the *love of God* found in the various religions of the world.[36]

Finally—as a third example—there is the degree to which the basic apprehension of the Divine includes a *moral* element. I think that R. Otto was rightly criticized by Dr. Oman, Streeter and others for failing to demonstrate adequately the interrelationship between the Holy and the Good in the *Idea of the Holy*.[37] Recent studies in anthropology have provided theologians and philosophers with very much important material. There can be no question but that religions such as the Egyptian, Sumerian, Vedic-Brahmanic and more especially Judaism, Islam, Buddhism and Confucianism are far from prescribing indistinguishable or purely negative solutions to this problem. Max Mueller was not altogether wrong when he jotted down in his *Chips:* "An intuition of God, a sense of human weakness and dependence, a belief in a Divine government of the World, a distinction between good and evil and a hope of a better life, these are some of the radical elements of all religions."[38]

All this goes to show that we have no right to treat non-Christian religions indiscriminately as a *massa perditionis*. The early Fathers of the Christian Church, especially the Alexandrians, were quite right in allowing for the notion of general revelation, and the Medieval Church was right to follow this lead. "The great pillars of the Catholic faith," says Otto Karrer in his *Religions of Mankind*,[39] "from St. Paul, Clement of Alexandria, St. Augustine and St. Gregory the Great, to Gorres, Mohler and Newman were no less convinced champions of Christian truth, because they combined their faith in the one holy Catholic Church with an open eye for all that was noble and worthy of reverence in the non-Christian world. . . ." As late as the seventeenth century, Karrer has shown, Cardinal John de Lugo upheld this notion. (In Protestant theology this view still has to wait for recognition.) Thus he can say "that the adherents of religions and philosophies outside the Church or Christianity have saved their souls within their respective creeds, and have done so by the grace of God" attaching it to their good

[36]Th. Ohm, *Die Liebe zu Gott in den nichtchristlichen Religionen* (1950).
[37]J. W. Oman, *The Natural and the Supernatural* (1931); B. H. Streeter, *The Buddha and the Christ* (1932).
[38]*Chips from a Workshop* (1867), Preface.
[39]O. Karrer, *Religions of Mankind* (transl. 1945), p. 292.

faith and teaching them "to cherish and put in practice those features of their worship, doctrine, philosophy and religious community which are true and good and from God."[40]

We have indicated above some criteria by which to evaluate the apprehensions of the Divine in other religions. Another criterion is the degree of *awareness* and *articulation* of these apprehensions. The Australian native (or the Bushman or Hottentot) is aware of a numinous presence as his behavior at the sound of the bull-roarer shows. He would not behave this way at the sight of any other finite object. But this awareness does not match that expressed by Iranian or Hindu men of God of the types of Arda Viraf or Manikka Vasaga. The highly sophisticated theological statements of a Moses ibn Maimun, an al Ghazali or a Ramanuja, exhibit the highest degree of awareness as well as articulation of their vision and notion of God. Indeed it will surprise even those somewhat acquainted with non-Christian religions to what degree the differentiation of theological views is carried and how fine the distinctions which have been made. I should like to refer to Gardet and Anawati's *Introduction à la theologie musulmane*,[41] recent studies in the Shaiva Siddhanta[42] and Lamotte's commentary on the *Prajnaparamita-Sutra*,[43] to name just these inquiries into and expositions of the development of doctrine in some major non-Christian religions.

We may also call "preparation" *worship* as it has been and is practiced outside of Christianity. First of all is the very fact *that* in acts of *reverence* man seeks God, waits for him and is aware of his own numinous unworth vis-a-vis ultimate reality, as R. Otto calls this feeling. We find that many a non-Christian act of worship has a closer resemblance to our own attitude of life if we be religious than to the indifferent one of the sceptic or the contemptuous one of the modern atheist. The laudable attempt to do away with all idolatory and idolatrous forms of worship may lead to the creation of a deplorable vacuum such as exists among many preliterate peoples who have been led to abandon their traditional ways, without having something better to replace them. The cultivation of a genuine sense of *awe* I should consider a very important *praeparatio*

[40]*Op. cit.*, p. 267.

[41]L. Gardet–M. M. Anawati, *Introduction a la theologie musulmane*, 1948.

[42]G. Matthews, *Siva-nana-bodham*, 1948, V. Paranjoti, *Saiva Siddhanta*, 1938.

[43]E. Lamotte, *Le Traité de la Grande Vertu de Sagesse*, 1944, 1949.

evangelica. Though it would be wrong to measure the nearness of religion to true worship by the complexity of its cultus—just as it would be wrong to measure it by the absence of any and all, it is true that certain genuine and meaningful ways by which communion with the Divine may be facilitated and preserved and which have been lost or are not shared in other religious communities, could well be regarded as "preparatory." Prayer, fasting, meditation, certain forms of discipline are some of these forms. History shows us that a purely *spiritualistic* interpretation of worship is difficult to maintain and easily leads to its evaporation. It is well and good to spiritualize the notion of *sacrifice*, but it may be asked if a sacrifice with the right intuition might not be more acceptable in the eyes of God than the complete absence of all sacrificial intention so often found in modern Western man. If the author of one of the finest books on worship, Evelyn Underhill, is right in stating that worship is the heart of religion, then, it seems to me, its presence, its degree of intensity, its nature and form would be of the utmost importance in evaluating cultus where we find it. Here too we may see a *praeparatio evangelica.*

There is, finally, wherever religion is found some form of *togetherness.* The Christian knows his fellowship to be unique as the Body of Christ. But here also we feel obliged to ask: is all other associating and covenanting just one *massa perditionis* or may we regard as "preparation" religious communities, communities of believers in the non-Christian world? It is easy to point out the heterogeneity of all natural religious groupings among men, be it on a basis of consanguinity, locality or any other such principle. But what do we have to say in view of the fact that the religious community which is legitimately referred to as the forerunner of the ecclesia, namely, the Hebrew *Qahal*, is of the type of natural grouping based on ties of blood whereas the Buddhist Samgha resembles much more closely the ecclesia by being a *specifically* religious association? This latter type actually occurs already on the level of so-called preliterate societies in the form of the secret—and even more the mystery—societies. This does not imply equating the Christian notion of the church with that of the mystery association of the ancient Greco-Roman-Oriental world—as has been done frequently in the past—if we see in the principle of *spiritual relationship and brotherhood* a *praeparatio* for the profoundest notion of the communion of saints. Or again we may find that the respect paid to the spiritual father, teacher, *guru*, in various parts of the world, contrasts favorably with the lack of reverence or understanding of what charisma means in our own supposedly Christian civilization. May not a true follower of Christ feel more at home in a *gurukula* in the midst of earnest disciples rather than in the typical bourgeois congregation or in any stereotyped cult-group?

All of this implies a criticism of Kraemer's stress in his *Christian Message in a non-Christian World*, upon the *monolithic* character of religious structures and institutions. These are, of course, in a sense, unified wholes: Judaism, Zoroastrianism, Hinduism, Buddhism, Confucianism, and the so-called primitive religions.

Nobody will regard these colossal institutions *in toto* as a "preparation for Christ." But Kraemer dispenses himself too easily this way from the task of carefully scrutinizing the *composing elements.*

The historian of religions will study them and, because he must be more than a registrar of facts and phenomena, he will attempt to *evaluate* them. Just as the Christian theologian will evaluate elements in the Hebrew religion differently according to their affinity to the Christian kerygma, so he will be impressed by various apprehensions, notions, or attitudes in Islam, Hinduism, or Buddhism in differing ways. Last year's *Journal of Bible and Religion* carried two interesting articles on "Reason and Experience" and on "Mutual Love" in Mahayana-Buddhism.[44] Once more we wish to take issue with Dr. Kraemer who criticizes sharply in his Madras paper the term "*fulfillment.*" "It is," he says, "mistaken . . . to describe the religious pilgrimage of mankind as a preparation or a leading up to a so-called consummation or fulfillment in Christ."[45] We agree with his designation of Christ as the *crisis* of all religion and with his statement that "God as he is revealed in Jesus Christ is contrary to the sublimest pictures we made of him before we knew of him in Jesus Christ," but we reject his formula: *continuity* or *discontinuity*—the title he gave characteristically to his contribution in the *Madras* volume. Of course, "the Veda, the Koran, and the Gospel do not make a coherent scheme" (as Chenciah admits to Kraemer),[46] of course they do not answer the same questions. We

[44]JBR, XX, 1952, pp. 77ff., 84ff.
[45]"The Authority of the Faith," p. 2.
[46]*Op. cit.*, p. 3.

would never claim that. Even Bultmann says rightly:[47] "The Christian faith does not criticize from its standpoint the quest for God in non-Christian religions, which it can only perceive and clarify, but rather the *answer* which is given by non-Christian religions." Dr. Kraemer disavows any right to see in the Persian religion, which even Brunner declares comes the closest of the non-Christian faiths to Christianity, anything related, because "the Mazdean believer is the courageous and self-confident fighter for God whereas the man who lives by the faith of Christ is a pardoned sinner."[48] This is right but does not prove that in other ways (insistence on truthfulness, purity, sincerity) Zoroastrianism would not represent a "preparation," compared to some of the crude and ethically insensitive notions of certain primitive religions or the questionable sensuousness of certain Hindu and Buddhist cults (Sahajiya, Tantrism).

Dr. David G. Moses suggests in his previously mentioned book that *fulfillment* need not signify *continuation.* Quite rightly he speaks of "fulfillment by repudiation." In the words of Alan Richardson, "Special revelation is not a concrete illustration of general revelation but a correction and transvaluation of it."[49]

What we are advocating here is not some sort of *syncretism*, nor are we *relativists.* Our allegiance is to *Christ* and we do deem him the crisis of religions, Christian and non-Christian. But we feel that in the physical and spiritual struggle which is going on in the world today, we simply cannot afford and should not even want to deny that general revelation of God includes the other faiths. In the words of a Catholic author (P. de Montcheuil): "Christianity need not adapt itself to successive philosophies but it must take into account the spiritual experiences from which those philosophies are born."[50] Dr. Kraemer says, "the problem whether and if so where, and in how far God, i.e., the God and Father of Jesus Christ, the only God we Christians know—has been and is working in the religious history of the world and in man—is a baffling and awful problem."[51] Indeed it is. We should therefore give it the most

[47]"Die Frage der naturlichen Offenbarung" (*Glaube und Verstehen*, 1952), II, 86.
[48]Kraemer, *op. cit.*, p. 48.
[49]Moses, *Religious Truth*, p. 130.
[50]Danielou, *Salvation*, p. 68.
[51]Kraemer, *op. cit.*, p. 3.

painstaking attention. Though we cannot anticipate the result of labors which will occupy scholars for perhaps the rest of this century at least, we should think that, to stay with Kraemer's two examples, we should side with Clement rather than with Karl Barth here. "General revelation," to quote him again, "does not mean to the Alexandrian father that all religious men have the true knowledge of God, but that all mankind is instructed and prepared for Christ when he comes, the religious history of mankind being a unity in which the Incarnation of Christ is the culmination point."[52] For Barth all religions are—we add: only—"*Unglaube*" because "they do not constitute a real response to God's self-manifestation in Jesus Christ." The history which for Schopenhauer was a "*semper eadem sed aliter*," is for the Swiss theologian and for his Dutch followers, the endless and manifold repetition of endeavors at self-justification. We think that it is not impossible to reconcile both the belief in general revelation and belief in the Incarnation.

In the last chapter of his book on *The Meaning of Revelation*, Prof. H. R. Niebuhr says, "Revelation means God, God who discloses himself to us through our history. As our knower, our author, our judge and our only Savior."[53] The way which man is traveling toward a realization of this insight is identical with the history of religions. In this sense all history is potentially "*Heilsgeschichte*," or as Dr. D. Moses puts it,[54] "all religions are 'continuous' in the sense that they are all attempts to meet the fundamental religious needs and aspirations of men everywhere." More accurate still is Dr. Farquhar's statement in his classic, *The Crown of Hinduism*, which Friedrich von Hügel quotes in the first volume of his Essays: "Neither is any one religion alone true in the sense that all others are merely so much sheer error; nor, again, are they all equally true; but while all contain some truth, they not only differ each from the other in the points on which they are true but also in the amount of importance of the truth and power possessed."[55]

One last word. An era in the history of our studies was marked when the attempts at construing a *unilineal* development in non-Christian religion, such as the eighteenth and nineteenth centuries

[52]Kraemer, *op. cit.*, pp. 16, 18.

[53]H. R. Niebuhr, *Revelation*, p. 53.

[54]Moses, *Religious Truth*, p. 158.

[55]Baron von Hügel, *Essays* I, p. 7; J. N. Farquhar, *The Crown of Hinduism* (1913).

had indulged in, came to a close at approximately the time of the First World War. It was followed by a period of resolute refraining from all tracing of progress, development or even growth. Where a registration of fact was deemed insufficient, typological schemes were suggested. We have mentioned G. van der Leeuw's *Religion in Essence and Manifestation* already as a highwater mark of these endeavors. Now the tide is turning again. Living in one world we wish to comprehend something of the religious history of man after having amassed so much material which concerns it, seeing it in its unity—without failing in our loyalty to Christ, our Savior and Redeemer. The Christian answer to the non-Christian religions cannot be disregard or contempt, it must be understanding. That is, as Christians, we are convinced that man is created by God and thus that man may seek and find him, the same God who revealed himself in Christ and is Redeemer as well as Creator. Because in the Incarnation and in the Crucifixion the supreme love of God is revealed unambiguously, as nowhere else, we have to see in this particular disclosure God's final revelation. Because God created not only Europeans and Americans but Africans and Indians, Chinese and Japanese, it will also take Africans and Indians, Chinese and Japanese to apprehend this truth fully. Much misunderstanding and scandal could have been avoided if that could always have been understood by Western Christians. Some Westerners and many Easterners had seen this, but many of the former thought that Christianity as such had failed. So they were ready to abandon it in favor of an Eastern cult or a so-called world-faith. Many and not the least gifted among the latter, after shedding their traditional beliefs are driven into scepticism, thinly disguised as "scientific world-view," because they are not made to feel that they too are called to help in the appropriation of the meaning of the Christian kerygma. "Christianity," Baron von Hügel has written, "can, never ought to, satisfy just simply what men of this or that particular race desire, that and nothing else; Christianity is extant chiefly to make us grow, and not simply to suit us with clothes fitting exactly to the growth already attained."[56] The great text of the historian of religions thus becomes the Epistle to the Hebrews (Chap. II), "So the God who revealed himself continues to reveal Himself—the one

[56]Selected Letters, quoted by N. MacNicol, *Is Christianity Unique?* (1936), p. 176.

God of all times and places."[57] Or, to quote Godfrey Phillips, "The universal religious life of mankind is the context in which Christian affirmations reveal their fullest meaning. The general revelation of God, partial and many-sided, which has given rise to multitudinous forms of religion on the earth, is the best preface to the special revelation in history of which Jesus Christ is the center."[58]

[57]H. R. Niebuhr, *Revelation*, p. 136.
[58]Godfrey Phillips, *The Gospel in the World* (1939), p. 63.

5.

The Paradox of the Gospel

In his book *The Quest for Holiness* Adolf Koberle has said: "The Jew whom the letter kills and the Greek who has been intoxicated by his own natural endowments both alike need the preaching of the Gospel, which in the preaching of the Cross, is power unto Salvation."

Two kinds of people are designated here as needing the preaching of the Gospel, two perennial and ubiquitous types: those who cling to words and letters, and those who believe exclusively in the power and strength of their own minds or wills as they strive after the perfection which they hope to accomplish. The first group includes a great many people who credulously trust in letters, laws or systems, be they Chinese, Hindus, Parsis, Muslims, Jews or Christians. They have once and for all shifted the responsibility for search and inquiry into amulets and talismans, into what is between the covers of sacred or legal volumes; with veneration of word or formula, of shells and images, they believe themselves invulnerable and fortified against the onslaught of change and meaninglessness, of temptation and evil. They have little trust in living experience, but they have a boundless if uncritical trust in letters which more often than not they cannot read—to say nothing of understand. The second group includes those who are "intoxicated by their own natural endowments," be they Greek, Roman, Assyrian, Japanese, Hindu, Persian, Chinese, or any national variant of Buddhists or Christians; be they naturalists or spiritualists, Epicureans or mystics. They may be enthusiasts of the senses, acrobats of the mind or athletes of the will, what they have in common is the happy conviction that they can and will victoriously master life by their own strength.

Thus the Jew whom the letter kills and the Greek who has become intoxicated by his own natural endowment—and we all err in one direction or the other—both need the preaching of the Gospel. If there is any redeeming feature in the dark age in which we live, it is the growing realization that where the Gospel needs to be preached, if not more than elsewhere, certainly not less, is to the Christians. In this sense the apostolic word: "Christ sent me not to baptize but to preach the Gospel" has acquired a meaning which St. Paul could hardly foresee. Soren Kierkegaard suggested about a hundred years ago that it is especially difficult for a Christian to become a Christian. "It is easier," he says in his *Concluding Unscientific Postscript*, "to become a Christian when I am not a Christian than to become a Christian when I am one." Yet at that time most Christians were probably more thoroughly Christian than they are today. It is high time that we stressed more than we do that it is not easy but difficult, and ought to be difficult, to be a Christian. "What is a religion," asks Baron von Hügel, "which costs you nothing?" Perhaps at no time has the "wisdom of words," of which the apostle speaks, been accorded such high esteem as in ours when we have at our disposal in expensive and cheap editions, in books and sermons, in newspapers and radio addresses, the words of all the sages from Confucius to Whitehead. If the kerygma of Christ is just aother "word of wisdom," will it not be drowned in the flood of words that is poured on us from all sides? A glance at the sermon topics posted outside some churches convince us that to a large extent such is already the case.

"Not with wisdom of words, lest the Cross of Christ should be made of no effect." How then can we preach if not by the wisdom of words? "For because by the purpose of God the world with all its wisdom knew not God, it pleased God by so foolish a thing as preaching to give salvation to those who had faith in him."

Let us consider briefly the paradoxical nature of this preaching. All religious experience confronts the difficulty of expressing itself adequately. In myth and symbol it seeks to render imaginative account of its encounter with ultimate reality; in doctrine and philosophy it attempts to formulate conceptually the vision of the prophets and saints. In all religions we find a struggle to safeguard the pristine apprehension of the numinous from the encasement in the letter that killeth and from the arbitrary reinterpretation which seeks to put it within the reach of man's own efforts. But the preaching of which the Apostle speaks is one which is even more difficult to express than religious truth generally is. We cannot and we ought not sell cheaply the great central Christian apprehension of the revelation of God's power in the manifestation of the weakest, the lowest, the lonely moment of deepest suffering. That, however, is the burden of the preaching of the Cross. "No Cross, no crown." On the secularized and ultraliberal mind of our day the existentialists have exerted a powerful attraction by stressing anxiety, suffering and abandonment as over against the all too cheerful anticipation of the utopia of human achievement, of progress and perfection. But would the attraction which the message of Kierkegaard, Heidegger, Sartre and the lesser prophets of existentialism exert over the minds, and to some degree, the hearts of many of the more thoughtful of our contemporaries have been as powerful, if the Gospel of Christ crucified had been really made known to them with all that it implies? That there can be, that there is a meaning to suffering, to sorrow, to loneliness? That once despair was turned to victory? We cannot believe that he who sees a hope would see that hope for hopelessness. Even so vigorous a critic of liberalism and its sins as Reinhold Niebuhr holds on to some of the genuine if secularized notions of liberal theology and would have to do so because a theology of despair would not be a Christian theology. Joy, hope, and victory, are the concomitants of the salvation of which the Apostle speaks in our text. This joy and hope is not the cheerful ease of the untroubled bourgeoisie of the nineteenth century, not the hope that in this generation we are going to establish the Kingdom of God on earth, not the victory which so-called Christians believed easy to win over the "pagan" religions. This victory cannot be won by clever reasoning, by making the best of our natural endowment or by the exertion of our will, because they depend on the *grace of God*, supremely revealed in the "humiliation" of Christ who became man and suffered for us. Both to the "Jews" requiring signs and to the "Greeks" looking for knowledge (and these "Jews" and "Greeks" are found among Christians and non-Christians alike), the ultimate paradox of the "good news of Christ on the Cross," of which the Apostle speaks, must be offensive, a hard and a foolish thing.

The paradox that God's powers and his love are revealed in his suffering servant points to a basic apprehension concerning the nature of ultimate reality. The Christian God cannot be the unconcerned blissful One of the Vedanta nor the alien god of the gnostic, nor the exclusively stern judge of the Talmud or the Quran, nor can he only be conceived of as the friend or comrade who suffers in terms quite like our suffering. He is neither unconcerned nor finite in terms which suggest the theology of Xenophanes rather than Biblical language. Granted that it is wrong to attribute to God the character of a despot separated by a gap from the world he created, we are equally wrong if, for sentimental reasons, we envision him as inextricably tied to the world and its sufferings. God is transcendent as well as immanent, as, among modern theologians, William Temple has convincingly demonstrated.

Rightly he says: "God and the world are not correlative terms." God as immanent is correlative with the world but that is not the whole nature of God. The more we study the activity of God immanent, the more we become aware of God transcendent. The truth that produces awe in the heart of the scientist is such because it is his thought; the beauty that holds the artist spellbound is potent because it is his glory; the goodness that pilots us to the assured apprehension of reality can do this because it is his character; and the freedom, whereby man is lifted above all other aspects of nature, even to the possibility of defying it, is fellowship with him; "Heaven and earth are full of his glory but he is more and other than all that is in earth and heaven." Could it be an accident that ever since the patristic age Christian theology has insisted that the passion is suffered by the second person of the Trinity? "Let this mind be in you," says St. Paul in the Epistle to the Philippians, "which was in Christ Jesus to whom, being in the form of God, it did not seem to be equal with God was a thing to be taken by force but he made himself as nothing, taking the form of a servant being made like man, and being seen in form as a man, he took the lowest place and let himself be put to death, even the death of the Cross." We reject the repristination of patripassianism which the early Church repudiated for excellent reasons.

The preaching of the Gospel with "the good news of Christ on the Cross" is the reminder that (1) suffering and pain are not mere illusions as the Hindus and Buddhists as well as the Christian

Scientists believe, nor are they meaningless and mere frustrations as they are for the Existentialists and the Freudians; (2) that they are not a lesser but to a greater degree the destiny of those who want to follow the Cross, and that the "more abundant life" for which they stand as a promise, ought not to be pictured in terms of the Californian cults; (3) that this news is the promise of salvation and freedom but that a Christian is saved and free only in the degree that he lives under the Cross. This freedom is qualified—the yoke of Christ. It cannot be a negative freedom from authority, from obligations, from service in the household, which is the Church of Christ. It is the authority of Christ, the obligation to follow his command and the clear decision for his cause that binds Christians. Christian "freedom" is not a freedom from but a freedom to. Above all it is the freedom to love. A pure heart, says Kierkegaard, is first and last a bound heart. A heart bound to God. "First, the infinite binding and then the talk about freedom may begin," he says.

Here again we see how those whom the letter kills and those who are intoxicated by their natural endowment are in need of the preaching of the Gospel, of the preaching of the Cross, and here it is that we find the answer to the question, how can we preach if not by wisdom of words? The simple answer is by "deeds of love." They are the most convincing argument there is, as the Christian Saints have known ever since St. John.

Christians should exhibit joy—it was Nietzsche who said that he would begin to believe in their redemption if they looked (and acted) more redeemed—but above all they will freely draw from the inexhaustible treasure of love. That they are their brethren's keeper, all their brethren's keeper, cannot be a question to them. "Love," says William Law, "is infallible, it has no errors, for all errors are the want of love." And St. Bernard, "Love is sufficient in itself, is pleasing in itself and for its own sake. It is itself a merit and is its own reward. Love seeks no reason or fruit beyond itself. Its use is its fruit. I love because I love; I love in order to love." "Blessed," says St. Augustine, "is the man that loves thee, God, and his friends in thee, and his enemies for thee." This is to preach the good news, the Gospel; to help to unfreeze the yet untapped resources of love in the hearts of men. Who would not, if only he were free to, rather love than hate? The tragedy of our time is, above all others, the undernourishment of this divine faculty in man. Above all appeals to our generosity to help our brother in need, next-door, and in far different parts of the world through material means, this appeal has first priority. Charity—and this word should be understood in its deepest sense—*caritas* begins with those next to us, with the companions of our life and work. "*Ubi caritas et amor, ibi Deus est*;" where this charity and this love is, there is God. But loving cannot mean merely sentiment or attitude; it means, as in the supreme example of Christ, deeds of love.

Not a few of us, called to action in behalf of worthy causes to which we are expected to contribute, are apt to think first when we hear the words "deeds of love" of organized action or support of some agency. These are necessary but it is necessary also to pierce the crust which many of us have grown—as often in self-defense or in fear as out of coldness of heart. It is material help that the masses need the world over, but other help is necessary for individuals who are lonely in the age of the "busy teeming multitude which as company is both too much and too little." In no way and at no time can we picture Christ as one of the crowd, and there is no record that he belonged to any "organization." He discouraged rather than encouraged sensational action. But he was empowered in and through the close communion in which he lived with his Father to do countless deeds of love. There was no sentimentality in the power of love by which Jesus knew how to banish fear and despair in the hearts of those he touched. The Apostle who perhaps understood him best has spoken most beautifully in the name of all who could not but yield to his power: "We love him because he first loved us." What is it that makes it so difficult for all of us to do deeds of love, in excess of affection and kindness, respecting those who belong to us anyway?

One of the greatest Christian thinkers of recent times, Soren Kierkegaard, in anticipation of discoveries of modern psychologists, pointed out that there is a profound reason why Christ commanded us to love our neighbor as *ourselves.* Without the right attitude toward ourselves, without being reconciled to ourselves, we are not free to love. "When a man," he says, "in self torment thinks to do God a service by torturing himself, what is his sin except this, of not willing to love himself in the right way?" The *triple reconciliation* to God, to ourselves and to our neighbor, has become possible through the redemptive work of Christ. The *duty* to love, which the divine covenant establishes, is equally repugnant to the legalist and to the naturalist, but the Christian knows that spontaneous affection is transitory whereas *caritas* abideth. "When thou *shalt* love, thou hast no right to harden thine heart." Such love, a love that abides, the pagan does not know. To him it must appear hard and foolish, indeed, to say: Thou *shalt love*. If the Christian has a deeper understanding of love than the pagan, it is not because he despises the sensual but because he is trying to overcome the passive and active selfishness that ensnares the natural man and makes even his liking an extension of his self. Such an attitude is alien to the spirit of Christ. Since he gave the supreme example of a selflessness that never before had been contemplated and never before or after achieved, it has become possible to conceive of a life of perfect love, to this day a scandal to the prudent and an impossibility to the pride of self. There is a need for preaching the Gospel, yes, but there is also a resource by which the good news can reach those who sit in darkness.

I consider the greatest deed of love to be the execution of the missionary command of Jesus Christ: by witness to him, by preaching of the Cross, to kindle the light, to fan it to a flame and thus to free the power of love in those who yet do not know Christ. "It is because we believe," says Peter the Precentor (*ca.* 1198), "that we hope, and because we hope that we love." Before us is a tremendous task. In a world which is lusting for power and which is sorely tempted systematically and mercilessly to use human beings as instruments for the building of more and greater power, in such a world only one kind of preaching can be effective, namely, that in which a greater and more abiding power is revealed to men than that of all the empires: God's love and his power unto salvation. He alone gives man the victory.

6.

Redeemer of Man

I

Reading the Gospels and Epistles of the New Testament or the sermons of the Fathers of the Christian Church, or even the theological treatises of the great Catholic and Protestant teachers of past ages, we realize the depth of conviction, the profundity of faith, which speak out of these documents. There is certainty of being redeemed; there is belief in God, in his creative and saving power, in the Mediator and the Holy Spirit, in divine grace and the communion of saints, in the Last Judgment and the Resurrection, and in the consummation of the Kingdom. What is at the heart of this certainty? Faith in Jesus Christ, the son of the Living God. Devotion to him drew together the little band of disciples; the experience of the risen Christ influenced Paul's zeal. In him the great Alexandrians found the epitome of truth; the great Africans, the peace for which their heart, soul, and mind were longing. After a thousand years had passed St. Bernard of Clairvaux, the crusading mystic, flourished, devoting his life to a passionate love for the bridegroom of his soul. In his ecstasy the saint of the poor in spirit, St. Francis, joined our Lord in his passion, while Brother Bonaventure, truly a giant in knowledge and understanding, traveled the road of the spiritual pilgrimage, illuminated by the light of Christ. Whenever the great minds were in danger of losing themselves in subtleties of speculation concerning the mysteries of the faith, the vision of Christ was given to a simple soul and the affections thus rekindled. "O faithful soul," the author of the *Imitation of Christ* so admonished his contemporaries, "make ready thy heart for this bridegroom, that he may vouchsafe to come into thee and to dwell within thee. For thus saith he: If any man love me, he will come unto him, and will make our abode with him. Give therefore admittance unto Christ and deny entrance to all others. When thou hast Christ, thou art rich, and hast enough. For men soon change and quickly fall; but Christ remaineth forever, and standeth by us firmly unto the end." That Christ be born again and again in every individual soul eternally, redeeming the fallen creature, was the fervent desire of Meister Eckhart, while the life of Heinrich Suso, a St. Bernard redivivus, was consumed in passion for the heavenly Friend. Nowhere is Luther more genuinely rooted in the great tradition of Christianity and at the same time nowhere is he more profoundly stirred in the depth of his being than in his experience of Christ, his "only God" as he once said. Through Christ alone could he who knew so well the terrible aspect of the *mysterium tremendum* become convinced of the holy love of God: a precious heritage the great reformer bequeathed to all his followers. Among those who cherished it and lived by it were at least as many poets and musicians as theologians. It is to the everlasting credit of Pietism, in which C. Schwenckfeld's devotion for the great physician of souls lived on, that it reoriented the Christian's life by infusing into it the love for Jesus. It is easy to point out the exaggerations and aberrations to which an unguarded emotionalism will all too easily succumb. But without the fervor which a Spener and a Zinzendorf displayed in their zeal for winning souls for Christ, we could have no St. Matthew's Passion and could not be moved by Handel's great aria, "I Know That My Redeemer Liveth." Here is the English poet whose power over the word is matched only with the flaming affection of his heart:

> Since Christ embraced the cross itself, dare I
> His image, the image of his cross, deny?
> Would I have profit by the sacrifice,
> And dare the chosen altar to despise?
> It bore all other sins, but is it fit
> That it should bear the sin of scorning it?
> Who from the picture would avert his eyes,
> How would he fly his praises who there did die?
> From me to pulpit, nor misgrounded law,
> Nor scandal taken, shall this cross withdraw,
> It shall not, for it cannot; for the loss,
> Of this cross were to me another
> Better were worse, for no affliction,
> No cross is so extreme, as to have none....
>
> (John Donne, *The Cross*)

Many a modern reader has returned to the poems of that other great troubadour of Christ, the Spanish John of the Cross. True devotion to Christ is neither a Catholic nor a Protestant monopoly. Whereas the former has often enough degenerated into a sentimental ritual, the latter has frequently developed into a sentimental reminiscence.

Faith in Jesus Christ of the kind which I have tried to illustrate with these examples has become rarer in the last three centuries. There is no time here to analyze all the reasons for that or to follow the curve of its decline. There have been movements to counteract this drift, the greatest single figures being perhaps John Wesley, Schleiermacher, William Booth, and Frederick von Hügel.

II

I want you to consider with me just *one factor* which has contributed to alienating the loyalties and affections of modern men from Christ. I mean the growing knowledge and interest in the figures of the founders of the great non-Christian faiths. Only slowly have the Christian people of the Western world become acquainted with the existence of Mohammed, of Zoroaster, of Mani, of the Buddha, of the Jina, of Confucius, of Lao-tse. At the time of the rise of Christianity a number of religious leaders in its narrower and wider environment were known to have enjoyed the high veneration of their followers. Pythagoras, Plato, Plotinus, Apollonius of Tyana, and Alexander of Abonoteichos were held in such esteem. The early Christian apologists, adverse to conceding divine honors to the apotheosis of the Roman rulers, refuted the claims of the adherents of the so-called "mystery cults," in which such mythical redeemers as Osiris, Mithra, Attis, and Hermes Tresmegistus were acclaimed. Some of the Fathers knew of Zoroaster; Clement of Alexandria perhaps had a notion of the great savior of the East, the Buddha. Special claims were made in the name of some of the great Gnostic teachers since Simon Magus. Montanus was at least regarded as a prophet. But the great dualist, Mani, was the first of the founders of a world faith against whom one of the Fathers of the Church, Augustine, had to take up the fight. The chief theologian of the Eastern Church, John of Damascus, himself living in a Moslem environment, was the first to defend systematically the Christian faith against the followers of Mohammed. For the West, however, it was a new discovery and, perhaps we can say, a shock to become, during the Crusades, acquainted with the masses of people highly inspired by and loyal to the founder of Islam. The Middle Ages saw in him, as even Luther still did, the Anti-Christ. We will not dwell here on the arguments which the Christian theologians through the centuries prior to modern times advanced to refute Islam and faith in Mohammed. Very few individuals, however, were ever shaken in their loyalty to Christ or induced to manifest attitudes of indifference which spread later on, first among scholars at the end of the seventeenth century. What missionaries of the mendicant orders reported to the head of the Western Church of Asia's faiths remained unknown except for those concerned with the strategy of Christian missions and had no influence upon the masses of the Christian population. The era of the Reformation brought no change. Bitter controversies among the various parties into which Christ's Church was broken were fought over the questions of how to serve Christ; no alternative except a skepticism nourished by antiquarian study was in evidence. Not the learned tomes written in the seventeenth century on the religious customs and institutions of non-Christian peoples but a fashion which spread in the eighteenth century marks perhaps the turning-point. Not a few "enlightened" people, in France especially, became, for all practical purposes, Confucianists. China was the great fad in the days of Voltaire and Rousseau, and Lao-tse came in for great admiration too. Voltaire was the first to present a dramatic play, *Mahomet*, which dealt sympathetically with the founder of Islam. Most eighteenth-century savants, however, preferred still to think of themselves as Christians, and a Western "Moslem" or "Buddhist" would not have been taken seriously. Of the outstanding non-Christian founders, the Buddha was the last to become really known to the Western world. But he found more glowing admirers among the romantically inclined intelligentsia of the West than any other religious genius. Whereas the mighty Hegel was still hazy in distinguishing between Hinduism and Buddhism, Schopenhauer is the first great Western eulogist of the Enlightened One. In the century of historicism the first real communities of former Christian Moslems and Buddhists constituted themselves in Europe and America. With the actual knowledge of Eastern cultures, religions, and prophets increasing by leaps and bounds, more and more of the intelligentsia of both continents, who had become lukewarm in their religious and ecclesiastical loyalties, began to flirt with the East. Nietzsche disguised his dream prophet who was to usher in the beginning of a no longer Christian era as "Zoroaster." Emerson, as before him Schopenhauer and Wagner, Edward von Hartman and Yeats, sought to blend the faith of the West with that of the East in a somewhat blurred synthesis. While, during the nineteenth century, the great figures of the non-Christian world began to exert their fascination in the West, the twentieth was to discover not a few minor prophets from the East: Baha-ullah, Ramakrishna, and others have found their fervent devotees. It was not everywhere a radical displacement (to use Professor Hocking's term) of Christian loyalties, though more and more instances of this were known, but millions have become uneasy, fearing, in cultivating loyalty to the person and ideals of Christ, to be thought provincial and wondering how to arrange the "pantheon" which modern polyhistory provides.

III

It is simple enough to look back longingly to the faith of ages in which these problems did not exist. Such longing may be justified if it is productive in urging modern man to search his soul, especially where it lacks depth; but it saps man's strength and makes him sentimental if it remains romantic infatuation with a dead past. It is simple also to play ostrich and to try to ignore the apostasy of millions which leads them to the much-bewailed skepticism, cynicism, and secularism of our age or to embrace one of the Eastern teachings of redemption. There are still millions of good simple Christians in the Western world, and we should remember how many of them have again become martyrs for the cause of Christ in this century. Should we sit back, watching their ranks and strength dwindling as inevitably it must if reconception and reinterpretation are not undertaken in time by those in responsibility? Julien Benda has written a forceful accusation directed against the sins of the modern intellectual, *La Trahison des clercs.* Let us consider what we can do to overcome the disastrous consequences of this great betrayal.

Our first question is: What are the reasons for the profound appeal of the various great non-Christian leaders? Of course, it is not surprising that, since the West, long ignorant of their nature and message, became acquainted with them, its people were attracted to the spiritual riches which they appear to, and actually do, offer. It is hopeless to speculate whether this attraction would have proved equally powerful if the Christian faith had not been so weakened by inherent developments in the West since the era of the Enlightenment, as actually was the case, by the time the Eastern saints and sages became really known. There is something disarming in the naiveté with which the pronouncement of truth and the discovery of methods of spiritual truth on the side of these non-Christian prophets are hailed by so-called Christians, totally ignorant of their own (the Christian) faith and its potentialities. How often have I asked some enthusiastic laymen if they had ever read the Fourth Gospel; the answer was quite frequently, "No." It seems ironical that the same interest and zeal with which some are prepared to study the message of non-Christian faiths are not applied to the documents of our own. However, I do not consider these two possibilities *alternatives*, for the simple reason that the very ignorance of the potential treasures of Christ's religion is, to a large degree, the result of a lack of knowledge concerning other faiths on the side of Christian ministers and teachers. This means that we have no choice but to meet the challenge which the various major religions of the world present, so as to be able to answer intelligently and satisfactorily the questions which a growing number of lay people are already asking and which a large number will ask in the future. This is one of the consequences which the Christian theologian has to face in the One World.

What, then, is the cause for the fascination which the persons and messages of Mohammed, the Buddha, Confucius, and Lao-tse exert? There is no doubt that there is one element present which we may call the appeal of novelty. Many are prone to forget that our Lord himself was one of the Eastern masters to whom the spiritually undernourished child of Western urban civilization looks with expectancy and trust. Cynics have commented, with a glance at exotic sectarianism (cultism), on the charm that a turban or a beard or a shaven head exerts on gullible souls. But there is much, very much, more to the attraction besides externals. There are, quite aside from the subjective disposition of souls and minds who have long lost contact with the powers inherent in the genuine Christian tradition, objective qualities in the spirituality, faith, and devotion to the Divine to which the words and lives of the Eastern masters witness. The sheer intensity and burning zeal of Mohammed's religion, his powerful witness to the omnipresent God, the utter truthfulness, serenity, and peace which are radiated by the Great Enlightened One, his insight into the human heart and its dispositions, his counsel to the lonely seeker; Confucius' sincerity and wisdom, his convincing rectitude and uncompromising moral courage; finally, the beguiling simplicity and profundity of the mysterious hermit author of the *Tao Te Ching*— are all these witnesses to the highest spiritual attainments *nothing*? I am afraid that those who say so among Christian theologians are not too well informed as to the facts and not quite as much imbued with the spirit of Christ as they themselves seem to believe. But should we conclude that those in the past or present are right who have enlarged this pantheon to worship, besides Christ, the Buddha and/or Confucius and Mohammed? Such a suggestion would imply that we, each of us, as individuals, are free and altogether autonomous without bonds and obligations to those before us and with us. Those living in the twentieth century might feel less confident with regard to too much freedom than some nineteenth-century individualists were prone to be. It is more than stating a fact to say that we are born and brought up in, hence deeply indebted to, Christian civilization. It means that it has claims on us. We are not free to renounce our responsibility. That is not to say that we are blindly caught up in a destiny which leaves us without freedom to think or act. It is rather the offering of a priceless heritage into which we are invited to enter, the charge of a great love which may release the last resource of power in us. Yes, some will say, "Surely we will not renounce Christ, but we don't find that Christianity, as we know it, is imbued with his spirit; whereas we recognize in the spiritual culture of the East the values for which Jesus stood." Both of these assertions we should take very seriously and think through all their implications. In our theological schools we are engaged in an unrelenting double effort to investigate the causes of the lack of vigor and efficiency of modern Protestant Christianity and at the same time to re-study and re-evaluate the tradition of Christian teaching and worship with the aim at re-conceiving the kerygma of Christ. While we are busy with efforts in this direction we ought not, however, neglect our second duty—to acquaint ourselves with the spiritual wisdom and practice of the great religions of the East. What may have been, or appeared to be, plain intellectual curiosity and a luxury of the scholar in the previous age is now an existential part of our task as theologians and ministers. You will easily see the reason why. We need all the insight available, all the resources, means, and techniques which we can muster, for our effort to translate the message of Christ to the Christian, former Christian, and non-Christian world. Furthermore, we owe it to our brethren of the younger Churches in Asia to help them in translating Christ into terms which make sense in their cultural heritage. Though we have come to know him in the context of the tradition of our civilization, we should jealously guard ourselves against identifying him with it. We see in the Palestinian Jesus the cosmic Christ; the Arab Christian and the Chinese or Japanese Christian will want to see him thus too. We have just begun to understand what an important task this sets for the new theologian.

The surprise at the existence of claims which could only appear blasphemous to a period of thinking in terms of "black" and "white" has worn off. A relativistic response to the challenge of a historic age satisfied with a listing of parallels is not possible in our own times, which have rediscovered the potential power of faith and a dynamic notion of God's revelation. It is not possible, though it has been tried, to demonstrate "scientifically" the superiority of Christianity over some of the other great world religions. A greater responsibility has been thrust upon us since "accepting Christ's message is not any more the natural, the conventional, the only option." If by God's grace we avail ourselves of the opportunity to hear Christ's word and accept him in our heart, a spiritual realm is opened to us whose laws can be formulated in different languages and terminologies.

We thus receive the power which can come only from a genuine encounter with the living Christ, and which we must bring to bear upon the wide world that the unrelenting efforts of many generations of adventurous explorers, missionaries, and scholars have opened to us. Without such knowledge, whatever force our faith may have, it will remain ineffective, just as such knowledge without commitment and loyalties remains stale and academic.

In unforgettable words the poet Rainer M. Rilke has said: "Religion is not knowledge, not conduct or feeling . . . it is not duty and not renunciation, it is not restriction: but in the infinite extent of the universe is a direction of the heart."

7.

Seeing and Believing

In the nineteenth century and at the beginning of the twentieth the Fourth Gospel, according to Luther *"das rechte, zarte Haupt-evangelium"* (the true, tender main Gospel), was unpopular with many a "progressive" student who took his cue from F. C. Baur who believed that it could not have been written before late in the second century. This error was tellingly refuted through the discovery of the papyrus Ryle from which we learned that our Gospel must have been current in Egypt at the turn from the first to the second centuries. Many questions as to its origins, authorship and relations to other writings of the New Testament still have to be solved. Yet whatever the conclusions of scholarship turn out to be, the Christian Church seems to be rediscovering the tremendous spiritual value of the Fourth Gospel in our own days. It is with one of the farewell discourses of the Johannine Christ (Chapter 14) that we shall be concerned in this brief meditation.

1. "Let not your heart be troubled: ye believe in God, believe also in me."

"Vain and brief," says Thomas à Kempis, "is all human consolation. Blessed and true is the consolation which is received inwardly from the truth."

Jesus knows that in the heart of those who do believe in God, none of the hopeless despair and utter despondency can arise which beset those who have not found him or deny him. He addresses himself to those who do believe in God. Our Lord and Master is our highest authority for the assumption that there is a world-wide congregation of those who "believe in God" though they do not know Christ. Theologians speak of general revelation by means of which an appreciation of the Divine is vouchsafed to the primitive, the so-called pagans, and to other peoples who may worship God though not under his true name. Through the history of religions we learn more and more how widespread this notion is and how manifold are the ways in which it has been expressed. Jesus extends his invitation to believe in *him* also, to all the multitudes of nations, peoples, congregations, and individuals who believe in God. He seems to read the minds of those who would not follow his invitation because they do not want any mediation between themselves and the ultimate or who pin their faith and hope on mythical mediators. The Johannine Christ destroys the illusion that there could be several gods. Out of his consciousness of his most intimate communion with the Father, he assures his hearers that he and the Father are one.

Believe in me. To believe in Christ does not mean in the first place an intellectual assent to a dogma; it means the opening of the heart to the life-giving influence which will grip and transform whoever comes to know him; it means a dynamic and existential relation with the living Christ. "He that followeth me walketh not in darkness." (John 8:12.) Again Thomas à Kempis has said in simple and beautiful language, "When Jesus is present, all is well, and nothing seems difficult; but when Jesus is not present everything is hard. When Jesus speaks not inwardly to us, all other comfort is worth nothing; but if Jesus speak but one word, we feel great consolation."

2. "In my Father's house are many mansions: if it were not so, I would have told you. I go to prepare a place for you."

Christ, our Lord, reveals in these often-quoted words the profundity of his insight into God's nature. He uses a startling metaphor—the Divine realms as a vast palace with spacious accommodations—to warn against too limited and too narrow a notion of the supreme Deity, thc Upholder of the Universe. We do not have to go as far in the literal understanding of this image, known already to the Hebrew rabbis, as the authors of the early mediaeval Jewish mystical Hekhaloth treatises which describe in great detail the heavenly palaces opened to the gaze of the ecstatic visionary. We may not agree with Joachim Lange who suggested that Christ might have pointed to the starry sky while referring to the heavenly mansions. But we know how difficult it is to abstract completely from the temporal and spatial imagery of religious language, aware as we are of the symbolic character of any statement which is other than a negative or a positive assertion. In an age like ours, when living quarters are so hard to come by, the value of a place of rest such as Christ promises us is easily understood. Millions of temporary or permanent migrants in this world of ours are looking for a spot where they can rest. It need not be crude anthropomorphism to envisage the state of nearness to God in terms of the dwelling prepared for us by the Johannine Christ.

Preparation is necessary in the sense that the place must be provided but there is also the necessity to create the right disposition on the side of those who shall occupy it.

3. "And if I go and prepare a place for you, I will come again, and receive you unto myself; that where I am, there ye may be also."

St. Thomas Aquinas in his commentary to the Fourth Gospel quotes St. Augustine[1] as follows: "The temple of God is holy, which temple ye are. This house of God then is now built, now being prepared. But why has he gone away to prepare it, if it is ourselves that he prepared? If he leaves us, how can he prepare us? The meaning is that, in order that those mansions may be prepared, we must have faith: and thou seest, there is no faith."

"Where I am, there ye may be also."

The founder of Buddhism, no minor psychologist of the human heart, enumerates in his discourses the factors which constitute misery and suffering in this life. One of these factors is: to be separated from what is dear to us and to be tied to what is not dear to us. We long for the company of those we love in earthly terms, so no analogy could be more fitting to express our desire and our hope as Christians than that we may be where our Master is. He promises that he will come again and reveal himself to those who love him, but he announces first that he will go away. It is the test, that we believe that which we cannot now touch, hear, or see: "Now faith is the substance of things hoped for, the evidence of things not seen" (Hebrews 11:1). It was Kierkegaard who raised the question of whether disciples at secondhand, which includes all

[1]*De Trinit.* 48, 1.

those who have lived in the last eighteen hundred years, have been the worse off the further they were removed from the time in which Jesus Christ lived among men. He rightly says that there is no difference in principle between the disciples and those who, following the example of Paul, accepted Christ on faith, and who in Kierkegaard's words have the "autopsy of faith." The eternal or perpetual condition is ever given in time.[2] The first generation were at an advantage not because they were nearer in time, but because they realized more fully the tremendous challenge, which was played down and obscured as time went on. The later generations had to discover that behind what seemed easy was concealed the tremendous difficulty of the decision. Disciples at first *and* secondhand receive the "condition" (faith) immediately from God who does not favor anyone by letting time decide.

4 and 5. "And whither I go ye know, and the *way* ye know. Thomas saith unto him: Lord, we know whither thou goeth; and how can we know the way?"

Three of the disciples ask questions of Jesus in this chapter, and each of the three questions reveals a profound lack of awareness of the meaning of both the life and work of their master. While Peter inquired about the goal, "Lord whither goest thou?" (13:36), Thomas seems doubtful about the *way* which will lead to the Fathers' house. It is the same Thomas Didymus who, according to our Gospel (20:24, 25), felt that he could only trust sensual verification. "Except I shall see in his hands the print of the nails, and put my finger into the print of the nails, and thrust my hands into his side, I will not believe." In his answer to Thomas' question Jesus substitutes for the *house* of the Father, the *Father himself*. "Because," as Frederic Godet quite beautifully states, "it is not in the heavens that we find God; it is in God that we find Heaven."[3]

6. "Jesus said unto him: I am the way, the truth and the life. No man cometh unto the Father but by me."

St. Augustine beautifully explains this verse in *De Verbo Domini*: "He said: I am the *way* whereby thou wouldst go; I am the

[2]Soren Kierkegaard, *Philosophical Fragments*, trans. David Swenson (Princeton, 1946), p. 57.

[3]Frédéric Godet, *Commentaire sur l'evangile de Saint Jean* (English translation; Edinburgh, 1880), p. 131.

truth whereto thou wouldst go; I am the *life*, in which thou wouldst abide. But he adds: the truth and life everyone understands; but not every one hath found the way." "Truth" we take to mean with Godet the revelation of God in his essence, in his holiness and love. "Life" refers to the Divine being communicated to the soul, giving it power and peace. Because Christ is truth and life, he is the way, *vera via vitae.* Hilary asked, "When it is said that 'the Son is the way to the Father,' is it meant that he is so by his teaching or by his nature?" The earlier centuries were greatly troubled by this question, and many today are making such distinctions, but the Johannine Christ does not permit us to indulge in them. Christ's teaching reveals his nature, and an understanding of the nature of Christ alone can make his kerygma meaningful. Because he is one with the Father, he is truth and life; and because truth and life are revealed for us in him, he is the way.

John 14:6 is a stumbling block to many today because of the exclusive character of the claim stated in the word "*I* am" and "nobody comes to the Father *but by me*." It is Christ anticipating his glorification who speaks. If in him the fullness of the power and love of God is becoming manifest, then he is, because truth and life are embodied in him, *the* way to the Father. As Christians we believe that God has revealed himself at sundry times and sundry places and that the great seers and teachers of mankind have apprehended him according to the light afforded to them. But there is a difference between the realization of this fact and the experience of transformation in and through the communion with Christ which comes to us by knowing him and loving him. But of this existential relation we can and must say: He is the way, the truth, and the life. Not by accepting his teaching or believing in his claims but by way of communion with Christ we "come to the Father."[4]

Westcott[5] in his commentary reminds us of Thomas à Kempis' paraphrase of *Ego sum via veritas et vita: Sine via, non itur* (without a way there is no walking); *sine veritas, non cognoscitur* (without truth there is no knowledge); *sine vita, non vivitur* (without life there is no living). *Ego sum via quam sequi debes* (I am

[4]George H. E. MacGregor, *The Gospel of John* (New York, 1929), p. 306: "Not by accepting my teaching, or believing in my claims, but only by way of mystical communion *with myself*."

[5]Brooke Foss Westcott, *The Gospel According to St. John* (London), 1908), II, 170. The quote from Thomas à Kempis is *De Imit.* III, 57.

the way which thou shouldst follow), *veritas quam credere debes* (the truth in which thou shouldst believe), *vita quam sperare debes* (the life in which thou shouldst put thy hope).

7. "If ye have known me, ye should have known my Father also; and henceforth ye know him, and have seen him."

We are inclined to see in the "henceforth" (ἀπ'ἄρτι) with some older (Chrysostom) and some newer interpreters (Lücke) a hint at the fullness of understanding which was to come to his disciples at Pentecost though we may not be altogether wrong in supposing that it is with a view to the last gathering itself, at which these words were spoken, that Christ expects his friends to come to a true realization of his intimate communion with the Father.

Now the second disciple asks a favor of his master:

8. "Philip saith unto him, Lord, show us the Father, and it sufficeth us."

It has been said that the desire for a theophany to which Philip gives expression with this wish was probably shared by all of our Lord's disciples.[6] Philip, prudent and cautious as in the story of the feeding (John 6), does not understand that the true theophany is found nowhere but in a holy life. With his physical eyes he sees the Lord, but the meaning which the sight reveals is hidden to him. Philip—here a symbol of us all—is, as one interpreter (Hengstenberg) subtly puts it, "*alius a se ipso*," not making use of the best powers that are in him.[7]

Jesus reproaches him in saying:

9. "Have I been so long with you, and yet hast thou not known me, Philip? He that hath seen me hath seen the Father, and now sayest thou then: Show us the Father?"

I think we have to understand this second request not so much as the desire to test the affirmation of the master through the experiences of the senses, as a Thomas demands, but rather as the impatience of the disciple who, ever ahead of himself and of his own spiritual growth and development, yearns for an experience, the total vision which is as yet inaccessible to him. The unique intimate

[6]Godet, *op. cit.*, see pp. 133–34.

[7]Ernst Wilhelm Hengstenberg, *Commentary on the Gospel of St. John* (Edinburgh, 1865), p. 200. ". . . alius a se ipso, an alien to himself. . . ."

communion of Jesus with his heavenly Father is the presupposition for Jesus' beholding God; and it is a crude mistake on the side of the disciple to expect to be "shown" to have "demonstrated" *ad occulos* the fruit of this sacred communion achieved in Christ's most holy life.

10. "Believest thou not that I am in the Father, and the Father in me? The words that I speak unto you, I speak not myself; but the Father that dwelleth in me, he does the works."

11. "Believe me that I am in the Father and the Father in me: or else believe me for the very works' sake."

Jesus' "I am in the Father" is rightly taken by a modern interpreter[8] to mean reading God's will and mind. And his "The Father is in me" is taken as God's communicating to Christ his knowledge and power.

Philip (and in Philip the disciples, and in the disciples all of us) is invited to open his eyes and heart to divine the meaning of the double revelation of Christ's true nature in the *words* he speaks and in the *works* he has done: his words, that is the teachings recorded in the Gospel, which we have to interpret as inspired by Christ's intimate communion with God, and his deeds, performed under the motivation of the indwelling power of the Godhead. Taking into consideration the very context in which Jesus speaks, we may be justified in surmising that he anticipates here the last and greatest of the "works," the supreme redeeming act of divine love in his suffering and death.

Through the ages men have pondered over the meaning of the words of Christ, contained in the next two verses.

12. "Verily, verily, I say unto you. He that believeth on me, the works that I do, shall he do also; and greater works than these shall he do; because I go unto the Father."

13. "And whatsoever ye shall ask in my name, that will I do, that the Father may be glorified in the Son."

How could it be possible for his followers not only to exhibit acts of supreme devotion and divine love such as the Redeemer

[8]MacGregor, *op. cit.*, p. 307.

was capable of performing but even "greater works"? Godet says rightly in his commentary on the Fourth Gospel that greater than any outward manifestation of "miracles" is spiritual communication, as is found in prayer supported by the glorified Christ. Thus, we cannot isolate the two verses just read because the second provides the way for the understanding of the first.[9]

Jesus living, thinking, willing in us, as God in Christ, enables us to do the "greater works," the Church's works of faith. "With Christ's departure," MacGregor explains, "the full power of the Holy Spirit will be liberated into the world."[10]

14. "If ye shall ask anything in my name, I will do it."

Tholuck, in his commentary to the Fourth Gospel, quotes from the *Yalkut Shimeoni* to Ps. 91: "The Jew's progress will not be heard in this aim because they do not know the true name of God, but God will teach it to them in the age to come, according to Jeremiah 52:6."[11]

Twice in these verses there is mention of the name of Jesus. Here as elsewhere the name, *pars pro toto*, stands for what it designates instead of for Jesus. But as if he had anticipated the misuse of his holy name by some who would claim to "stand in Christ," Jesus adds, apparently without a close connection with the preceding words:

15. "If ye love me, keep my commandments."

Through the ages and in our own days there have been advocates of a brand of mysticism, according to which whosoever is filled with the Spirit becomes free from the yoke of all obligation, and cannot sin. The Montanists, the Brethren of the Free Spirit in the twelfth century, and our modern antinomians and orientalizing mystics have all assumed this position. The first epistle of John (2, 3) rebukes them as does our Gospel: "And hereby we do know that we know him, if we keep his commandments." To this

[9]Godet, *op. cit.*, see pp. 136–37.

[10]MacGregor, *op. cit.*, p. 308.

[11]V. Tholuck, *Commentar zu den Evangelio Johannis* (Hamburg, 1827), p. 255. "R. Joschua Ben Leir sagte: Die Juden werden in dem עולם חבא (im der vormessianischen Zeit) nich erhört, dann sie kennen den שם הפורש (den besonderen Namen) Gottes nicht, ober im zu kümftigen wird Gott ihnen denselben lehren, nach Jer. 52, 6."

Dodd remarks very finely in his commentary on the Johannine Epistles, "The Gospel of Christ is essentially a declaration of what God, in his grace toward man, has done through Christ; the Law of Christ is a statement of what God requires of those who are the objects of this gracious action."[12]

This is Christ's promise:

21. "He that hath my commandments and keepeth them, he it is that loveth me: and he that loveth me shall be loved of my Father, and I will love him, and will manifest myself to him."

These words St. Augustine explains: "He that has them in mind and accepts them in life, he that has them in words and keepeth them in works, he who has them by hearing and keepeth them by doing: he that has them by doing and keepeth them by persevering, he it is that loveth me."

Our chapter opens with a word of comfort: "Let not your heart be troubled;" the first half of it ends with a promise: "I will manifest myself." Whereas the first is addressed to the disciples the last is a direct promise to the individual lover and doer: I will manifest myself to him. The second half of the chapter begins on the same note: consolation. Preparing his disciples for the approaching separation, Jesus assures them that in the Spirit he will abide with them.

16 and 17. "And I will pray the Father, and he shall give you another comforter, that he may abide with you forever. Even the spirit of truth whom the world cannot receive because it seeth him not, neither knoweth him, and ye know him for he dwelleth with you and shall be in you."

In two other main passages in our Gospel (Chaps. 15 and 16) which, according to some critics, may have at one time preceded the Fourteenth Chapter, the coming of the comforting spirit of truth is said to be contingent upon Christ's leaving his disciples: "It is expedient for you that I go away for if I go not away, the comforter will not come unto you, but If I depart, I will send him unto you" (16:7).

God's Holy Spirit proceeding, as we believe, from the Father and

[12]Charles H. Dodd, *The Johannine Epistles* (London, 1946), Introduction, p. xxxi.

the Son, Supporter and Counsellor, will abide after the Lord Christ, according to the First Epistle of John (2:1); our advocate with the Father has returned to him. Therefore, the "Spirit of Truth" is called another comforter, sent (*paraklytos*) to strengthen and to represent the orphaned (the comfortless—*parakalon*). Didymus the Theologian explains, "the Holy Ghost was another comforter, differing not in nature but in operation." In order to receive him, we have to know him; that is, we open ourselves to the awareness of God's power and God's love manifested in his redeeming purpose. We have to see him and identify him, both of which are impossible for the "world," which, as MacGregor aptly puts it, "has neither the spiritual vision nor the mystical experience which alone can make the action of the Spirit intelligible."[13] In order to receive, the right disposition is a condition. Already in human teaching such presuppositions prevail, as St. Gregory says (30. Homily), "Let none then attribute to the human teacher the understanding that follows in consequence of his teaching: for unless there be a teacher within, the tongue of the teacher outside will labor in vain." The Spirit, so Christ tells his disciples, is present for them outwardly (παρ' ὑμῖν μένει) in the present Christ; it will be in them (καὶ ἐν ὑμῖν ἔσται): "he dwelleth with you and shall be in you."

18–20. "I will not leave you comfortless; I will come to you. Yet a little while and the world sees me no more; but ye see me; because I live ye shall live also. On that day ye shall know that I am in my Father and ye in me and I in you."

"I will come" (ἔρχομαι): In the Spirit, Christ is ever coming into hearts ready to receive him. We do not want to think here only of the manifestations of the risen Christ. We understand that his resurrection marks the preparation, as his appearance on the last day will be the consummation of his coming.

The world did not respond to the divine invitation extended in the life and teaching of Christ while he could be seen with fleshly eyes. Those he leaves behind are told that they are not "orphans" after he is lifted up; neither are we. Those who "see" him are promised that they shall live, with the realization of the indwelling of God's spirit in Christ and through him in us.

[13]MacGregor, *op. cit.*, p. 309.

22. "Judas saith unto him, not Iscariot, Lord, how is it that thou wilt manifest thyself unto us, and not to the world?"

For the third time one of the disciples, this time Judas Lebaeus or Taddaeus, the "energetic one," poses a question indicating that he does not follow his Master. His error is that he also longs for a miraculous manifestation of power to convince men without the spirit of understanding, not realizing that a disposition is necessary to perceive the things of the Spirit. His disappointment is akin to that of the Jews who expected the Messiah to come in earthly pomp and power. It is significant that he is not directly answered. Jesus, though addressing him, continues in his discourse as if the question had not been voiced.

23. "If a man love me, he will keep my word: and my Father will love him, and we will come unto him, and make our abode with him."

There is no manifestation except in that of the indwelling spirit which abides and illuminates and which is the gift of divine love and grace which rewards the keeper of the divine covenant.

As we read in the *Imitation of Christ*, "The doctrine of Christ exceedeth all the doctrines of holy man; and he that has the spirit will find therein the hidden manna. . . . Whosover then would fully and feelingly understand the work of Christ, must endeavour to conform his life wholly to the life of Christ."

24. "He that loves me not, keepeth not my sayings: and the word which ye hear is not mine, but the Father's which sent me."

St. Chrysostom explains: "Christ says: to love me, is not to be troubled but to keep my commandments: This is love: to obey and believe in him who is loved."

The end of this discourse resumes the theme of its beginning. "Let not your heart be troubled." Having prepared his disciples for his parting—

25. "And now I have told you before it came to pass, that when it is come to pass, ye might believe."

Christ imparts his blessing:

27 and 28. "Peace I leave with you, my peace I give unto you: not as the world giveth, give I unto you. Ye have heard how I said

unto you: I go away, and come again unto you. If you loved me, ye would rejoice, because I said, I go unto the Father, for my Father is greater than I."

It is in their attitude in the hour of parting, in the face of permanent or temporary leave-taking, that people reveal by which faith they live. To some it means hopeless despair, to others, the Stoics, it means composure in the face of hopelessness; the followers of Christ can be expected to understand their Master's exhortation, "if you loved me, ye would rejoice," rejoice for his Lord's sake (he is going to the Father) and for his own sake. With Christ, they know that the world cannot harm them. The peace of Christ is not like the negative "peace" in this world which means an intermittent ceasing of strife. As we read in the *Imitation*: "Peace is what all desire, but all do not care for the things that pertain to true peace. My peace is with the gentle and humble. In mild patience shall thy peace be."

30 and 31. "Hereafter I will not talk much with you; for the prince of this world cometh and has nothing in me. But that the world may know that I love the Father, and as the Father gave me commandment, even so do I. Arise, let us be going hence."

As the time of his passion draws nigh, Jesus, in setting his face to the coming trial, can proclaim in utter serenity that the great tempter, the prince of this world, has "nothing in him," no hold on him, meaning that no element in Christ's nature responds to him.[14] There is no denial of the existence and of the power of evil, an error of which not a few of Christ's followers have been and are guilty. The prince of this world cometh, and he ever cometh into what he well might consider his own. He cannot be appeased, but he can be confounded with the only power to which he has to yield, and that is power from on high. "I love the Father." Having lived in this love and testified to it by his works, Christ leaves, as his legacy, the great new commandment by which it will be known who are his disciples as he prepares himself and his disciples for his passion.

[14]*Ibid.*, p. 313.

8.

Belief and Witness

I

> Matthew 28:19-20: "Go ye therefore and teach all nations, baptizing them in the name of the Father and of the Son and of the Holy Ghost:
> Teaching them to observe all things whatsoever I have commanded you: and, lo, I am with you alway, even unto the end of the world. Amen!"

There is no characteristic of the Christian religion which is more enigmatic and obnoxious to the civilized and the uncivilized pagan than its propagandistic nature. Why, so the ancient and modern Stoic, Cynic or Epicurean asks, should anyone want to inflict his personal religious experiences, views or judgments upon any one else instead of minding his own business, according to the rules of polite society. This question is asked, with a modicum of surprise and irritation, quite often among people at large but also in academic circles, among adepts of the humanities as well as among those of the sciences; the "philosophers," who, in earlier days, were themselves not altogether adverse to proselytizing, tend to become actually annoyed with what has appeared all through the ages to the skeptical philosophical temperament as the misplaced zeal of the "religionist." The criticism leveled at Christian missionary efforts has been voiced on various grounds. There is the objection from *aesthetic* considerations: It is not in good taste to pry into another person's religious attitude, much less to turn on him in a desire to change him, his view or his conduct. The objection may also be based on *ethical* considerations: Is it morally right, is it defensible on moral grounds to invade another person's privacy, as you inevitably do if you approach him with a propagandistic motivation? Should we not rather have him err in his fashion than to see him subjected to outside pressures? It is only one step from this ethical concern to religious doubts as to the legitimacy of propaganda when it comes to religious truth. Very definitely the members of certain Asiatic cults insist in the name of conscience that there should be no invasion of religious premises, no interference with the individual search for truth. Certain individuals and some Christian groups have in more recent times been inclined to take a similar attitude, sometimes with the implied understanding that an "enlightened" Christianity must be expected to foresake all "fanaticism." Everybody, so it is said, must be tolerant of everybody else.

It does not take a prophet to see that we are faced with a genuine dilemma. On the one hand, we cannot but sympathize with the desire to protect in this day, when so little privacy remains to Western man, his right to be master within his inner four walls. In fact, it is in the very interest of this, his true freedom, that we are going to argue here, taking the word freedom to mean, as Bishop Gore once defined it: "power to realize our true being." But in order to be able to do that, we have to see very clearly that some sham freedom will have to be given up: namely, that of following the enticement of those who try to reach us on the level of the lowest common denominator (modern advertising) or the beguiling lure of our individual inclinations and desires. Peoples of aesthetic and moral sensitivity know that. That is why some would defend purely on aesthetic and ethical grounds the right to prevent a person from ruining his health by too literal a response to advertisement for alcohol, or the right to acquaint an unrepentant egotist with the Christian notion of *caritas*, a healthy respect for individual liberty nothwithstanding. But too much freedom, we have learned, is just as bad as not enough of it. There was a time when people took seriously the claim of some that they wanted for themselves and for others the freedom to go to hell.

Are we, then, ready to say that the critics of Christianity are wrong in objecting to the propagandistic zeal of its followers? Or should we go further and suggest that a Christian without the desire to convince others that in Christ is to be found the truth, is a truncated, an invalid Christian—in other words, no Christian at all? To the all-too-tender minded such a statement may appear wrong; it reminds him of inquisition, indoctrination, intolerance. Let us examine the three "ins" for a moment. There is nothing wrong with inquiring into one's brother's state of physical or spiritual health; in omitting to do that we should rather be guilty of indifference and of lack of brotherly affection. We should even take the initiative in bringing to his consciousness and helping him to make articulate the principles which guide his actions. However, all coercing pressure is to be avoided. But we feel compelled to tell him of Christ. Where should we draw the line? Granted that we feel that we enrich his life in sharing with him our experience of the power of Christ, should we leave him to "think it all out by himself" for fear of "indoctrinating" him, or should we attempt to articulate the meaning of this experience? Surely there must be many ways to lead one's life. Are they all equally good? As Christians we have preferences. Is it "intolerant" of us to make them known? Does "tolerance" mean to be frightened of that little sign on the study: "please do not disturb"? A Christian minister ought to have a somewhat "disturbing" effect; he is not true to his vocation if he tries to blend too smoothly into the social and ecclesiastical surroundings. Tolerance in the name of indifference is a bourgeois virtue. Neither Jesus himself, nor St. Paul, nor St. Francis, nor Luther, Wesley, nor Jonathan Edwards were in this sense tolerant. Do we then advocate "intolerance"? In one of his books, the well-known Indian philosopher, Sir Sarvepalli Radhakrishnan, lauds modern Christianity for having abandoned the missionary attitude—this he considers a sign of maturation. If we do not agree with this judgment we have to do two things. First, we have to state clearly how much and exactly what it is in our religion we want to impart to others; and secondly, we have to see to it that "religious minorities" are protected. If we do try the first, we may become fanatics; if we do not care about the latter, we should be rightly called intolerant. Professor O. Cullmann in his study of the incipient development of the Christian creed has shown what the earliest Christian confession of faith "entailed." "Jesus Christ is Lord"—in this formula his followers found the epitome of their belief. The Lordship of Christ—this formula has metaphysical, ethical and social implications. In other words, I do not mean to profess merely that Jesus is my Master or Savior, my favorite saint, as it were, but that he is the "Light of the World." In acknowledging the cosmic dimension of his redemption work, I pledge myself to help to establish his dominion ("that in his name every knee should bow and every tongue confess"; Phil. 2:6–11). Only a generation who saw in him exclusively the Carpenter could be satisfied to look upon Jesus as their personal guiding star irrespective of how he might appear to the individual neighbor or the neighboring nations. If the subjective reaction to the cosmic Lordship of Christ is worship, that to his moral demands is imitation: "Be ye perfect, as your Father in heaven is perfect." It is in this realm that even a highly secularized Christian society did not altogether surrender to the spirit of the age: in the realm of morals, Christian ideals continued to be propagated through the end of the nineteenth century though they became frequently blended with Victorian conventions.

Our acknowledgment of the Lordship of Christ will of necessity, in addition to its metaphysical and ethical, have its *social* implications. Here past generations have grievously erred in their interpretation of the nature of Christianity, and we have barely begun to rediscover what such terms as the "Body of Christ" or "the Church" really mean.

II

Now if all of us acknowledge the Lordship of Christ, notwithstanding differences in our understanding thereof, can we refrain from *proclaiming* it? The proclamation of the Kerygma (Gospel) is only in part to be thought of as a *verbal* one. Sermon, preaching, teaching are all good and useful. But they are much less indispensable than many Christians think. In this sense Dean Inge has said, "Religion is not taught but caught from someone who has it. We learn about the spiritual world from those who have been there." It does not take too much imagination to envisage a state of affairs for the future in which verbal expression will play an even less important part than it does now. We rather hope for it. It is not altogether a weakness of Catholicism that in its worship and its total life preaching is not as prominent as it is in Protestantism. Promulgation of the Kerygma (Gospel), in addition to being work, is action. The good deed is the most persuasive argument, and it is one of the real merits of modern Protestantism to have rediscovered this emphasis especially in its social implications: "Be ye doers of the word." But now, both word and deed are means of promulgation which are open to the suspicion of implying an invasion of the sanctity of another person's private life. All of us, at times at least, don't want to be talked to and urged on. Everyone knows how difficult it has become in the modern world to defend oneself against propaganda, direct or indirect, and against the coercive methods of those who want professionally to do good. But there is a third method of promulgation besides word and deed: by the exhibition of a disposition, a disposition which can best be characterized by the presence of the so-called theological virtues, faith, hope and charity. Of course, we modern people are very apt to think immediately of an expression of all that in action and not as an Easterner would, of the disposition which is really meant by *agape* or *caritas*; and yet, it is perhaps the most effective means of promulgating the Kerygma. "Men," says Meister Eckhart, "should not think so much of what they ought to *do* as of what they ought to *be.* Think not to lay the foundation of thy holiness upon *doing* but rather upon *being.* For works do not sanctify us, but we should sanctify the works. Whoever is not great in his essential being will achieve nothing by works whatever he may *do.*" There is nothing offensive or coercive in such a method of demonstration. The difficulty is only that there are not as many ready techniques to acquire it as there are for learning to speak and to act.

T. S. Eliot in his address on "Education and Religion" has warned us how easy it is to mistake one's own zeal for the truth. That is why those of us who will teach and preach need a vigorous education and training in critical methods to be applied to all that which claims our assent. A naive person is inclined to feel that he is always right, the other always wrong, and he finds it difficult to distinguish between: "This is my inclination or persuasion" and "Thus says the Lord." His strength is the vigor of his conviction; his *weakness*, the lack of discrimination between that which is valid in it and that which is not. The over-critical student, on the other hand, distinguishes all too well, but dares not any more to espouse a cause the relativity of which makes it lose all value in his sight. Yet education and devotion are not mutually exclusive. The learned skeptic and the ignorant zealot are extreme caricatures, if you will, of tendencies of which one or the other prevails in each of us.

While the skeptic will never be exposed to the temptation to violate the sacredness of another person's inner life, the zealot rushes in where angels fear to tread. Against his attack we need, what otherwise would not be necessary, the protection of "religious minorities." It is not against the Gospel of Jesus Christ that protection is needed for Jews, Hindus, or Buddhists as well as for other non-Christians, but against those who compromise it by ways of promulgation which, to say the least, are not adequate. Non-Christians often have a good feeling for such inadequacy. They must be reassured that they will not be coerced or compelled or bullied. Let me quote the words of Jeremy Taylor, a great Anglican divine of the seventeenth century: "But, whatever you do, let not the preference of a different religion make you think it is lawful to oppress any man in his just rights: for opinions are not, but laws only, and 'doing as we would be done to' are the measures of justice and, though *justice* does alike to all men Jew and Christian, Lutheran and Calvinist, yet to *do right to them* that are of another opinion is the way to win them: but if you, for conscience sake *do them wrong*, they will hate both you and your religion."

III

Is it not a terrible responsibility to preach and teach Christ? That is why in the word of our text the exhortation to baptize is so intricately linked with that of teaching: "Go ye therefore and teach all nations, *baptizing* them in the name of the Father and of the Son and of the Holy Ghost." The motivation is that it does not suffice to reason somebody into Christianity, to convince him intellectually, but that it ought to be rather the *fullness of the spiritual* and the sacramental life of the body of Christ into which he must be expected to enter. Here modern Christians have another reason for self-examination. For a long time now, the teaching of the Kerygma had been fragmentary, half-hearted, and half-convincing, and all too often has been insufficient with regard to the dimensions of the Christian life into which it meant to initiate. It is *one* thing to be an Aristotelian and to urge others to form a study group for the reading of the writings of Aristotle, and another to invite to enter, by the act of baptism, the common life of the body of Christ which is the Church. In the recent past, Christian people and the whole Christian groups have made the mistake of believing that they could take the sting out of the challenge they were supposed to present to non-Christians by selling the Christian religion, as it were, at reduced costs. The word was passed around that you do not need the *Church*, or, for that matter, the *sacraments*, if you had only the right notion of or the right feeling about Jesus. In nearly all branches of Protestantism there is now evidence of repentance for this mistake, though the degree to which changes have taken place varies. The fact that conversion to Christianity implies *participation in the sacramental life of the ecclesia*, not only intellectual assent, makes it, at once easier and more difficult to promulgate Christianity; easier, because we do not try to out-think the philosopher, out-prove the scientist, out-argue the skeptic merely by beating them at their own game. True enough, questions and arguments have to be met but the demonstration which a Christian life and a Christian fellowship represent will speak its own convincing language without a noisy tournament of intellectual arms. The task is *difficult* because it is so exacting, reaching as it does in practically all the dimensions of life. Yet Abbe Hugelin, Baron von Hügel's friend, was right when he said, "The true means to attract souls is not to attentuate Christian doctrine, but to present it in full force, because then we present it in its beauty"—and, we may add, in its most convincing form.

Perhaps we are now in a better position to see why our Lord and Master exhorts us in the passage of Matthew which is our text to "observe all things whatever he has commanded us." That is a more detailed rule than the great summary which he himself outlined, in the exhortation to love God and to love one's fellow man. Such observation of duties fulfills the double task of testing our sincerity and loyalty and of helping to witness for our Christian faith. In this day and age we have to say that there is no danger in too close an observation of rules because there is generally so little observance of the things commanded. It is easier to laugh off and feel superior to the austerities and frugalities such as an earlier age of Christians knew than to replace them in their function, to arrest the flighty thoughts of an unconcerned world, and to focus and integrate the religious life of those who practiced such asceticism.

Re-reading our text, we cannot help but be stuck by the observation of how clearly it reflects the three great Christian tenets of faith, charity and hope. Somehow, we feel, every Christian sermon should rest on them. What, if not faith, would impel us "to go, to teach and to baptize," what would it avail, if it was not done in the spirit of charity—not in pride, not in a bellicose or polemic spirit—and, if it could not be done in hope? "Lo, I am with you alway, even unto the end of the world." This is the promise of Christ in the words of our text. The assurance of this presence which is not only to be understood eschatologically, is the ground for the confidence with which we undertake the missionary task. And this is the reason why we dare not slacken in it. In his last written words, the great English mystic William Law, the teacher of the man whose parish, it has been said, was the world, comments on our text: "All that Christ was, did, suffered, dying in the flesh, and ascending into heaven, was for this sole end: to purchase for all his followers a new birth, a new life and a new light, in and by the Spirit of God, restored to them, and being in them, as their supporter, comforter and guide into all truth." *And this was his "Lo, I am with you alway, even unto the end of the world."* Without this presence of the comforting and guiding spirit of Christ any teaching and preaching concerning him would be an exceedingly difficult and lonely venture. But as Hugh of St. Victor says: "*Non est solitarius, cum quo est Deus*" (None is lonely with whom God is).

Have we answered the questions of why the Christian cannot be expected just to mind his own business; what it is that compels him to propagate his faith, his love and his hope, and in what kind of spirit he should carry on his missionary task? John of the Cross has put it very simply and very grandly: "It is clearly true that compassion for our neighbors grows the more according as the soul is more closely united with God through love; for the more we love, the more we desire that this same God shall be loved and honored by all."

III

Faith and Knowledge

9.

The Meaning and Task of the History of Religions (Religionswissenschaft)

On special occasions . . . a discipline has the right and the duty to look about and to examine the correctness of its path, to ask about the well-being of its method, and to ascertain what shall be the purpose of its task. What is the meaning of *Religionswissenschaft*? There is an old traditional discipline already concerned with religion, namely, theology. Why need there be a *Religionswissenschaft* at its side? When this discipline took shape during the nineteenth century in a very fascinating process of development, there were many—and they still may be found now and then—who thought that *Religionswissenschaft* was called to supplant theology. Recent *Religionswissenschaft*, insofar as it need be taken seriously, has definitely departed from this error. At this point it is widely separated from the work of a meritorious scholar such as Ernst Troeltsch. Theology has its own task in identifying its own confessional norms, and none may take this task from it. Theology is concerned with understanding and confirming its own faith. Foreign religions, to a certain and not inconsequential degree, belong to its realm of study; namely, as they exhibit close or distant relationships in their respective histories or in their concerns. But this can never be the reason for ascribing to theology the immense task of studying and describing the foreign religions in their manifold fullness. At the same time, the development of religious studies tells us that the proposition "he who knows one religion knows all" is false. Thus, theology has every reason to show and to cultivate a lively interest in the results of studying other religions. It nevertheless leaves the study itself to the discipline which has come into existence especially for this purpose. Quantitatively and qualitatively *Religionswissenschaft* thus has a field of study distinct from that of theology: not our own religion but the foreign religions in all their manifoldness are its subject matter. It does not ask the question "what must I believe?" but "what is there that is believed?" According to this definition, it may now seem that the question raised by *Religionswissenschaft* is a superfluous, idle, even harmful curiosity—for the satisfaction of which we can waste neither time, nor energy, nor motivation today—especially at this juncture when we ought to concentrate on what is absolutely necessary. It is good that difficult times now and then compel people to recognize the superfluous for what it is and to throw it overboard and then to limit themselves to what is essential. For us this means that if *Religionswissenschaft* is only an aesthetically interesting or purely academic matter, then, indeed, it has no right to exist today.

The religions of exotic or primitive peoples have often, as has their art, been regarded as curiosities. This is an insufficient, as well as an improper, motive for occupying oneself with them. But even the pure, academic study of foreign religions, which ethically can be fully justified inasmuch as it rests on a broad desire for truth, must today be prepared to defend its right to exist. It cannot be denied that many a recent attempt in *Religionswissenschaft* is more or less exposed to the threefold criticism of lifelessness, intellectualism, and historicism. This accusation is often brought against the scientific disciplines in our own time. But it is an empirical, not a basic, shortcoming. *Religionswissenschaft* can as little do without learned research as can any other discipline. Nevertheless, this purely learned pursuit stands in the servitude of a higher purpose. Where research in religions, as a consequence of individual inability or from a basically false attitude, appears in the guise of a herbarium—a collection of and for linguists, ethnologists, and historiographers of religions—and where it appears as an occupation with theoretical and abstract formations of thought which dissolve values in unlikely comparisons, there it misses the purpose of *Religionswissenschaft.*

Religionswissenschaft, as we think of it, is alive; moreover, it is positive and practical. It is a living concern to the extent that it remains aware that the religion with which it deals is the deepest and the noblest in the realm of spiritual and intellectual existence, although, to be sure, it is difficult to see into the dark depth of that inwardness. *Religionswissenschaft* is alive, further, in that it recognizes the dynamic nature of religion, in that it knows that its goal will never be reached, and in that it can never sufficiently express that which it hopes to express. For the study of religious expressions, this means a never-ending task. *Religionswissenschaft* is also positive. A rather justified suspicion to the contrary has repeatedly been expressed—and not on the part of insignificant people. This suspicion has been nourished by the sounding from within our own realm of negative, overly critical, destructive, and nihilistic opinions. These tendencies could not help but produce justified defensive reactions since the enemies of religion disguised themselves as scholars.

However, *Religionswissenschaft* in its true intention does not dissolve values but seeks for values. The sense for the numinous is not extinguished by it, but on the contrary, is awakened, strengthened, shaped, and enriched by it. And as research in religions discloses religious feeling, desire, and action, it helps to reveal more fully the depth and breadth to which religiosity may radiate. A history of religions (*Religionsgeschichte*) which is inwardly connected with the history of cultures can accomplish much in this respect. When we have at last stated that *Religionswissenschaft* has a practical aspect, we must however protect this assertion against a possible misunderstanding. The practical benefit which justifiably is to some degree also demanded of all scientific disciplines must not be seen and sought too directly—which happens now as ever and which is supported by the spokesmen of contemporary need. How far-reaching in its often broad and indirect effects has been what appeared at first to be a very abstract philosophical investigation! The practical aspect must not be understood too narrowly. *Religionswissenschaft* cannot and must not serve the current moment in this bad sense.

What then is the practical significance of *Religionswissenschaft*? It broadens and deepens the *sensus numinis*, the religious feeling and understanding; it prepares one for a deeper conception of one's own faith; it allows a new and comprehensive experience of what religion is and means. This is as true of the religious experience as such as it is of the doctrinal and dogmatic aspect of religion, of its practice in the cult, and of the organization of the congregation. The effectiveness of the religious genius, the power and the formation of the religious community, the shaping of culture by religion—all these are experienced in new and manifold ways which do not paralyze but rather strengthen and fortify religious impulses.

Let us here remember the comparative approach; it has been much too overworked in the past, and too great expectations have been held concerning it. Now, in turn, it is easily underestimated. To observe the multiplicity of religious life and of religious expression, to discover similarities and relationships, need not, as some fear, have a sobering or paralyzing effect on one's own religiosity. On the contrary, it could become a support and an aid in the battle against the godless and estranged powers; it ought to lead to the examination and preservation of one's own religious faith. The value and significance of this may be recognized more clearly through that which is related but not identical. As Christians we have no reason at all to shy away from comparison—at any rate, not insofar as the idea and the impulse of our religion is concerned, although more, perhaps, in regard to practice. But there, precisely, the results of *Religionswissenschaft* could have very enlivening and encouraging effects. Precisely because the young person of our time has often very little living knowledge of the final and decisive religious experiences, the detour through examples and analogies from other religions may serve many a purpose.

Personally, I have many times seen young and open-minded students, in the study of the great subjects of *Religionswissenschaft*, attain, to their own surprise, a new understanding of the essentials of their own faith. The study of our various creeds—not as the dry enumeration of various doctrinal opinions, but as actual introductions into the piety of particular Christian movements—may accomplish something new. For example, in understanding the meaning of the cultic expressions of Catholicism, we may effect a richer and more forceful unfolding of our own religious life. As an instance from the general history of religions, the understanding of the immense role which the ethical aspect plays in the life of Buddhists will in theory and in practice lead increasingly to a more intensive unfolding of the motives contained in the imperative of the Christian ethic. *Out of life and for life*—even though it is to be understood in the above-described sense—is the motto of every scientific discipline and consequently also of *Religionswissenschaft.*

It is of course especially clear that the discipline concerned with religion must be inwardly alive (more, perhaps than the disciplines concerned with economics, law, language, and art), that it can proceed finally only with the austerity and sacred depth appropriate to its great subject matter, with an ever renewing openness, with enthusiasm and thoroughness. It is an exaggeration, but nevertheless understandable, when some people in principle and because of the depth and delicacy of religious matters question the possibility of a *Religionswissenschaft* or of "understanding" religion. Perhaps there is here a greater justification than there is for those who seek to interpret the documents of religious life no differently from documents of a business nature or than there is for those who cast judgement from the ivory tower of a modern intellectual enlightenment upon the customs and beliefs of the primitives. In any case, *Religionswissenschaft* would choose to assert rather less than too much. Happily, at least among us, it has freed itself from the pathos of optimistic positivism.

However much the work of *Religionswissenschaft,* as research, will always be careful about particulars—for here the meditation on the insignificant, of which Jakob Grimm spoke cannot be thorough enough—the goal of *Religionswissenschaft* remains to understand and to present as living totalities the religions studied. After they have been disclosed and studied, its desire will always be to place the individual beliefs and ideas, the customs and communal modes, into that context in which alone they live; to connect them and to show them together with the spirit of the entire religion, with the basic intention that animates them, and with the creative religious intuition at their source.

Schleiermacher has said that every religion represents one aspect of the divine and develops a certain attitude toward it, an attitude which unfolds within the major spheres of religious expression, in doctrine, and in community. It is the task of *Religionswissenschaft* to show how strong, how weak, how enduring, the spirit (*Geist*) of a religion is, or how in ever new beginnings it manifests itself externally. The hermeneutic circularity in this need not frighten us. This spirit must be understood by means of its dogmatic, cultic, and sociological expressions so that it may then be presupposed in the interpretation of these same manifestations. Religious language in the broader sense of "expression" (*Ausdruck*) is always a code which points beyond itself. This is the truth of the hermeneutic of depth-exegesis, which we encounter in all great religious complexes and which—however arbitrary and unprovable its interpretation of the particulars may seem—has an eternal right over against all rationalism in the understanding of religious expressions.

In a religious doctrine, or in a cultic act, there is always more intended than can be recognized (because expressions in word, pitch, and gesture always limit that which is to be expressed). And then again in excess of what is intended, there is also something in an expression of the religious totality which is represented by it and hinted at by it. The demand to do justice always to all these relationships is put on the student of religions. It is exactly the decisive trend, the central motivation of a given religiosity, which is often very difficult to grasp, to trace, and to describe. And still, this apparently theoretical and abstract undertaking is of special practical significance. It is significant for missions; they are just as much entitled to make use of the work of *Religionswissenschaft* as the latter will always thankfully accept for study—and this does not exclude criticism—the results of missionary reports about other religions. For the sake of contact (*Anknüpfung*), it will be very important to recognize the primary motivating forces of the religiosity which one confronts. These forces are definitely not always expressed in the ideas and beliefs of the primary official doctrine. It is important to identify them, to determine where and to what extent a religion is alive and has power to live. It is important to determine where the negative and sensitive spots are that require considerate care and to determine where positive values appear, the admiration of which is required for contact and communication to occur.

From what has been discussed, it should be clear that the central concern of *Religionswissenschaft* must be the understanding of other religions. Before we speak about this understanding proper, we shall venture yet a few words toward the further clarification of what has been said. Today, especially, the study of religions which are not our own is obliged to defend its ambitions. First, it has to defend itself against the theological objection that "he who knows one religion knows them all." Then, further, it must defend itself not only with respect to external opportunity (Can one afford to occupy oneself beyond the present concerns of our nation and our hemisphere with the religions of distant lands and times?) but also against skepticism that knowledge is possible about that which transcends one's own vital and spiritual life, feeling, thought, and will. To the point respecting opportunity, we may add that *Religionswissenschaft* in its presentations and in its research has to distinguish between what is important and what is less important, what is interesting and what is peripheral, what is necessary to know and what is worthy of knowing. But this is essentially a didactic matter. It is understandable that today in lectures and in courses it is primarily the religions which appeal to the wider public that must be discussed: those which stand prior historically to our Christianity—as for example, the Germanic religion as the early faith of our people—or, in another way, the high religions with which our own struggles today at so many places. In this, *Religionswissenschaft* will have to claim the totality of religious phenomena as the task of its research—to study them and to understand them—but it will also have to claim penetration into most distant realms. A discussion of the final reasons for this would lead us deeply into the systematic problem of philosophy of religion, on the one hand, and into the methodology of the intellectual disciplines, on the other. Therefore, in the present context we must omit such a discussion. But since again and again in the course of time the possibility of understanding other religions has been doubted, *Religionswissenschaft* has a fundamental interest in this question.

The student of religions must be clear about the difficulties to which critics have rightly pointed. We refer here to the difficulties contained in the very naive assumption that religious phenomena, if only sufficient materials were available, could readily be understood through the scientific approach. This assumption still plays a great role among the various types of Positivism, as well as in that study of religions which is determined by it. Of course, a radical skepticism as a consequence of either religious indifference or of agnosticism or as a result of historical skepticism (where the history of religions, as all history, is a *fable convenue*) must be rejected just as must be any naive optimism concerning phenomenological imagery.

The difficulties in our understanding are of various types. First, they are quantitative in nature: for example, the often considerable distance in time and space, especially serious with respect to the "dead," the exotic, and the primitive religions. With the consequent lack of information, with the discontinuities and transformations among the traditions or source materials, may one still hope at all to attain a more or less true picture of the religions from the distant past and from distant realms? One need only think for instance of the religions of Egypt, Babylonia, China, and Mexico. Second, there are the qualitative difficulties that hinder our understanding: the uniqueness of foreign inwardness, which is likewise inherent in its expressions. Spengler, to name only one widely known thinker, has recently pointed especially to the uniqueness of ancient thought, feeling, and perceptivity. Who is there who has not felt the unfathomable depths that inhibit the religious representations of the Far East or the demonic so typical of African religions?

However, not only *Religionswissenschaft* is burdened with both of these types of difficulties; rather, all intellectual disciplines concerned with cultures, especially the historical disciplines, share them. In long and toilsome work they have sought to develop methods and criteria which would allow to some degree the mastery of these difficulties. If one looks to the results of these labors, one will have to admit how astonishingly and how extensively they have been crowned with success. We actually have a body of knowledge about the religions of peoples long since past as well as of distant places. This knowledge can withstand the most exacting tests and controls; it completes, broadens, and extends itself continuously, and it constitutes more than a subjective picture of particulars. Moreover, we are even able to test against the certain results of research the false pictures which are based on insufficient and one-sided information; here the error of poor subjectivity appears to be eliminated to a very great extent. Nevertheless, nobdy will therefore underestimate the difficulties that have been mentioned.

We continuously have reasons to examine within an ever-extending problematic the possibilities, the chances, and the limits in understanding other religions. How difficult it is even to obtain a clear picture of the religiosity of a person near to us—still within the realm of common faith and familiarity! How difficult it is to comprehend the piety of our predecessors of perhaps only a few decades, of the faiths of neighboring lands, of the faith of Islamic people who still have certain religious influences in common with Europe, and finally of the people of India and China.

With this we actually have arrived at the third major difficulty with which the understanding of other religions must struggle. This difficulty is unique in that it concerns the nature of the religious. It will certainly be less difficult to obtain a picture of the legal customs and of the linguistic and artistic expressions of a people than of their religion. The last is above everything else kept in high esteem. It may even be fearfully hidden from foreign eyes and guarded as an arcanum. And even when it is possible to look into it, it is really not easy to grasp its meaning. A simple example will point this out: a Roman Catholic mass, in which so much is interrelated and unfamiliar, even foreign, to the Protestant who attends. If it is a church service according to the Greek, the Coptic, or the Armenian rite, the strangeness is immediately greater. This foreignness grows again as we encounter no longer a Christian but, for example, a Jewish, or an Islamic, or even a Buddhist worship service. How difficult for consequent understanding are the religious root-conceptions and root-customs of taboo, totem, nagual, and others. How different the baroque mythology of Japanese Shinto, the orgiastic cults of certain Indian Shiva sects, the fanaticism of the Islamic Shi'ah, appear to us. Here our discussion closes in on a great and serious problem: the secret of plurality among religious experiences. We can only lead up to this problem, for its consideration is a concern for philosophy of religion and for theology. Here we shall deal only with the question whether and how it is possible for *Religionswissenschaft* to understand other religions. We have already seen that many practical proofs of its possibility are available. Hermeneutically, on what does this possibility rest?

We have spoken above of what is generally representative of spiritual, and therefore also of religious expressions. The expression then becomes transparent; it allows something to shine through of the specific and perhaps unique spirit (*Geist*) of a certain religious context. Thus it is that views into the depths (*Tiefenblicke*) become possible. Not always and not to everybody do they open themselves. But it is amazing how much a small and peripheral aspect, taken from the conceptions and customs of a faith, can disclose to a gifted and trained mind. Actual intuition (*Divination*) here, as always, is the exception. Synthesis (*Kombination*) stands in the foreground of all intellectual endeavors, as it does in *Religionswissenschaft*. If then, perhaps, in a happy and fruitful interplay of both avenues to knowledge, some decisive characteristics of a foreign religiosity have emerged for the researcher, he may then dare to grasp and describe its basic intention. In this it is a great help for the human understanding that in the structure of spiritual expressions (of such great and deep experiences as are the productively religious ones) there is inherent an amazing continuity (*Folgerichtigkeit*). Nor is this continuity absent in the structures of the historical religious systems.

It is not very difficult for one who has really comprehended the central intuition of Islam, its experience of the deity, as this is expressed in the original revelation to the prophet Muhammed, to discover it again in the doctrine, theology, cosmology, anthropology, soteriology, and cult. In spite of all other influences, this central intuition develops within the framework of these expressions. The experience of suffering within a world of change, fundamental for Buddhism, is displayed with such a continuity in its doctrine, is presented in its symbols, and is shaped within its ethic, so that the understanding of this may, like a great key, unlock an otherwise strange-appearing world of expressions.

Such considerations certainly ought not minimize the difficulties; they ought not delude us about the levels and degrees of understanding, about the differences involved among its various risks. But by considering and by honoring differences, an old truth must not be forgotten. As Goethe and Wilhelm have formulated it, in every man there dwell all the forms of humanity. Novalis asked at one time: How can a man have an understanding of something of which he does not have the seed within himself? This insight in no way implies the lack or the weakness of him who does the understanding; rather, it implies the conviction that in all of us is contained more than becomes manifest in the co-operation of circumstances and fate.

Only very recently Eduard Spranger in his illustrative investigation of the primary levels of reality-consciousness (*Abhandlungen der Akademie der Wissenschaften* [Berlin], 1934) has proven that in all of us there are latently present certain more primeval structures of consciousness. What is called "mind" has the ability to activate these and to understand, so to speak, the atavistic and distant expressions of our soul, the expressions which are alien to our present consciousness. Novalis again says: We stand in relationship with all parts of the universe, with the future and with the past. What relationship we shall primarily develop and what relationship for us shall become primarily effective and important depend only on the direction and duration of our attentiveness. This means that in principle there could resound in each of us something of the ecstatic, the spectral, the unusual—something of that which to us, the children of another age, of another race, and of other customs, appears strange among the religious expressions of distant lands. Where this natural disposition is developed through training, there also the prerequisite for an actual understanding of foreign religiosity exists.

This can be illustrated through the example of myth. In myth, religious experience is expressed in unique categories. As recent ethnological and psychological research has shown, our logical norms are not necessarily valid for these categories. Thus the myths of primitive peoples with their identifications, their theriomorphisms, and so on, at first seem abstruse to the uninformed, contemporary reader or listener. And still, it does not seem impossible to sense something of the intended reality of the myth. Such immersions into archaic modes of consciousness are generally more easily attained by young people. Such modes of consciousness are almost self-evident and present for them. I am reminded of our youth associations and their experience, their symbolism and their customs; in them the world of primitive man (*Naturmensch*) is not only imitated externally but actually felt in participation, and it becomes clear that their experience of it is not a purely intellectual affair.

In the human understanding, as the excellent hermeneutics of Wilhelm Dilthey has shown, the totality of mind and soul (*Totalität des Gemüts*) is effective. Concretely stated, the religious content of myth cannot be found alone in a careful and thorough, though necessary, analysis of its ideological elements and motives; rather, the entire personality of him who studies and understands is spoken to. If he wishes to understand the attitude from which the mythological faith and custom have issued, he must respond. An inner aliveness and broadness is necessary if we actually wish to understand other religions. In this connection it should be stated explicitly that the one-sided advancement of a particular point of view is bad for the understanding. As justified and fruitful as may be the co-operative approaches of psychology, sociology, and typology, pure psychological, pure sociological, and pure typological answers do not help us to understand foreign religiosity. Unfortunately, our discipline is rich in one-sided attempts that have been based on false, narrow, and oblique conceptions of the nature of religion.

It appears to be a truism to say that hemeneutics demands that he who wishes to understand other religions must have a sense (*Organ*) for religion and in addition the most extensive knowledge and training possible. Many still think that one of these two prerequisites is sufficient. While all sorts of dilettantes (a famous example is the interpretation of Lao-tse's *Tao Te Ching*) err in one of these directions, often philologists, ethnologists, and other specialists go amiss in the other. The first demand is stated by some in a still more strict and narrow sense. Well aware of the abovementioned difficulties in understanding other religions, they think that one must actually belong to a community of believers if one wishes to grasp its actual concern. This is a significant assertion, and it must be seriously examined. If it proves to be fully correct, the ground on which *Religionswissenschaft* builds will have been withdrawn. Here, too, a glance at the results of a century rich in religious studies of the most varied kinds will reveal in fact that even those who have not studied another religion as a member of that particular religious community may be successful. The same can likewise hardly be denied of knowledge concerning the entire realm of expression, that is, of the doctrine, cult, and constitution of the religious community concerned.

But the matter gets more difficult when we are dealing with the inner experience, the understanding and intention to which such expressions bear witness. There can be no question that growing up within a tradition, belonging to the community of faith, can be a favorable precondition. However, the effect of habit, the absence of distance, and so on, may certainly also be negative influences. Standing within a tradition is nevertheless important. It could perhaps be an advantage in certain situations for the convert over the outsider. It could enable him to grasp the conscious ambition of the community which he joins. But one would want to ask, with respect to understanding Buddhism, for example, whether he who through conversion has been accepted into the community actually has a greater insight than the outsider, perhaps a Westerner, who for a long time has immersed himself in Buddhist studies. We may admit without reservation that standing in a tradition is something that is difficult to replace and that—provided the other prerequisites which we have found necessary are also present—the chances for understanding the actual intention of a religious community are increased. But in practical confrontation with the multiplicity of phenomena, with which the student of religions must deal, such a participation will not be possible. Thus, the demand that one belong to the religious community which one wishes to understand cannot be made a prerequisite—not to speak of the new errors which could arise under these circumstances. The problem of knowledge and faith, of faith and understanding, cannot be discussed here. Only this much must be summarized: being rooted in a personal faith—a faith which may well blind one to other things but which, in contrast to the opinion of many, need not do so—does not necessarily mean a disadvantage for him who seeks to understand. The demand of a *tabula rasa* has long been recognized as utopian; and even though such objectivity might be desirable, it is actually impossible. Schleiermacher has seen that we must learn from our personal religious life in order to encounter the foreign. We need not a blank sheet but an impregnated one, one that will preserve the pictures projected onto it.

Is it at this point that *tout comprendre c'est tout pardonner*? In other words—and in connection with the above—is not the result of *Religionswissenschaft*, then, a hopeless relativism? Is it of such a nature that in its own best interests the Christian mission should be warned against a closer touch with *Religionswissenschaft*? I hope that with the foregoing I have succeeded in showing that contemporary *Religionswissenschaft* no longer pays obeisance to the historicist fallacy which in its time has fettered the so-called *Religionsgeschichtliche Schule*, namely that norms may be attained from history itself. If history of religions were supposed to tell us what we ought to believe, we would wait for such information for a long time. No, since it no longer thinks about giving such advice and since it has recognized that its field of study is sufficiently large as it is and that it has many concrete tasks that can ambitiously be attacked, we would be doing it a grave injustice to have this sort of suspicion. Certainly, it seeks to understand foreign religiosity. We have also seen that its motivation for this is ethically beyond reproach. How does it stand now with respect to forgiveness? Does the study of *Religionswissenschaft* weaken the sense of value, the courage and the ability to decide?

The ability to decide "what must I believe?" lies—and this we have repeatedly emphasized here—outside the sphere of a scientific discipline. We no longer are good enough rationalists and Positivists to believe that an intellectual discipline can replace religion, not even that it necessarily limits it. In practice, it is, however, still the case, as we can see among those peoples who have not yet emerged from their susceptibility to the scientific faith, that an Eastern student graduated from a Western university returns to his home region and deems himself toweringly exalted above the "superstition" which "still" prevails there. As we have said, with us this is no longer the case. It is not a good sign for a faith if it allows itself to be shaken by an intellectual discipline. True decision for a faith, I would like to say, is not only not impaired but is aided and deepened by *Religionswissenschaft.* But what about the sense of value? Nietzsche, who must be understood not only as a dogmatist but also as a critic, has said in his famous discussion of the advantages and disadvantages of historiography, in behalf of the life of the concrete force (*plastiche Kraft*), that it would be impaired if the great museum of human history—and thus also that of history of religions—were spread out without choice and distinctions before the people of today. The nineteenth century, to which Nietzsche held up the mirror, was stuck deeply in historicism; its anarchy of values was destined to have its full effects only at the beginning of the twentieth century.

We now have found again the right and the courage to evaluate. *Religionswissenschaft* will seek to grasp with understanding all that foreign religions produce of faith, cult, custom, and community. It will seek to grasp the actual meaning, the religious intention, out of which spring all these; otherwise, and this it knows well, it will have only empty shells to tinker with. *Religionswissenschaft* does not abstain from using scales and standards; on the contrary, it makes much use of them. It seeks to overcome all superficial presuppositions, all the binding tendencies; it attempts to see the phenomena of other religious life; it tries to understand and honor this life in its actuality. For once, the student of religions looks at a particular religion immanently, from within. He asks himself what a conception or a characteristic looks like, how it integrates within the totality of the religion concerned. He asks further—and here the reference to value in his study becomes quite clear—about the amount of religious productivity and vitality which speaks from within the specific phenomenon. If, for example, we consider the faith in a god (*Gottesglauben*) of a certain African tribe, we must determine the degree of perfection to which this belief in a god is expressed by this particular community; then we must honor the level of theistic experience which appears attained therein. This certainly is no easy task. Good sense, manners, and experience are needed in order to appraise correctly, to appraise, beyond all naive absolutizing of one's own personal beliefs and feelings, the religious quality among the particular phenomena of religious life. This is so precisely because standards which are taken from elsewhere, from the realm of aesthetic and ethical evaluation, very easily creep into the place of the only decisive religious point of view. It is understandable that from a didactic point of view, the more history of religions increases the amount of data and the more data it pushes into our horizons, the more the separation of the important from the unimportant, the great from the small, will have to be worked out.

An introduction to *Religionswissenschaft* should not consist of a non-selective enumeration of encyclopedic facts—as is said to be the case occasionally in academic presentations. Rather, it should be concerned with describing the great and classic figures in the history of religions, and of these, again—for each of these great inspirations, too, represents something typical—there should be pointed out the typical and the significant, the personal and the characteristic. The world religions have a claim to a special and thorough consideration. To this introduction also belongs the study of the history of a particular religion—perhaps the history of a significant one from among the more advanced as well as one from among the primitive cultures; then, further, the structure of that religion (its central point of doctrine, the major aspect of the cult, the hinge-point of the organization) and the major phases in its development must be identified clearly enough to make a comparison possible. For this, the role of the leading religious personalities, as well as the transformation of the official religion by popular piety, must also be presented. In all this the decisive thing is to make visible that in which true religiosity is present—a religiosity which may further be cultivated to determine secondary formations, for example, where petrification and degeneration have set in. An exemplary model for training oneself to grasp the significant from the fullness of the materials of *Religionswissenschaft* is still Rudolf Otto's *Das Heilige.* This study, besides being important for the phenomenology of religion, also has great methodological significance.

We have spoken of scales and of choice. It becomes readily clear that here again there is an important starting point with practical consequences. The missionary will find it valuable to have worked out for himself scales of the type hinted at here. From his point of view, he will know well the religion of the nation or tribe with whom he primarily deals. But he gladly and in addition would also like to acquire the greater background against which he can still more deeply understand this religion. In this context we cannot talk in detail about the various relationships between *Religionswissenschaft* and the study of missions. To cultivate and to deepen this knowledge has already been the special task of this periodical.[1] The more the insight spreads and deepens—as has happened especially in recent times—the more in all Christian missions one motive must stand decisively in the foreground: that behind the religious motive all other motives must retreat to the background, and that the people whom we missionize ought to be led to a religiosity appropriate to themselves and to their uniqueness. So the thorough study of their uniqueness becomes an increasingly important task; to this, too, *Religionswissenschaft* can contribute its share.

> I invite you to observe every faith which human beings have ever confessed, every religion which you have designated by a certain name or label and which perhaps has long since degenerated into a codex of empty customs, into a system of abstract concepts and theories; and when you investigate it at its source and through its more original constituents, you will discover that all this dead

[1]That is, the *Zeitschrift für Missionskunde und Religionswissenschaft*, where this article first appeared in 1935. [Ed.]

slag at one time was a red-hot pouring of the inner fire, the fire which is contained to a greater or lesser degree in all religions; you will discover in their true nature that, as I have presented it, each of these unique formations has been the one which the eternal and never-ceasing Religion had necessarily to assume among finite and limited characteristics.[2]

[2]Friedrich Schleiermacher, *Über die Religion. Reden an die Gebildeten unter ihren Verächtern* (3d ed.; Berlin: G. Reimer, 1821), pp. 364–65.

10.

Religious Commitment and Tolerance

It is a very great pleasure for me to be with you here in India and to have the privilege of sharing some thoughts with you about matters which concern both the minds and the hearts of many of us, both Westerners and Easterners. It has been an old and ever present wish of mine to visit India sometime, the home of a great civilization and of so much that fascinates and attracts a student of the history of religions. Having followed closely and with a lively interest the momentous developments which have, under inspired and wise leadership, culminated in the establishment of a new, free India, it is an incomparable satisfaction for me now to be able to visit India and to be with you thanks to the generosity of my home university. I want you to understand very definitely that I have come as one who wants to *learn* and there is no doubt in my mind but that I shall be able to bring back with me to America and to my students invaluable impressions and information. True, we in this modern world live closer together than we used to, but even so there is a very great need everywhere for true and genuine information. Certain preconceived notions, favorite prejudices and cliches interfere to prevent the genuine meetings of minds and hearts which result in true understanding on the basis of mutual respect.

But there are certain things I want to say to introduce myself to you. I was born and brought up in Germany. I studied and taught at the University of Leipzig, a center of Indian studies. My major interest was the history of religions with philosophy and Oriental studies as auxiliaries. I was brought up a Lutheran. When

I was a high school student, I met Professor Deussen, who was well known in this country as well as a scholar of Indian thought. After eleven years of teaching at the University of Leipzig I left Germany in 1935 to accept an invitation to come as a guest professor to the United States. Here I taught another eleven years at Brown University, one of the oldest schools in America and one founded in a spirit of tolerance. I joined the American Episcopal Church. In 1945 I was called to be Professor of History of Religions at the University of Chicago where I have since been teaching as a member of the Federated Theological Faculty.

One of the problems which has always interested me and one which I have written about is the problem of *understanding*, or more technically, of interpretation. What does it mean to understand other people, people different from ourselves, other civilizations, other religions? What is the nature of this process which we call understanding? Are there grades of understanding? What are the presuppositions of the interpreter? Are there kinds of understanding? And how about the limitations? In Germany this was an important practical question. I imagine it is in India, too.

A second problem to which I have tried to devote some thought and some writing has been the study of religious groups, the *sociology of religion.* My German teachers, Max Weber and Ernest Troeltsch, led the way, and when I ascertained that in America there was no textbook on the sociology of religions, I wrote one in which I attempted to give a typology of religious associations and to analyze the interrelationships of society and religion. My questions were: How do they interact? And, what are the different forms of religious authority? In many instances I drew examples from the Indian scene.

The third and most important problem which I should like to mention here is that of *religious experience.* At first there seem only to exist two alternative attitudes with regard to religion: fanatical partisanship and indifference. It has always been my conviction that this need not be. Fanaticism wherever it occurs is a product of fear and the contrary of that freedom to which the pursuit of truth entitles us. Indifference is a mortal enemy of religion; a people that allow it to take possession of them is most certainly on the downgrade. A degree of width and breadth is fully compatible with strength of conviction. The breadth I have in mind is not born of skepticism: it is a necessary ingredient in all enlightment faith. The problem of what constitutes genuine religious experience is not easily answered: it naturally leads one into another, that of religious *truth.* I have always felt that contempt, disregard or even hatred for convictions, opinions or views differing from mine was objectionable, not because I did not have any convictions myself but because I considered all and everyone's opinion as of equal value. If I am today a Christian, it is not because I was born and brought up as such. There was a time in which I felt highly critical and was looking for guidance and edification elsewhere. But as I looked around and as I delved deeper into the study of the varieties of religious experience, I became persuaded that Jesus Christ was my Lord and my Saviour, the light of the world. Far from spoiling me for scholarship and study, this insight immeasurably helped me and encouraged me. It also did not mean that now I would find Christianity all correct and the non-Christian religions all wrong. The contrast between what Christianity ought to be and what—in all its forms without exception—it actually is, has been very vivid in my mind ever since I consciously adopted him as my norm. Inversely, I became deeply convinced that there was so much Christ-like, so much thought and done in the spirit of Christ, in the non-Christian religions, that black-white paintings never had any appeal for me. Impressed increasingly upon my soul and mind was the understanding that it is the modern cardinal sin to despair of the truth, to embrace with the skeptics doubt that any one thing could be proved to be better or more valuable than any other. We are made and called, all of us, to seek for the truth and to receive as much of it as is accessible to human beings. Truth is a universal option. No country, no people, no individual has a monopoly—and none is exempt from its binding claim. Whether I am born in Europe, or in India, in America or in Africa, the same truth is truth, and it will take a tremendous cooperative effort on the part of all to do justice fully to it. It was a preposterous mistake to believe, as the West did, that the meaning of Christ and of the Christian message could be understood without the contribution of all peoples and all races of the world. The notion of a Christ seen through African eyes or in Asiatic garments exerts great fascination on me. In no case so far have I found it difficult to discern the spirit of Christ in what I read by and heard from Indian Christians.

You have so far patiently borne with me as I have tried to acquaint you with some facts and ideas which have made me what I am. Let me just add one more consideration. Christianity, we realize, is badly split. There are historical reasons for this. Yet many Christians are grieved by this fact and are most seriously concerned with bringing about changes. The most important difference is that between the Catholic and Protestant wings. On both sides we have strengths and weaknesses. The Anglican communion, into which this lecturer entered when he came to live in the United States, conceives of itself as a via media. It is a rich witness to the early Church and to the Fathers of the Church, which it considers as its norm. Its great age was the sixteenth and seventeenth centuries. There followed a decline which lasted until the end of the eighteenth century. After the Evangelical and the Catholic revivals in the early nineteenth century the new ecumenical and incarnational theology of Maurice, Gore and Temple endeavored to combine sound principles and sound learning with an ecumenical width and social concern. This movement points to the future by preserving the best in Anglicanism.

In this series of lectures entitled a *New Era in the Comparative Study of Religions*[1] I shall attempt to do three things: *firstly* to acquaint my audience with the recent developments and major contributions in our field; *secondly*, to outline a theory of religion which allows us to do justice to universal or general features in the expression of religious experience the world over and throughout the ages, without prejudice to the particular faith which each of us adheres to and wishes to make known; and *thirdly*, to indicate the direction in which we may find that the relations between religions everywhere in the world should be developed.

It would be presumptuous to explicate to you any aspect of the traditional religion of India on the one hand or, for other reasons, the basic tenets or applications of the Christian religion. I have rather chosen to present to you an analysis of religious experience which, if valid, would serve as a kind of *natural theology*, to allow a greater understanding between the religions of mankind.

[1]See Joachim Wach, *The Comparative Study of Religions*, Edited by Joseph M. Kitagawa (New York: Columbia University Press, 1958).

11.

The Problem of Truth in Religion

Our inquiry into the nature and structure of religious experience inevitably leads us to the problem of truth in religion. It is widely held that "tolerance" demands that the comparative study of religions should not raise the embarrassing question of truth on the ground that one religion is as good as the other and that one's affiliation with a particular religious tradition is more often than not the result of accident. Such indeed is the opinion of so outstanding a thinker as Sarvepalli Radhakrishnan. His theory of religious truth has been effectively refuted by D. G. Moses.[1] And although I have also taken issue with Radhakrishnan's view on the subject already,[2] it may be worthwhile for me to reiterate some of the arguments involved at this point.

We might recall that the quest for truth was at one time dismissed by historical, psychological or sociological determinism and relativism. It was the reawakening of a systematic interest among philosophers and theologians in the early twentieth century that revived the problem of truth as a prominent issue. For example, in the field of the comparative study of religions the work of Rudolf Otto greatly stimulated the question of truth in religion. It is significant to note in this connection that despite Karl Barth's negative attitude toward non-Christian religions, his influence has been widely

[1]See David Gnanaprakasam Moses, *Religious Truth and the Relation between Religions*, Madras, 1950, Part II, Chapter I, "Professor Radhakrishnan and a Parliament of Religions."

[2]Joachim Wach, "Radhakrishnan and the Comparative Study of Religion," in Paul A. Schilpp (ed.), *The Philosophy of Sarvepalli Radhakrishnan*, New York, 1952, pp. 443–458.

felt among those who are concerned with the relation between Christianity and other religions through the writings of Emil Brunner and Hendrik Kraemer. Both of them have rendered great service by vigorously protesting against the reigning relativism in religious questions. However, their approach to the problem of truth and their concept of the relation between religions are not satisfactory from our point of view. Admittedly, they are entitled to their Christian convictions on these questions, but their theories betray some unfortunate misconceptions which have serious implications.

Brunner is absolutely right in his insistence that the problem of toleration should not be confused with the solution of the question of truth. "Tolerance is a human attitude, which respects the personality of the other, but it has nothing to do with the truth or falsity of the 'other's' opinions and ideas."[3] Unfortunately, we cannot agree with Brunner in his radical opposition to all attempts to define the general nature of religion. It is simply not true to say that any formulation of the general "nature of religion" is bound to be irreconcilably opposed to the Christian faith, and that it is impossible for a Christian "to accept the view that there is a universal 'essence of religion' of which Christianity has a predominant share."[4] The notion of "discontinuity" between the Christian faith and other religions is even more sharply stressed by Hendrik Kraemer.[5] As over against those who acknowledge continuity between the Christian faith and other religions in their essential tendencies and aspirations, Kraemer maintains "discontinuity" as the starting point, rejecting all natural theology as well as theories of "fulfillment" and general revelation.[6] His whole argument hangs in the air if it can be shown that he is wrong in establishing such arbitrary alternatives—that one must either start from a general idea about the essence of religion, or derive solely from the revelation in Christ the standard of reference regarding what religion is and what religion ought to be.

It seems to us that these two conceptions are actually on quite

[3]Emil Brunner, *Revelation and Reason: The Christian Doctrine of Faith and Knowledge*, trans. by Olive Wyon, Philadelphia, 1956, p. 219.

[4]*Ibid.*, p. 220.

[5]See his *The Christian Message in a Non-Christian World*, London, 1938, and "Continuity or Discontinuity," in *The Authority of the Faith* (Madras Series, Vol. I), New York, 1939, pp. 1–21.

[6]See *The Authority of the Faith*, p. 14.

different planes. For instance, our understanding of the nature of religious experience and its forms of expression is not an act of faith but a result of empirical observation and investigation, whereas our faith, be it Christian, Muslim or Hindu, is based on an affirmation of reality which cannot be provided by phenomenological study of religions. Kraemer asserts that the Bible testified to divine acts and "not to religious experience or ideas."[7] But how do we know of these acts if they have not been experienced and interpreted? Kraemer himself has to admit that religious experiences are not absent from the Bible. It may be true that "preparation" and "fulfillment" are not the only categories under which the relation between religions has to be seen, but it does not follow that the "discontinuity" is the only term to be applied to the relation between the Christian and other religions. Quite rightly, D. G. Moses, in his criticism of Kraemer's views, affirms that all religions are continuous.[8] While Moses is aware that in some religions the fundamental religious needs of man are inadequately or wrongly expressed, he asserts that all religions are attempts to meet the religious aspirations of men. The final criterion, in his view, is thus the adequacy of the solution offered to the perennial religious needs of mankind. It follows, then, that although there are degrees of truth, the reduction of this problem to a simple true-false alternative is unsatisfactory in dealing with different historic faiths. What is at stake is the question of whether or not a particular historic faith reveals adequately the nature of the Divine, and not the strength or fervor of belief as such.

One of the most important characteristics of truth is its universality. We have learned to become suspicious of local, ethnic or parochial limitations of truth. As over against such provincialism, in whatever guise it may appear, it is necessary to emphasize the *universal availability of true religious insight.* In fact, it is this notion rather than a relativistic indifference toward truth which should determine the character of relationships between religions. That is to say, because everywhere certain questions are asked concerning the Ultimate, there is everywhere potentially the possibility of hearing and apprehending the truth. This view in no way implies that one answer is as good as another, of course, for even the manner of the

[7] *Ibid.*, p. 1.
[8] Moses, *op. cit.*, p. 158.

asking of the questions is not identical. It is well said that "The supreme longing of the Hindu, to escape from *samsara*, Christ does not satisfy, and the Lord's gift of rebirth does not appeal to the Hindu. Thus the correspondence of longing and satisfaction fails."[9] Indeed, it will not be easy to reduce the expressions of need in various religious traditions to a common denominator. On the other hand, it is not a completely hopeless task to translate the language of the human heart from one version into another. William Ernest Hocking has convincingly shown how the universality of religion with its urge for communication necessitates its particularization. In his words: "Communication is never to human beings in general; it is to *specific human beings*, having specific difficulties in seeing what is meant, having specific languages and histories with whatever resources of legend and reflection are there to be drawn upon for explanation, also with specific ethical and social questions to meet."[10] He rightly stresses the fact that because religion is universal, it must become particular. The basic question that confronts us is not Hinduism or Christianity, but the universal truth particularized for this country or that, this continent or that, or this individual or that.

In his well-known book, *The Crown of Hinduism*, J. N. Farquhar states: "Christ is already breathing life into the Hindu people. He does not come to destroy. To Him all that is great and good is dear, the noble art of India, the power and spirituality of its best literature, the beauty and simplicity of Hindu village life, the love and tenderness of the Hindu home, the devotion and endurance of the ascetic schools."[11] On the other hand, he rightly points out that "however faithful any single country might be to Christ, it could not interpret Him fully. He is human; and the riches that are in Him can be set forth only by the united efforts of the whole human family."[12] He was convinced that Christ would be more fully understood and interpreted after meeting the religious genius of India. Similarly, P. Chenchiah holds that the Indian convert of today "regards Hinduism as his spiritual mother who has nurtured him in a sense of spiritual values in the past. He discovers the

[9]The statement of P. Chenchiah, quoted in *The Authority of the Faith*, p. 5.

[10]William Ernest Hocking, *Living Religions and A World Faith*, New York, 1940, p. 16. (My italics.)

[11]J. N. Farquhar, *The Crown of Hinduism*, Oxford, 1913, p. 54.

[12]*Ibid.*, p. 63.

supreme value of Christ, not in spite of Hinduism but because Hinduism has taught him to discern spiritual greatness."[13] It seems to us that both Farquhar and Chenchiah correctly understood the manner in which, in the case of a particular religious tradition, a special way of "preparation" should be recognized. This does not imply that a historic religious tradition in its entirety should be regarded as *praeparatio evangelicum*. But in none of the religions of the world are such "points of contact" lacking. In this respect, we agree with the view of Alan Richardson who acknowledges the necessity and value of general revelation. He rightly reminds us, however, that "general revelation is not and can never be the consummation of man's knowledge of God; it is only God's 'point of connection' with men, and this is its essential character and raison d'etre."[14]

Let us assume, for the time being and without any further inquiry, that we have found the truth in Christ. What does that mean for our concept of, appraisal of, and attitude toward other religions? Our analysis of the nature of religious experience and its forms of expression has led us to the view that all religions are based on an apprehension of Ultimate Reality, expressed in theology, cosmology and anthropology, and that all religions have developed forms of worship as well as religious fellowships.[15] In this respect, Christianity, which happens to be our own faith, is no exception. Indeed, Christianity has a great deal in common with other faiths, even as to the kinds of questions asked regarding the nature of Ultimate Reality. It follows, then, that there is not only the universal religious consciousness but there is a "convergence" of types of doctrines, forms of worship, and patterns of religious organizations, as Rudolf Otto has so clearly suggested. For instance, it is rather obvious that there is a high degree of similarity among the mythical elements of various religions.[16] Basically, each of the major re-

[13]P. Chenchiah, "Jesus and Non-Christian Faiths," in *Rethinking Christianity in India*, by G. V. Job *et al.*, Madras, 1939, p. 49.

[14]Alan Richardson, *Christian Apologetics*, New York, 1947, p. 130.

[15]See Joachim Wach, *Types of Religious Experience—Christian and Non-Christian*, Chicago, 1951, Chap. II, "Universals in Religion."

[16]Whether or not a mystic is a genuine representative of his religious tradition remains an interesting and complicated problem. We are convinced that there is a great deal of correspondence between the mystic's vision and the non-mystical tradition of any religion transmitted in doctrines, devotions, and religious fellowships.

ligions, here including both mystical and non-mystical dimensions, represents a fundamental existential concern with the totality of life, based on its central religious apprehension and affirmation, even though every religion suffers to a greater or lesser degree from distortions, misapprehensions and misdirections. In this respect, too, Christianity and other religions must come under the same indictment.

It has become apparent that the relation of Christianity to other faiths cannot be dismissed simply by the principle of "discontinuity." Far more fruitful is the approach advocated by A. J. Appasamy in his *The Gospel and India's Heritage*. In the section, "Why should we use the Heritage of India?" Appasamy rightly says: "It is now felt that all the non-Christian religions cannot be simply dismissed as heathen. The growing science of religions has made it quite clear that there is much truth in all the religions of the world."[17] We do not come to know Christ better by denigrating the non-Christian religions instead of distinguishing carefully between the genuine and the false. This is not a matter of missionary strategy; we must recognize light wherever it is found if we seek for truth, beauty and holiness.

Of course, it is not a simple matter to make distinctions between the genuine and the false. We must first separate the genuine religion from its historical, cultural, economic, political and other contexts, and distinguish its various factors. Secondly, it will be desirable to assess the adequacy of any theoretical, practical and sociological expression with regard to the experience to which it is meant to witness. Thirdly, we must ask to what degree there is a consciousness of the provisional character of all expressions of religious experience. By asking these questions, and seeking for answers, we will find that the attitude toward the relation to the different religions will have to be different. All religions, if they truly seek religious truth, must be ready to disavow demonic elements which in the course of history have crept into their religious communities. Furthermore, in all religions the problem of meaning cannot be overlooked not only with regard to the intellectual expression but with reference to worship and fellowship as well. Only if the religious meanings which were once adequate can be retranslated into contemporary language or spiritual power can a

[17]A. J. Appasamy, *The Gospel and India's Heritage*, Madras, 1942, p. 16.

religion claim to be regarded as genuinely religious. Here modern existentialism with its insistence on authenticity has much to teach every religious community.

Ultimately, the relation of Christianity to other religions, or between any one religion and another, for that matter, might be regarded as one of a contest of spiritual power, which is another way of saying that the criterion of truth can only be religious. It has to be a contest rather than a sentimental parliament because of the claim to universality which is the characteristic of all religions' attempts to apprehend truth, and also because each religion has the obligation to witness to its understanding of truth. We hasten to add, however, that this contest cannot be carried out except by means of demonstration and persuasion. That has been the way of all great religious teachers, including Christ.

The questions before us are many. What is it that your faith can do? What has it done, what can it be expected to do? What can it do for you, for those related to you, and for all men? Does it bring that peace higher than understanding, that felicity greater than happiness? Does it explain the riddle of existence, does it interpret the nature of Ultimate Reality, the nature of the world and the destiny of man? Does it provide by its forms of worship a continuous and fruitful communion with God, and also provide the necessary incentive to action in his service for the purpose of transforming the world as well as one's own life according to the great vision? Does it create and recreate a fellowship inspired by this vision and acting, in worship and in service, to witness to the truth vouchsafed in the revelation on which it is built? Who are the initiators and prophets, saints and seers it has produced? Who is entitled to speak in its behalf today? It is most certainly impossible to give simple yes or no answers to these questions. The major religions of the world without exception give answers but on different levels, with different scope and different power. To say that religions ought to learn from one another is not to advocate relativism or to betray one's own allegiance. It simply means the recognition of universal character and obligation of genuine religious experience. Thus, some among Christians advocate the establishment of Christian Ashrams, convinced that certain methods of concentration and meditation of Hinduism could be profitably adapted by the followers of Christ, who long to express their faith with an ardor comparable to that of the great Bhaktas of the Hindu faith. Similarly, some Christians have become deeply impressed by certain features of the faith of the Muslims, especially their devotion to the One God and their consistency in practicing brotherhood irrespective of race and color. Some Christians who have delved into the study of Buddhist scriptures have been inspired by the vision of that great tranquility which has been the aim and goal of so many of the saints of Buddhism, and by the serenity and beauty which has been radiated by them, and with some of their methods for achieving the life of the spirit.

There is no need for us to focus our attention upon features of other religions which may be regarded as weaknesses or falsifications of an initial vision. So much apologetics, perhaps in every religious group, has consisted of extolling its own faith, often at the expense of the other claims. It seems neither commendable nor helpful to compare one's best qualities with the worst qualities of others, or to make generalizations based on artificial categories, comparing Westerners and Easterners *en bloc*, thereby subsuming a religion under the heading of a civilization.

If, then, we assume we are right in rejecting "discontinuity" as an inadequate term for describing the relation of Christianity to other religions, how are we to interpret the famous passage in the Johannine Gospel: "I am the way, and the truth, and the life; no one comes to the Father, but by me" (14: 6, RSV), or Peter's statement in the Acts: "And there is salvation in no one else, for there is no other name under heaven given among men by which we must be saved" (4:12, RSV). It is our sincere conviction that these passages should be given inclusive rather than exclusive interpretation. That is to say, if the great spiritual principle of reconciliation and redemption which we affirm in the name of Christ is the truth, then no other can be truer or equally true, at least from the Christian point of view. But it should be remembered that it is not Jesus but the Cosmic Christ who is speaking in the Gospel. Wherever his spirit prevails—and who can say that it cannot prevail anywhere outside the community named after him—he is actually reigning. This is no narrow, dogmatic claim but the recognition of the spiritual reality that only by way of reconciliation and redemption can the house of the Father be reached. Peter's statement in the Acts likewise should be interpreted to mean that there is no salvation through another name, that is, through any secondary entity, than that of the Cosmic Christ.

In actual practice, it is true that choice and decision are necessary in regard to the great paradigmatic figures in the history of religions. Neither birthright nor tradition are substitutes for decision. The nature of religious experience demands a personal and an existential commitment. In this sense, the universal option of truth is open to all.

Seen from the perspective of the Christian faith, there cannot be "discontinuity" between Christianity and other faiths because wherever there has been or is truth there Christ was or is present, and he is coming into his own where his spirit triumphs altogether. To conceive of Christ worthily all races and all nations have to do their share. The symbol of the Magi bringing their gifts and worshipping the holy child in their own ways seems very apt, for Christian faith affirms that all men are called into that universal fellowship known as his Body, the Church.

12.

The Christian Professor

I

> Thou therefore that teacheth another, teachest thou not thyself? (Romans 2:21.)
>
> For one is the true master who alone has not learned what he taught all; but men learn before they teach, and receive from him what they may hand on to another. (St. Ambrose.)
>
> All are not fitted to teach, would that all were apt to learn. (St. Ambrose.)

The life of any Christian, we claim, will have more breadth and more depth, and it will have more structure to it than that of another person—"agnostic," "pagan," or "religious." Because he has met Christ, he will test all his experiences in the light of the purpose which such an encounter necessarily engenders. Such orientation will make for unity, coherence and purposiveness, that is, for integration. It will once and for all determine his attitude: (a) to himself and his work, (b) to other individuals, (c) to his closer associates (colleagues, students), (d) to society. This attitude will be reflected in his conduct. Instead of being irresponsible, impressionistic, egotistic, and erratic, he will be responsible, consistent, altruistic, and directed in dedication to his central purpose. Moodiness, despair, cynicism—the result of the former attitude—will give way to joy, love, patience, hopefulness, and serenity (Gal. 5:22–25). "It is because we believe that we hope, and because we hope that we love" (Peter the Precentor, *ca.* 1198).

The difference does not result from any initial desire to be different from others; it is rather the result of the observation that those concerns which matter most to the Christian are not necessarily shared; they may meet with indifference, scorn or hostility in his environment. A Christian would try to live his ideals even on a lonely island. In a secularized world a Christian and a Christian teacher will find a challenge in addition to the imperative to live a Christian life: that is, to win others to this way. These others may be agnostics, pagans or members of non-Christian religious communities. He will by word and action encourage the agnostic to risk "the movement of faith." He will by the same method help the "pagan" to discover the limitations of a "naturalistic" view of life, freeing him to experience the quickening effect of spiritual graces. With his fellow-believers he will, in the mutual exchange of insight and experiences, search for increasingly deeper apprehension and appropriation of religious truth. Moreover, in and through his testimony for Christ he may hope to win others already strengthened by some faith to Christ Jesus. All this requires, firstly, certitude and conviction on his own part; secondly, thorough familiarity with the tenets of the Christian faith ("*Nemo autem amare potest quod nescit*," says Hugo of St. Victor, "*et ideo si Deum amare cupimus, primum eum cognoscere satagamus*"—"Nobody can love what he does not know, and therefore if we desire to love God let us first make it our business to know him"); thirdly, absolute sincerity (no "ulterior" motives); fourthly, sensitivity and respect for the integrity and individuality of others.

A genuine encounter with the redeeming love of God in Christ is, as we saw, on the part of any Christian (and Christian teacher) the presupposition for his testimony through act and word. Merely having been brought up in Christian ways is not sufficient. ("*Fiant, non nascuntur Christiani*"—"Let them become Christians, since they were not born thus.") Though it would certainly not be required of anyone to look back upon and give an account of a "conversion-experience" (day, hour, minute), a conscious decision and commitment to Christ, implicit in our life, and explicit in our testimony, is indispensable. It alone will guarantee the consciousness of the purpose of a Christian life and the determination to integrate it in accordance with this ideal.

Only if an individual's life reveals this purpose ("orientation"), will it have the radiating power which alone can affect, attract and convert others. All a man can do or say is merely an expression of his character. This character, formed in the interaction between his nature and his experiences, will be the criterion by which his words as well as his actions will be tested. Unity, coherence and purposiveness are brought about by a constant check of an individual's inclinations, feelings, and thoughts, a process which shapes his nature and coordinates his experiences. Most of us are threatened by the concerted impact of heterogeneous influences (modern education and advertisement[1]) and hence tend to live in the state which Soren Kierkegaard has called the "aesthetic" stage. On a higher level the same impressionism, that is, openness to any trends or "winds of doctrine"—political, intellectual, religious—exists in intellectual and academic circles. This is one reason why all kinds of esoteric, semi-esoteric, and substitute religious cults find an echo, frequently among the emotionally or spiritually starved "scientists" in both the natural sciences and humanities. The egocentric attitude, so frequent among the educated in modern society, is not by any means necessarily constitutional but more often than not is the result of the pressures and exigencies of practical circumstances and of contemporary political, philosophical and religious teachings. Inasmuch as the latter are apt to find the mind and soul of modern man little prepared for any "value judgment" and decision (the result of the "positivism" of the nineteenth century), we see more and more that individuals withdraw into their shells, asking only "to be left alone." It seems hardly necessary to point out how much of the cynicism, now so widely spread in the intellectual centers of the old and the new worlds, is due to disappointment and disillusionment after one or the other or many of the conflicting ideologies were tried and found wanting. Because a cynical attitude and a cynical philosophy do not render anyone incapable of high intellectual achievement, brilliancy of teaching and of tremendously successful research have continued to distinguish the centers of learning in the modern world. In nearly all academic pursuits it would be possible to mention distinguished scholars and teachers whose intellectual achievement compares favorably with that of the greatest minds of the past. But at least since the turn of this cen-

[1]"America is," according to Santayana, "the country of the greatest possibilities and the worst influences."

tury, we have also been warned by candid critics from the West as well as from the East, that while knowledge among us was increasing, wisdom and spiritual discernment were not. No finite purpose, not even learning, or the acquisition of skills, will achieve the unity, consistency and integration of personality which is the presupposition of an effective and radiant life. Though concentration of will and mind upon the achievement of such a relative purpose may lead an individual to mighty accomplishments, resulting in great blessings for his fellow man, this will be done at a price. This price may be what Christians call a man's soul, the highest of all his possessions. Though it may be nobler to sell it for great knowledge than for great possessions or great power or great pleasure, a man without a soul has died a spiritual death (Rom. 8:1–6). This of course is not to say that this must happen to anyone engaged in a wholehearted effort to advance the boundaries of man's knowledge. There were times—and not a few individuals prove that it can happen today—in which scholars could say in full conviction with Johann Gerson: "*Anima nostra facta est ad Deum cognoscendum et amandum*"—"Our spirit was created to know and love God." Great achievements of whatever kind they may be will always elicit respect and admiration though both may be cold and distant. Now there are, no doubt, men who would rather be respected than loved and if we had to choose between them, that might even be our choice. But we do not have to choose.

The difference between the learned expert and the sage is like that between the teacher and the master. Cultivation of the spirit is something different from the training of the mind and from the development of bodily, technical, or intellectual skills. It is possible to possess the latter and to impart it to others in the impersonal way which alone is open so long as a person is a house divided against itself. Integration of will, emotions, and intellect, modern psychologists such as Jung, Horney, Menninger, Fosdick, and Ligon have shown to be possible only on a religious basis. Such integration alone sets the individual free by removing the frictions and conflicts existing within these areas. Thus a person is rendered capable of a total response in which not only his intellect or his emotions or his energies but his integral personality react. Such freedom makes spiritual experience possible, and with it, creative living. "*Anima spiritualiter cadit et spiritualiter resurgit*"—"The soul falls spiritually and spiritually rises" (St. Augustine). In and through divine encounter, the comforting spirit of Christ enters our life and makes it whole and sustains it. Moods, despair (Kierkegaard's "objective" sickness unto death), cynicism will give way to the joy of which the apostle speaks (Phil. 4:4; cf. the moving novel of Bernanos, *Joy*). Christians, and especially Christian teachers, should exhibit this joy. Nietzsche was right in saying: "I should begin to believe in their [the Christians'] redemption if they would look more redeemed." Very naturally the desire will arise on the part of one thus freed to share this joy, and, on the part of others, to participate in it. St. Paul exhorts the Philippians (2:4): "Look not every man on his own things, but every man also on the things of others." These others will, in their new frame of mind, not be judged harshly or treated indifferently, but with patience, a virtue especially important for those who teach. Another "virtue" even greater is often spoken of and little practiced in the society in which we live. "Knowledge," St. Paul tells the Corinthians, "puffeth up, but charity edifieth." It pays to reread the famous thirteenth chapter of the second letter to the same community, if we wish to know what is required of a Christian teacher. Intransigence and fanaticism do not become him. He will agree with Francis of Sales: "Whoever preaches with love preaches sufficiently against heretics though he may never say a controversial word." The *humilitas* which adorned the greatest master of the past and which is exalted here, flows naturally from a charitable disposition. "We cannot prevail against Satan by pride," according to St. Vincent de Paul, "he has more than we have, but through humility we can conquer him, for of that he has none." The English mystic William Law was of the same opinion: "Look not at pride only as an unbecoming temper, nor at humility only as a decent virtue; for the one is death and the other is life; the one is all hell and the other all heaven."

II

An academic community is constituted by those who teach and those who learn. If what the student unconsciously or knowingly is looking for is more than technical skills or mastery of subject matter, it will be his professor to whom he will look for orientation. The professor who lacks integration in his own life and outlook will usually not be willing, or if he is willing, he will not be capable of contributing to this end. Or the professor may have his philosophy but consider it his private business and say so. Of course nobody can live another's life or make his decisions for him. Students who expect easy and ready-made formulas from their teachers will be disappointed.

There are *two ways* by which a professor may, if he is a Christian, fulfill his obligation to win students to Christ (cf. Rom. 11:14, 15). He may, without any explicit statements or references to Christianity, act, and act consistently, in accordance with the commands of our Lord ("indirect witness"). The student who is eager to find an orientation for his thought and life will without great difficulty discover *why* his teacher is *what* he is. The student may then feel confident enough to ask questions. These offer the opportunity for the professor to "profess." There is no doubt in my mind that such a way is open to teachers in all fields of instruction.

A second way consists in definite and articulate statements, where they are appropriate, of the axioms of the Christian faith on the part of individual professors, faculties, and administrative leaders ("direct witness"). There is no reason why objective search for truth or the communication of results arrived at by such inquiry should be prejudiced or jeopardized by a procedure which is paralleled by the normal teaching of mathematics, physics, etc. It is customary in these fields to proceed from well defined axioms. By this term we mean primary basic assumptions, consciously made and explicitly stated (methodological, delimiting and selective considerations are secondary). If there is a God and if man's chief end is to glorify him, it may be said that this spiritual truth cannot be affected by psychological, sociological or other factors. The latter may condition the forms of apprehension and the modes of expression of these truths but they do not affect the realities of these spiritual truths. (Psychological and sociological factors should not be classed as axioms. A criticism of the method and results of the so-called *sociology of knowledge* from the Christian point of view seems overdue.) To understand that knowledge is socially conditioned does not necessarily mean that what is apprehended is invalid or limited ("relative").

But will such procedure not destroy the freedom of thought and research upon which the modern university is built? The university has often been defined as a community of free seekers after truth (teachers *and* students). We should understand that we cannot have our cake and eat it too. "Freedom" should be rightly understood and defined. It certainly cannot mean that anyone is "free" to formulate his own logic. He is bound by the traditional categories of thinking in our culture. If Christianity is understood to be at least one of the basic forces which shaped our Western civilization, and if it is, as we belive, a "live option," then we must strive to arrive at a clear articulation of its tenets. These would have to be understood as having "axiomatic" character, and freedom would be meaningful only in the sense of appropriating these values for our own and society's life in an effective manner.

Such orientation does not seem to make much difference as long as we think of what may be called penultimate concerns, that is, technical work, the kind of work which looms largest and is most necessary in all scholarly pursuit (engineering, philology, biology, law, etc.). Here "objectivity" has its right place. But no field and no worker in any field of studies is excused from facing *basic questions* such as "knowledge—that is, always, knowledge concerning one definite subject matter (engineering, philology, biology, law)—for what?" Here, in relating his necessarily relative efforts to the needs of man and society, the orientation which we are advocating does make all the difference. What we conceive of as the nature and destiny of man and the meaning and goal of societal life, will determine for good or for ill our choices, preferences and omissions and thereby the direction of our whole endeavor. If these basic questions are answered in the light of the Gospel of Christ we will come out somewhere else in the end than would be the case if an explicit or implicit hedonistic or will-to-power philosophy supplied the answers. No man's work will be better than the man himself. The depth and quality of the Christianity of the Christian professor is of profound importance to himself, his students, and the future of the total body of scholarship.

13.

The Crisis in the University

A Review of *The Crisis in the University*, by Sir Walter Moberly. Student Christian Movement Press, London, 1949.

This is an important book because it presents a clear diagnosis of the situation of the University in the Western world by a man equally distinguished as a scholar and as an administrator, and because it includes hints at a "therapy" suggested on the basis of certain fundamental convictions of the author which are Christian in character. A very wide audience will welcome warmly and discuss eagerly this contribution to the theory of education by the former Chairman of the University Grants Committee in the United Kingdom. It will include all the scholars and students who are vitally interested in the problem of higher education, in the role of the Universities in society, in the quest for the aims and the function of higher learning, in the problems of norms, the nature of science, and academic freedom, and in the role of religion in the process of higher education, to say nothing of a host of practical questions with regard to academic and student life. It will include, of course, the large number of avowedly Christian students and educators the world over who will be familiar with the name and fame of Sir Walter Moberly.

Sir Walter's task has been far from easy, for it will always be difficult to present an "objective" analysis of the state of a body politic, ecclesiastical, or academic, which satisfies *all* the "experts" and *all* the "lay" folk. The very choice of features and trends selected for discussion, and the emphasis placed on each of them and on their relations, is controversial. Even more debatable in detail will appear the necessary attempts at establishing a causal nexus between the phenomena singled out for diagnosis. What the author of *The Crisis in the University* sets out to do, however, is much more than to present an "objective" analysis of the characteristics of the modern university. His is a normative quest. He himself is at pains to show how much people differ in questions of evaluation and norms, in Weltanschauung or philosophy of life. And yet, what he wants us to do is not only to "see developments" and "tendencies" in modern higher education but to assent to a diagnosis of ailments and to do something about a therapy for them.

Sir Walter will have many an opponent—as, for example, the skeptics for whom there is no good or bad that can be bindingly identified—who will *evaluate* the dominance of "scientific" thinking or the potential "contribution" of moral or religious reflection quite differently; he is fully aware of that. However, the main source of disagreement will be in the field of remedies. Will more of this, less of that (e.g., in the interrelationships of the Universities, in the function of the teacher as a "moral" guide, in lecture-courses) do away with the "symptoms" (provided we agree what they are symptoms of)?

Sir Walter Moberly himself feels keenly that the crisis of academic institutions is only to a small degree indigenous, for it is really a reflection of the crisis of modern life and thought in general. Therefore, to complete his task the author would have to be not only ahead of all sociologists, economists, scientists and technicians, but also of all the philosophers and theologians to whom we customarily look for the articulation of what ought-to-be with regard to individual and collective life. In a word, he would have to be a major prophet, not in the sense of one who foretells what *will* happen, but of one who "reveals" a scale of values with a claim to *universal* assent.

An author who does *not* raise any such claims will easily be accused from two opposite directions: of going too far in what he advocates and of not going far enough. It is not difficult to see that that will be the case with regard to at least the last six chapters of Sir Walter's book. It is a cautious, not a radical procedure, which its author advocates. What will appear to some as wisdom, seasoned by long and wide experience, will be indicated as lack of determination and courage by others who will attach to it as negative characterizations such catchwords as too "liberal," "conservative," etc. And yet in its moderation this programmatic study is both British and academic, and *both* in the best sense of the word. And let us add a third epithet in the same vein—it is Christian.

Some would hotly deny that moderation is a Christian virtue, and it is not if it were meant to exclude zeal. But as opposed to fanaticism, purposeful moderation is both a Christian and a classical virtue. Again we narrow down considerably, not the number of those who will find *The Crisis in the University* highly stimulating and interesting, but of those who will agree in full with the principles hinted at by the author. He himself shows, and could have instanced even more, the degree to which education in the ancient classics has receded. All those who lack it at least will show themselves "color-blind" to the assets which accrue to Sir Walter's *modus procedendi* from his being steeped in this tradition. After a long period in which complete harmony of the classical and the Christian philosophy of life was postulated, we hear today serious objections to this identification. That he desires neither a classicist (93ff.) nor a Christian University as such (99ff.) is another instance of the moderation characteristic of his approach.

That the University be truly the university is Sir Walter's chief concern. Fewer will quarrel with him for asking the question, "What can Christian insight contribute to enable the University to be the University?" (p. 26), than for the answer he gives; here "maximalists" as well as "minimists" will object. It is, however, highly significant that the justification by the author for expecting a most vital contribution from Christians for this purpose is not based primarily on the historical argument—significance in the past—but on the intrinsic vitality, power of insight, and moral force of the Christian religion.

Sir Walter Moberly is at pains to distinguish between what might be called—though he does not use this term—the essence of Christianity or the Christian ideal and the forms under which it has been effective in the past and still is effective. There is, however, no discussion of the sources of our apprehension of what is Christian and their relation to each other. Jesus Christ is rarely referred to directly. We are not told how the author assesses the role of traditon, of the Scriptures, the Church and the individual experience of the follower of Christ (but cf. p. 103 on "authentic" Christianity). The concern of the author is not primarily with Christianity as an ideal or as a way but with its function as a philosophy of life with integrative power. Yet at times the reader will miss a clearer distinction between ultimate principles and what may be called "middle axioms," that is, the articulation of the former in terms of concrete reality mediating between the ultimate demand and casuistic application.

The introduction to Sir Walter Moberly's treatise poses the question as to the position of the Universities in a world in which "mentally and spiritually, most persons are 'displaced persons.'" The special role of Great Britain with its "greater political maturity" and of its Universities and of the peculiar "malaise" besetting them is discussed; finally, the problem of the contribution of Christians to a constructive solution is raised.

The second chapter reviews the three dominant "schools" which have consecutively determined the spirit of the age during the last century—the Christian-Hellenic, the Liberal, and the Technological-Democratic—and analyzes their conceptions of the nature and task of the University. The characteristics of each "ideology" are succinctly and, so it seems to the reviewer, adequately stated. This section is in itself a valuable contribution to a critical history of the theory and practice of education of the nineteenth century. In the third chapter some of the main features of the "chaotic university" of our own day come in for discussion, namely the shirking of fundamental issues, false neutrality (in politics, religion and morals), fragmentation (the student "never faces as a whole the social problem or the problem of his personal life" [p. 61]), uncriticized presuppositions (here the important analyses of Max Scheler should have been adduced) and, finally, the neglect of moral and spiritual factors.

The concern of the fourth chapter is with some of the "spurious remedies" as suggested by scientific and by classical humanism and by Christian repristinators. The criticism of scientific humanism is of special interest and may well be carefully pondered by its adherents in the United States who are by no means limited to scientists proper. Sir Walter takes exception to their shirking of three major problems: that of values, that of power, and that of the transcendental. "Scientific humanists" do justice neither to the heights nor to the depths of human experience (p. 88). The assets and deficiencies of classical humanism (it lacks in "catholicity" [p. 91]) are briefly reviewed.

For those who have followed or taken a part in the discussions which the S.C.M. has stimulated (e.g. in its University Commission) on the role of the Christian in the University, Sir Walter's reasons why Christians ought *not* to want an all-Christian University (99ff.) will be of singular interest. Christian politics for the present age, according to him (28f.), will be "very unlike what it has generally been in the past" (p. 28). "Much as we have to learn from our Christian predecessors, we have some things also to unlearn" (*loc cit*). A repristination— the author does not use this term—would be "impracticable, inequitable, disastrous" according to Sir Walter, who is repelled by all that could smack of "exploitation" of the Christian religion. Domination by theologians he finds no less objectionable than domination by any other group (p. 104). He no doubt very rightly feels that "even" the heretic has to teach us a lesson; he is "needed as a text and a contributor" (p. 105). Marx, Nietzsche and Freud are named in this connection.

Some will see the "heart of the matter" in the discussion in the fifth chapter, entitled "Aim and Basis." What can we, after rejecting alternatives, state positively to be basic requirements for the University today? Its neutrality, Sir Walter says, should be "positive," not "negative"; it should be a community in which solidarity and personal fellowship exist and hence where a living encounter of different and differing people is possible. Tension is necessary. "At the university stage there is no excuse for depriving students of the means and responsibility of judgments or of sheltering them from its difficulties" (p. 110). The author does not regard it as the "primary concern" of the teacher to "make proselytes" though he should not "suppress his convictions" (p. 110). The religious issue must enter; "no students should go down without having been confronted by the Christian challenge" (p. 111).

Besides being an open forum, the University should make true communication possible, even if the attainment of specious agreement is illusory; it must guard certain basic values and virtues some of which it shares with the larger community. Hence, to Sir Walter, any "special colour," "whether Christian, communist or bourgeois-individualist" would be "illegitimate" (p. 120). To this reviewer these three are, however, not quite on the same level, hence he would be inclined to qualify this statement. Virtues and values to be fostered by the "ideal" University are: intellectual passion, thoroughness, accurateness in dealing with empirical evidences, fairmindedness, freedom of thought and publication. Sir Walter refers in this connection with assent to Toynbee's distinction between "creative" and "dominant" minorities.

The University must, finally, focus the community's "intellectual conscience." That is its social responsibility (p. 126). After a brief, but lucid and extremely pertinent, discussion of universal, Western and British communal values, the Christian ingredient in them is analyzed. In dialectical fashion the positive, the negative and the critical case is stated with regard to the question, "Are Britain and her Universities Christian?" This is the conclusion: "The British people today is not Christian, except in a debased sense of the word. . . . But its imagination, its ethos and its sentiment are . . . Christianised" (p. 140). The important task is therefore, today, to "deepen the Christian colouring" and to "bring into consciousness the Christian background of the basic values on which the University is built" (p. 171). Again Sir Walter's cautious realism becomes manifest when he says that the "Christian" unity can only be a "minimal" unity; one not of faith and religion but rather of orientation (p. 145). It is easy to imagine that this restraint might be criticized.

The sixth chapter of this treatise is dedicated to the problems of freedom and integration and exhibits again the quest for "balance" so characteristic of the author. Dialectically it sets forth two sets of claims, those on the side of the state and on the side of academic community, and the right *and* wrong inherent in both extreme conceptions.

The second part of the book is on the whole the application of the viewpoint and principles exposed in the first to certain concrete topics, situations and problems: studies, corporate life, religion and theology, the university and the world. Many fine observations are included in the discussion of immediate and more distant goals and tasks. Everywhere in these chapters we meet the sanity, balanced moderation, width of knowledge and experience so characteristic of the author. They are instanced by his fair treatment throughout the book of the three types of British universities, Oxbridge, Redbrick and Scottish. Because many of the topics touched upon in the second part of the treatise are of a technical, administrative, or generally practical nature—though Sir Walter's suggestions are never purely pragmatic—we cannot go into any detail here.

I should like to add a few remarks with regard to the tenth chapter which deals with "Religion and Theology." It is indeed a salutary emphasis which Sir Walter places upon the deepening of our Christian obedience rather than upon techniques of communicating it (p. 261). *In concreto* that means forming real communities of Christians to enable us to carry out our work in the spirit of the Master and to become lay-theologians who know their Bible, and Christian doctrine, and understand the world today and the implications of their faith for life in it. With regard to theology the question of its legitimate role in the University as a faculty and its own concept of its competence are taken up. The short section "What is Theology?" is not quite satisfactory in the eyes of this reviewer; the problem of the relation of general and special revelation or of the claims of non-Christian religions receives no attention. But I agree wholeheartedly with the argument for the inclusion of theological training in the University and the criteria by which standards are to be measured.

Enough has been said to accomplish the task of the reviewer of a book such as *The Crisis in the University*: to urge teachers and students the world over, especially Christian teachers and students, to read it, ponder over it and discuss it. I am sure that this is the purpose for which it was written and that such would be the best "success" and "reward" for its distinguished author.

14.

A Translation Hugo of St. Victor on Virtues and Vices

CHAPTER I. WHAT THE FIVE SEVENS ARE IN THE SACRED SCRIPTURES[1]

I have, dear brother, found five series of seven things in the Holy Scriptures which I will distinguish. I will enumerate them first briefly, as you request, and then show in what relation they stand to each other. In the first place we put the seven vices: pride, envy, wrath, sadness, avarice, gluttony and opulence.[2]

We contrast with these the seven petitions included in our Lord's prayer: Hallowed be thy name; Thy kingdom come; Thy will be done as in heaven so on earth; Give us this day our daily bread; And forgive us our trespasses as we forgive those who trespass against us; And lead us not into temptation; But deliver us from evil.

[1]Hugonis de St. Victore, *Opera Omnia* (ed. nova, Migne), Tomus I (Patrologiae Cursus Completus: Series Latina Prior. Tomus CLXXV, Parisiis, 1880), p. 406ff.

[2]Cf. also "De Fructibus Carnis et Spiritus" (*op. cit.*, II, p. 998ff.), "Summa Sententiarum," Tract III, Chap. XVI, XVII (*op. cit.*, II, 113ff.); "Allegoriae in Novum Testamentum, Liber II in Mattheum" (I, 763ff.); "Exposito in Abdiam" (*op. cit.*, I, 402ff.). Cf. also Émile Mâle, *Religious Art in France, XIII Century*, tr. by Dora Nussey (London, New York: 1913; New York: Harper Torchbooks, 1958, under the title *The Gothic Image*), Book III, and Ludwig Ott, "Untersuchungen zur Briefliteratur der Frühscholastik" (*Beiträge zur Geschichte der Philosophie und Theologie des Mittelalters*), 1937, 433ff.

Then follow thirdly the seven gifts of the Holy Spirit:[3] The spirit of the fear of the Lord; The spirit of devotion; The spirit of knowledge; The spirit of fortitude; The spirit of counsel; The spirit of understanding; The spirit of wisdom.

In fourth place we have the seven virtues:[4] Poverty of spirit or humility; Clemency or benevolence; Compunction or pain; Thirsting after righteousness or good will; Compassion; Purity of heart; Peace.

Finally in fifth place, we have the seven beatitudes: The Kingdom of heaven; Possession of the land of the living; Comfort; Attainment of righteousness; Compassion; Vision of God; Divine sonship.

Therefore try to understand even the faults as some striving of the soul, or as wounds of the inner man: man himself as sick, the physician as God, the gifts of the Holy Spirit as the antidote, the virtues as health, the beatitudes as the joy of happiness.

CHAPTER II. HOW MUCH DAMAGE THE SEVEN SINS DO TO MAN

There are seven principal or cardinal sins and from these originate all evils.[5] These are the fountains and abysses of darkness from whence the rivers of Babylon flow which, flowing all over the world, divert into rivulets of iniquity. Of these rivers the Psalmist sings in the person of the faithful people: "By the rivers of Babylon did we sit and weep as we remembered thee, O Sion. We hanged our harps upon the willows in the midst thereof." We will speak as much as we deem necessary of these seven sins . . . which ravage and corrupt the whole integrity of nature and produce the germs of all evils. There are seven of these:[6] three of them rob

[3]On an independent version cf. Ott, *op. cit.*, p. 440. For the number seven: "Quid in septenario numero nisi summa perfectionis accipitur?" Gregorius Magnus, *Moralia* (Migne, Patr. Lat., LXXV, 534).

[4]Cf. De Sacramentis (*op. cit.*, II), liber secundus, pars. XIII, Chaps. I, II. Cf. Adolf Katzenellenbogen, *Allegories of the Virtues and Vices in Mediaeval Art* (London: Warburg Institute, 1939).

[5]Allegoriae, 774ff. Cf. Beda Venerabilis, *Opera Paraenetica* (Migne, Patr. Lat., XCIV, 533, 556); Alcuin, "De Virtutibus et Vitiis" (Migne, Patr. Lat., CI, 613ff.). Also Mâle, *op. cit.*, p. 110, tracing the concept of the Virtues from Plato to Ambrose and St. Augustine, and from him to the Carolingian authors (Alcuin, Rabanus).

[6]"Vitium autem est corruptis naturalis affectus praeter ordinem et extra mensuram" (Allegoriae 174 B).

man; the fourth flagellates the robbed; the fifth throws the flogged man out; the sixth seduces the ejected; the seventh subjects the ejected to servitude. Pride removes God from man, envy removes his neighbor from him, wrath removes himself from himself, sadness flogs the robbed, avarice ejects the flogged, gluttony seduces the ejected, opulence subjects the seduced to servitude. Then we can explain, in reversing the order, the individual by the series. We have said that pride[7] removes God from man: pride being that love of self-glory in which the mind is overfond of the good it has, that is: without reference to the One from whom it receives the good. O pestilential pride, what are you after? Why do you persuade the rivulet to divide itself from the fountain? Why do you persuade the beam to turn away from the sun? Should it dry out once it ceases from being flooded and the other be adumbrated as it turns away from the source of light, both will, as they cease to receive, continue to lose also that which they still have. When that is done you act, as you teach to love the gifts without the giver, so that who ascribes perversely a part of the good that was given by Him, loses all the good that is in Him. So it happens that he will (even) not really possess for use that which he has while he does not love that in the giver. Because, as all good really comes from God, so can nothing good be put to use without God. Moreover this way even that which we have will be lost because it is not loved in Him and with Him from whom we have it. Because if someone does not know if that which he has of good has to be loved in itself so that he views some good which he does not have in another, so much the more will his imperfection pain him in the degree that he does not love Him in whom all good subsists. Hence envy[8] ever follows pride; because if someone does not postulate love where all good is, meanwhile extolling perversely his own, he is tormented more severely by someone else's good. Right indeed is the punishment for one who wants himself, that is envy which he produces from out himself which because he does not care to love the common good, rightly eats itself with envy of the other's good. The success of another's fortune would indeed not burn if he would possess by love the One in whom there is all good. And he would not consider as alien another's good if he loved his own as he possessed his own together with another's good. Now in the degree to which he

[7]Cf. De Fructibus, Chap. III.
[8]Cf. De Fructibus, Chap. V.

vaunts himself, in that degree he falls under his neighbor through evil and to the extent to which something is exalted falsely, it will truly fall down. For he cannot resist once corruption has set in; for straightway as of pride envy is born, it procreates wrath from itself; because the wretched soul is incensed from its own imperfection as it does not rejoice over somebody else's good in love. And even that which he posseses begins to displease him because he recognizes in another that which he cannot have himself. But who can, in love, have all in God, loses also that which he tries to possess by elevating it without God, through envy and wrath:[9] because, after losing God through pride, he will lose his neighbor through envy and himself through wrath. Because after all is lost, nothing remains in which the unhappy conscience could rejoice, it sinks through sadness within itself and, as it does not want to rejoice in another's good, will suffer rightly from its own evil. Pride, envy and wrath which rob man are then continually followed by sadness which flogs the despoiled. It is succeeded by avarice which ejects the flogged because he is, once the inner joy is lost, forced to seek outward consolation. Later on gluttony is added which seduces the ejected because it tempts to excess through the natural appetite as it were the soul absorbed by externals. . . . Finally comes opulence which violently subjects the seduced to servitude because after the flesh has been inflamed, the mind weakened and rendered feeble, it cannot prevail against the burning lust which comes upon it. So the ingloriously vanquished mind serves most basely as a tyrant and if the unspeakable love of the Redeemer would not intervene, the liberty lost would not yet be given back to the subservient slave.

CHAPTER III. TO WHICH GIFTS OF THE HOLY SPIRIT THE THREE PETITIONS OF THE LORD'S PRAYER CORRESPOND AND WHICH VICES THEY CURE

Seven petitions follow to help us against the seven vices, which were used in prayer by the One who taught us to pray (Luke xi)[10] and who promised what spiritual good he would give when we pray to the healing of our wounds and to the alleviation of the yoke of our captivity. We will, before we come to explaining them,

[9]Cf. De Fructibus, Chap. VI.
[10]Cf. Exposito in Abdiam 403f., and Allegoriae Lib. III, Chaps. III-XIV.

first show by another parable how great a corruption the above mentioned vices produce in us so that, the more dangerous the sloth is shown to be, the more necessary medicine will be required. Through pride then the heart is inflated; through envy it is dried out; through wrath it cracks; through sadness it is worn-out, and it is as if it were pulverized; through avarice it is scattered; through gluttony it is infected and so to speak moistened; through opulence it is trodden upon and turned into mire so that already the unfortunate could say:

> I am tied in the depth and there is no hold. I come in the height of the sea and the storm submerges me. (Ps. vi.)

When the soul becomes fastened to the depth and developed by the mire of pollution and impurity, it cannot emerge if it does not cry to Him and ask for His help. Of this the Psalmist says:

> I waited patiently for the Lord and he is inclined unto me, and heard my cry. He brought me up also out of an horrible pit, out of the miry clay. (Ps. xxxxi.)

Therefore He Himself has taught us to pray, for all good is of Him and that which we ask and what we asking receive is by His gift and not by our merit.

In the first petition, against pride, we say to God: "Hallowed be thy name." We ask him to let us fear and revere his name inasmuch as we are, in humility, his subjects—we who are by our pride rebellious and obstinate. On the ground of this petition the gift of the fear of the Lord is given so that He (God) may come into our heart, create in it the virtue of humility which heals the illness of pride: that is the kingdom of heaven, which the proud angel lost by choice. The humble man can achieve this end. In the second petition, against envy, we say: "Thy kingdom come." The rule of God is the salvation of men. That is called God's rule in (the hearts of) men when men surrender themselves to God by adhering to Him by faith and afterwards by inhering in Him *sub specie*. Whosoever prays that God's Kingdom come seeks truly the salvation of men and thus demonstrates while he asks for the common good of all that he reprobates the vice of malevolence. On the ground of this petition the spirit of devotion is given and comes to the heart that kindles it in benevolence, so that man himself attains to the same possession of the eternal heritage which he would like others to arrive at. In the third petition, directed against wrath, we say: "Thy will be done on earth as it is in heaven." Who says "thy will be done" does not want to command but indicates that he will be contented with whatever the Will of God decrees according to the judgment of its choice for him or others. On the ground of this petition the spirit of knowledge is given, and comes into the heart, illuminates it and healthfully purifies it so that man knows that the evil he suffers is due to his own fault but that whatever good he has proceeds from the compassion of God and that he thus learns by the evil he experiences or the good he lacks not to become incensed against God his creator but all the while to display patience. Wrath and indignation in the soul are softened by the compunction of the heart (which is under the operation of the spirit of knowledge born within from humility), as, conversely, wrath kills the fool who does not understand, then he is excited in misfortune, and blinded by the vice of impatience, that he has merited the misfortune he suffers. This fool does not accept the good he has by the grace of God. The price of comfort follows this virtue of compunction or grief so that he who by his own volition is contrite here in the sight of God in his lamentation will deserve there to find joy and happiness.

CHAPTER IV. TO WHICH GIFTS THE FOUR LAST PETITIONS REFER AND TO WHICH EVILS THEY PROVIDE A REMEDY

In the fourth petition, directed against sadness, we say: "Give us today our daily bread." For sadness is the loathing of the soul with mourning when the mind is as it were dwindling and embittered by its faults, does not strive after the inner good and, with all strength gone, is not gladdened by any desire for spiritual refreshment.[11] In order to heal this vice it is necessary for us to implore the mercy of God so that He will provide His constant kindliness to the soul which languishes with weariness, the nourishment of inner refreshment so that it can begin to love what it does not know how to strive for, admonished by the foretaste of what is present. On the ground of this petition the spirit of fortitude is given to raise up the languishing soul so that it regains the virtue of

[11]Cf. De Fructibus, Chap. VII.

its former vigor, may recover from the defects of its weariness and attain to the desire for inner nourishment. The spirit of fortitude creates in the heart hunger after righteousness so that he who strengthens the desire for devotion will earn as reward the fullness of blessedness.

In the fifth petition, directed against avarice, we say: "And forgive us our trespasses as we forgive those who trespass against us."[12] It is right that he who does not want to be stingy in asking, should be anxious to pay back his debt. And as, by the grace of God, we are liberated from the vice of avarice, we are taught by the proposed condition of our salvation how we have to be absolved from our debts. On the ground of this petition the spirit of counsel is given to teach us who freely sin that in this aeon mercy is established, so that as we are going to have to give account for our sins in the future, we may deserve to find mercy.

In the sixth petition, directed against gluttony, we say: "And lead us not"—that is: permit that we may not be led—"into temptation."[13] That is temptation by which the allurement of the flesh often strives to lead us through the natural appetite to excess, and it secretly subjects us to lust while it openly flatters us. Into this temptation we are actually in no wise led if we make sure that according to the measure of natural necessity help is near, so that we always remember to bridle the appetite from the allurement of lust. The spirit of understanding is given us as we pray, so that we may be able to fulfill this. Then the inner strengthening of the word of God restrains the outer appetite so that the bodily desires may not break the mind fortified by spiritual food, and the lust of the flesh may not triumph. Therefore the Lord himself answers to the tempter while he makes to the hungry a fraudulent suggestion concerning refreshment by external food and says: "Man does not live by bread alone but by every word which proceeds from the mouth of God" (Matt. iv), so as to clearly show that when the mind is refreshed by inner food, it does not greatly care if it suffers at the time fleshly hunger. Against gluttony the spirit of understanding is given: it comes into the heart, cleanses and purifies it, and makes the inner eye, through the knowledge of the word of God healing it as it were with an eye-salve, luminous and clear so

[12]Cf. De Fructibus, Chap. VIII.
[13]Cf. De Fructibus, Chap. IX.

that it becomes transparent for the vision of the clarity of the divine. As against the vice of gluttony the spirit of understanding is thus set as a remedy: out of the spirit of understanding the purity of the heart is born: to the purity of the heart the vision of God is promised, as it is written: "Blessed are the pure in heart for they will see God" (Matt. v).

In the seventh petition, directed against opulence, we say: "deliver us from evil."[14] Suitably the slave craves freedom. On the ground of this petition the spirit of wisdom is given which restores lost liberty to the captive and lets him leave behind the yoke of unjust dominion, which he himself is not able to do by his own strength but by the help of His grace. For "Sapientia" is derived from *sapor* "taste": as the mind, touched by the taste of inner sweetness, collects itself entirely within through desire. And it does not become dissolved in the lust of the flesh outside because all its delights in it possesses inwardly. By the same token the inner sweetness is opposed to exterior pleasure so that to the degree that it begins to taste and to be pleased it becomes subject to condemnation the more freely and gladly; whereas, the mind which is contented in itself so long as there is nothing outside it craves, reposes wholly through love, within itself. So the spirit of wisdom touches the heart with its sweetness and tempers outwardly the ardor of lust, and the lust when lulled to quiet produces peace within. In the degree to which the mind is totally collected in inner joy, man becomes fully and perfectly restored to the image of God, as it is written: "Blessed be the peacemakers because they will be called sons of God" (*ibid.*). See, my brother, I have fulfilled thy petition not as I was bound to but as much as I was able to meanwhile. Accept the little gift of the Five Sevens which thou requested and as you contemplate it, remember me. The Grace of God be with you.

CHAPTER V. ON THE SEVEN GIFTS OF THE SPIRIT, ESPECIALLY[15]

It is written: "If ye then being evil know how to give good gifts unto your children; how much more shall your heavenly Father give the Holy Spirit to them that ask him" (Luke xi.13). So the

[14]Cf. De Fructibus, Chap. X.

[15]Cf. Allegoriae, 763. For the dependence of Hugo's concept of the Seven Gifts on St. Augustine and Gregory the Great: Ott, *op. cit.*, 433ff. John Gerson

heavenly Father will give the Spirit to those of His children who ask Him. For those who are His children, ask not for anything else; those who ask for something else, are mercenary servants, not sons; those who seek silver, seek gold, seek the transitory things; who seek not the eternal, seek the ministry of slavery, not the spirit of freedom. What is sought, is given; if thou seekest the material, thou wilt not receive more than thou seekest. If thou seekest the spiritual, it will be given what thou seekest and what thou dost not seek, will be added. The spiritual is given, the fleshly is added. "Seek ye first the kingdom of God and all this will be added unto you" (Matt. vi). So pray to the Father and ask the Father who is in heaven for heavenly not earthly gifts; not material substance but spiritual grace. He shall give the good spirit to those who ask Him; He shall give His spirit to heal thy spirit; He shall give the Holy Spirit and shall heal the spirit of the sinners. This one is sick, He is the medicine. So if thou wishest that one be healed, ask Him. If thou askest for the spirit, ask the Spirit. Do not be afraid to apply the medicine to the illness; the illness does not corrupt the medicine, but the medicine disrupts the illness. It does not stain it but is bare of it. So be not afraid to invite the Holy Spirit of God to thy sinful spirit, being a sinner and His unworthy consort: it is done not because thou art worthy but so that thou shalt be made worthy. It comes to thee to dwell in thee.

It shall not find when it shall come but it shall come in order to achieve. First, it shall edify, then it shall indwell. First, it will heal, then it will illuminate. First, to heal, then to delight. If you are a son and seek the Father, be confident and not afraid. God hears, the Father shall understand. He cannot but listen because He is God: He cannot but understand because He is holy. He shall give thee what thou askest if thou askest rightly, and thy prayer shall not be in vain, if it should be worthy to be heard. Thou hast prayed for the healing of thy illness: accept the medicine. Thine are the vices, thine the illness; the spirit of God is their healing. Against the illness of pride the medicine of the spirit of fear will be given thee to heal the corruption and elation, and restore health and humility.

---

preached in 1402 a series of Sermons on the Seven Capital Sins, the Seven Petitions, the Commandments, the Seven Gifts of the Holy Spirit. In his private devotions he prayed each day for the Gift suggested by his meditation: James L. Connolly, *John Gerson, Reformer and Mystic* (Louvain: Libr. Univ., 1928) 148f., 269; Jean Gerson, *Initiation à la vie mystique*, ed. P. Pascal (Les Arcades; Paris: Gallimard, 1943), p. 241.

Individual vices have individual medicines; seven vices, seven spirits; as many medicines as there are illnesses. Which are the seven spirits? The gifts of the spirit are seven, and the gifts are the spirits and the spirits are the gifts: the gift of the spirit is spirit; the spirit gives itself: the one spirit gives itself sevenfold. Hence there is one spirit, that is seven spirits because it is given sevenfold and striven for. Seven breathings and one spirit: one nature and seven works; one substance and a sevenfold operation.[16]

The first spirit is the spirit of fear, the second is the spirit of devotion, the third the spirit of knowledge, the fourth spirit is the spirit of fortitude, the fifth spirit is the spirit of counsel, the sixth spirit is the spirit of understanding, the seventh spirit is the spirit of wisdom. All these operate as one and the same spirit (I Cor. xii); the same is fear, is devotion, is knowledge, is fortitude, is counsel, is understanding, is wisdom. All this happens to thee who are one in thyself, accepting Him who is not divided: thou art made to diversification. Hence is multiplied in thee the One who is ever one and the same. He who is thy love, the same is thy fear. Jacob swore to Laban by the fear of his father Isaac (Gen. xxxi). He who finishes, the same begins. At first He comes to thee to make thee fear, later to make thee love. It is the same light that pricks the watery eyes and caresses the clear ones; He does different things because He finds different things, yet He is one within Himself. And He would be one in thee if He had found thee unified. If thou hast healthy eyes, thou perceivest light without penalty, but if the eye is ill, its coming is painful. Nevertheless it is necessary that it comes thus because if thou art not tormented, thou shalt not be enlightened ("*quia si non cruciaris, non illuminaris*"). Two opposite forces struggle, the medicine and the illness, the medicine for thee, the illness against thee. If there be no resistance to the illness, health cannot be restored. If there be no resistance to the medicine, no penalty would be felt. The struggle of the opposite forces is thy penalty: thou shouldst not plead the medicine but the illness, the pain which the two inflict, attribute to one: medicine wants to help, illness to hurt. Hence illness alone has peace, not health. Only medicine has health; it has no penalty. But when they are together, penalty is a conflict of opposites—of one that wants to come to

[16]Cf. Gregorius Magnus, *Moralia* I, caps. XXVII and XXXII (Migne LXXV, 544, 547).

contribute and of another that does not want to leave in order to do harm. In this penalty, however, the illness is to be accused, not the medicine, because what torments come from the illness which if it did not exist would be health and there would be no penalty.

Thus comes the spirit and by blowing becomes infused into thee; thou, on account of what is contrary to it in thee, comest not immediately to be contented in it but contradictest it so that it could not peacefully enter thee. Yet it comes and illuminates thee, so that thou seest in thyself what thou hatest before but did not see because thou did not attend to it. With its coming thou art illuminated and vivified: thou art illuminated in order to feel; thou seest and divinest, thou seest and foreseest.

Thou seest evil and foreseest evil. Thou seest present and foreseest future evil. Thou seest guilt and foreseest punishment. Before, however, the Holy Spirit came to thee, thou didst not see, being blind; and thou didst not sense, being dead; and hence thou didst not see because thou didst not look and didst not feel because thou didst not listen. But after the good returned, thou becamest excited by its taste and illuminated so as to recognize evil. First, the evil which thou didst suffer, that is guilt, then also the evil which thou didst deserve from it and for it, that is a punishment. Both teach the coming good that the present evil be sensed and the future foreseen. Thereafter arises that wholesome penalty as thou beginnest, sensitive of the evil thou sufferest, to feel pain in order to amend, and, illuminated as to the evil thou deservest, to fear, in order to take heed. Because if thou dost not feel pain, thou wilt not amend and if thou dost not fear, thou wilt not take heed. First, therefore, thou art illuminated as to the guilt so as to see it, then as to the penalty so as to fear it. So as to become sensitive to the last punishment, thou feelest pain for thy guilt and amendest it because thou wilt not feel pain keenly if thou dost not fear. Because if the penalty which is feared is not seen, nobody would feel pain for the guilt which he indulged. Hence the penalty which will follow the guilt is shown to you so that the very guilt which may be pleasing in [actual] experience at least may displease in tribulation, so that thou beginnest to attend to it what evil is, namely that which appears sweet in it as that also is evil what appears bitter in it and after it. So thou art illuminated and afflicted because thou seest what terrifies and possessest what pains. If thou wouldst not be illuminated thou wouldst not be tormented because thou wouldst not see what thou fearest. Again if there would not be in thee what belongs to the flames, the fire would appear not a penalty and thou wouldst receive illumination so as not to sense affliction. Penalty terrifies, guilt fears; all that comes through the help of the light by which penalty is shown so as to be seen, guilt makes felt so as to be recognized. There is a difference between what thou seest and that by which thou art illumined; what is revealed in illumination terrifies. But the terror is, as it were, attributed to the light because, before thou wert illuminated, thou wert not terrified, it is necessary that the terror comes because if the penalty would not frighten, the guilt is not amended. Hence the light is beneficial for thee while it shows what torments, because it amends through it what evil pleases. So thou art illuminated in order to be terrified. First the light is terrible, even the shadows are terrible which are seen by the light inasumch as it cannot be seen without terror and this cannot be felt without pain, especially by him who does not understand that he deserved it so that he may feel what he sees impending and what cannot be avoided. From that fear is born as the danger is foreseen, fear which has penalty against that evil which torments, not evil in that it torments, not evil in that it liberates, an evil, I say, but not evil. All penalty is an evil but not all penalty is bad. Whatever contributes and is useful to something is good even if it is not in itself. Hence a minor penalty comes so that a major be avoided and that is a good however [flowing] from that which is not good. For through penalty we are liberated from the penalty and it is beneficial at a time to feel what is burdensome so that it never becomes necessary to feel what is intolerable. This thy good works from what is not thy good, the One who is really thy truest good; He will act after the fashion of another of thy good which does not exist only out of itself but out of Him. First thy liberation will be worked out of thy penalty then out of its sweetness thy joy. Everywhere, one and the same is the One who operates, here and there, and out of which He operates.

15.

To a Rabbi Friend

The anniversary of a religious leader is occasion for reflection on the function of organized religion in society. In times like ours it is not necessary to stress the individual's need for the support and comfort only religion can give to him. But some doubt the necessity of organized religion, interpreting religious freedom as an invitation to everyone to make up his own religion. These we have to remind that there is, in each religious community, a rich heritage which every generation is called upon to make its own. The religious tradition of the Hebrew people has miraculously survived the vicissitudes of many a struggle through many centuries, but it succeeded only because it has never lacked the inspiration of spiritual leaders who were able to interpret this tradition to each succeeding generation so that it could make it its own. Such a heritage could be considered a liability or an impediment to the freedom of individual experience only if the key to the understanding of its rich meaning should become lost. As long as it is preserved, an inexhaustible fountain of strength, the strongest possible tie to bind the members of the community, will be found in it. Every Jew and every Christian has, today more than ever, the sacred duty to make the principles of his faith his own. As we have to try to acquaint our youth with the political and cultural heritage of our nation, so we have to see that they grow into an understanding of their religious tradition. We rejoice in the thought that these principles of the two great religions are to so great an extent identical.

Modern man is the happy heir to a fight for freedom which his fathers waged against a dead weight of superstition and tyranny, a fight renewed in our own lifetime. Such a fight can be waged only on the basis and in the name of principles which will guide and direct the never-ending struggle for freedom. The idea of the dignity of the individual and the brotherhood of man is such a principle, but one that in turn rests upon the concept of the fatherhood of God which both Jews and Christians share. Without such a firm foundation chaos and anarchy threaten to turn emancipation and freedom into a travesty. I come to you from the state of Roger Williams, a great liberator but one whose fight for liberty was dictated by strong convictions and firm principles. He would have seen no contradiction between faith and freedom. The community he founded and which was the first to grant the right to worship without coercion or interference from the side of the state has maintained this precious heritage. Brown University, of which you are a distinguished alumnus, does not admit religious tests but expects its students to make their own religious heritage really their own, as something that counts in their lives and enables them to make their personal contribution to the academic community, the state and the nation. It provides not only an atmosphere for growing into the tradition of both religion and democracy but also through teaching and guidance encourages youth to follow the greatest commandment: to love God and to love one's neighbor.

How are we going to do it? A great deal of very serious thought these days is given to the question of education in and for a democracy. After a period of a steady increase in subject matter to be absorbed by the young, we have turned to a thorough reexamination of the aims and goals toward which we wish to educate our youth. Several leading universities (Chicago, Harvard, Yale and my own) have revised their curricula with a view to fostering integration in the body of knowledge to be acquired and in the individual who is expected to absorb it. Sciences and Humanities are confronted with the same problem: "knowledge for what"? The answer to this question invites philosophical reflection and again: religious orientation. In our Hebrew-Christian faith we pledge ourselves to a concept of God, of the world and of man, his nature and his destiny, which does not allow for callousness, indifference or defeatism, but provides a strong urge and motivation to contribute of our best toward the betterment of man, mindful of the prophet's words: "I, God, have called thee by thy name, thou art mine." We feel that youth trained in and committed to these principles will be well prepared to shoulder its burden of responsibility in the reconstruction of society on the communal, national and international levels. It will not only be immune to ideologies not in harmony with the teaching of the great Hebrew and Christian tradition but will actively work for a deeper understanding among men of good will.

You have done much to help those who look to you for guidance and leadership in a manifold way. On the deepest level you have contributed to better understanding and appreciation of the core of Hebrew religion, that of mystical experience. A magnificent volume, containing translations of the profound wisdom and insight of religious and ethical teachers, bears witness to your scholarly work. In conducting the worship in your synagogue, you have impressed your congregation with a consciousness of the interrelation of the values of beauty and holiness. In years of tribulation which brought in their wake persecution and suffering for millions of Jews and Christians, you have, as a true humanitarian, exerted the finest leadership in charitable and reconstructive activities and you have brought messages of spiritual uplift and comfort to audiences of various character and persuasion. Notwithstanding the manifold personal gifts and qualifications which equipped you for all these activities, it was possible for you to exert such leadership only because you are deeply rooted in and thoroughly committed to the religious heritage of organized Jewish faith. May you have the satisfaction to see for many years to come the fruits of such labor and may they be blessed by the giver of all success and happiness.

16.

On Felicity

With these words the great English metaphysical poet, Thomas Traherne, remembered his days at Oxford:

> There was never a tutor that did professly teach felicity, though that be the mistress of all the other sciences. Nor did any of us study these things but as aliens, which we ought to have studied to our own enjoyments. We studied to inform our knowledge but know not for what end we studied. And for lack of aiming at a certain end, we erred in the manner.

I think Traherne expresses very well the conscious or unconscious disappointment which many a student has felt during and after the time spent at a great seat of learning, where every subject under the sun was taught. Many a student would just leave it at that: a vague feeling of something lacking, of being cheated of something which he would find hard to name. Traherne was more articulate. He named that something which he had missed in the instruction he received at the Athens of Britain: he called it "felicity." Nobody taught felicity. Yes, perhaps by implication or a reference here or there, but not "professly," not putting it in the center where it belongs. The "mistress of all the sciences"—what is that? Is it mathematics which Traherne's great contemporary Newton represented so gloriously? Is it philosophy, that supreme entertainment of so many great minds of the metaphysical century? The nineteenth century would hardly have thought so, but we in the second half of the twentieth know again where we have to look when we want to know about "felicity." With all the satisfaction which may be derived from scientific endeavor, with all the gratification which a subtle epistemological inquiry may yield, felicity is still something else.

It must be concerned with the ultimate if it is to be the highest of all pursuits. It must affect more than just mind or intellect. It must affect the total being which is man. It must be practical and affect not only thought but life as well, if it is to reveal that certain "end" for all our study of which the poet speaks. We studied to inform our knowledge but "know not for what end we studied." Is it wrong to seek information? Certainly not: there is a great thrill in finding out, in ferreting out, things hitherto unknown or unknown to us. But there is also something melancholy in amassing a vast store of information. The danger of a subtle skepticism lurks near. Traherne and his friends did what so many "students" have done and so many still do: they studied as "aliens," that is, indifferently, without "enjoyment." To this danger you and I, who are lovers of books and lovers of learning, are not exposed. We do get pleasure out of manscripts and many-volumed works of scholarship. But do we know and do we always remember in the poet's words, "for what end we studied"? Or are we in danger, "for lack of aiming at a certain end" "to err in the manner"? Here we ourselves are responsible and cannot well shift the blame. It is bad if we did not have tutors who taught us felicity; we must blame ourselves if we did not trouble to find out for what end we studied. For how can we do better as teachers of others than we have fared ourselves at the hands of our instructors? We in the academic world are unusually well equipped for imparting to others from the considerable treasure of knowledge which we have acquired by patient and industrious work. May we never forget that we will be judged—by our own students first, and by a higher tribunal afterwards, as to whether we taught them felicity.

When we turn to the book which more than any other book in the world shows us the way to this felicity, we read the words: "The fear of the Lord is the beginning of wisdom and the knowledge of the holy is understanding," and in the same book "Wisdom" speaks to us (Prov. 8: 23–31, 35).

17.

A Prayer

Our heavenly Father, Thou hast given us the privilege of gathering here at this beautiful spot in the heart of Europe as brothers who have come together from different countries and from different backgrounds. Enlighten our hearts and our minds so that we may be able to understand each other's words and thoughts, but beyond that Thy Will and Purpose. Let us forget even our dearest thoughts, philosophies and theologies if they do not reflect our apprehension of Thy majesty and Thy love. Make us ready ever to review and revise each theorem and doctrine which stands in the way of our adoring Thee rather than any concept or image of Thyself. Save us from both coldness of heart and sterility of mind, and touch us where we live most deeply. But help us to translate our feelings, affections and aspirations into articulate thinking that is mindful of Thy Word and of the teachings of Thy Son and in keeping with the great tradition of Thy Church and our fathers. Let us remember their insights and their exhortations lest we foolishly deprive ourselves of our most precious heritage, and follow our own light rather than the Divine Command. Awaken in us some of the gratefulness which we owe Thee for having made us members of the Christian community, but preserve us from falling into the sins of pride, self-righteousness and smugness. Make us thankful for the gift of the *depositum fidei* but guard us against narrowness and stubborness in its interpretaion, so that with deep convictions we may combine width and breadth. Fill us with a sense of the urgency of our task as teachers, as Christian teachers, as Christian teachers in our day. Prevent us both from despair or resignation in confronting the gigantic task of the Christian teacher today and from over-optimism and easy belief in the efficaciousness of mere techniques and institutional changes. Help us to continue daily and hourly the self-examination which prevents us from sinking into the mere routine of the professional, and enables us to see clearly and to understand fully the ever new quest for truth and light with which our students come to us. As we need an infinite amount of patience, of humility, of self-denial to guide the young, we come to Thee who hast given us the supreme example in Thy Son, our Master, asking for encouragement not to falter in light of disappointments and difficulties. We also turn to Thee when, in the confusion of this day and age, so often the distinction between good and evil, right and wrong, seems terribly hard to make. So guard us against all the subtle temptations to conform, to keep silent, to take the easy road when we should stand up and speak and act as Thy saints have done through the ages. Though there is a danger of neglecting our own personal need for salvation, preoccupied with the needs and demands of the world around us, there is a greater danger for the intellectual to withdraw from all the outside clamor into his study, into the sacred fortress of his own quest for truth and happiness. Our heavenly Father, make us hear the voice of our neighbor in all the narrower and wider communities of which we find ourselves members: the family, the local community, the academic community, the nation, the Church. Confront us day after day with living beings, different from ourselves only in color, or nationality, or in economic circumstances or intellectual capacity, to try the seriousness of our desire to be followers of Christ. Let us ask ourselves in each instance: what do I do for this my brother?

Again we ask for Thy blessing upon the special task which we have set ourselves to do in this week: illuminate our hearts and minds so that we may search for a meaning in history and try to understand the lesson which Thou teachest us. Let us find ways and means by which to communicate a sense of Thy presence in history to those who are entrusted to our care. Help us to render some service to the great movement which has brought us together here and to which many of us owe inspiration and encouragement: the World's Student Christian Movement. Bless its leaders in their responsible task and bless each of us here. All this we ask in the name of Thy Son, our Redeemer, the Lord Jesus Christ. Amen.

18.

Bibliography of Joachim Wach (1922-55)

A. BOOKS AND PAMPHLETS

1922

"Grundzüge einer Phänomenologie des Erlösungsgedankens." Unpublished Ph.D. dissertation (April 5, 1922), University of Leipzig. Excerpts were printed in *Jahrbuch der philosophischen Fakultät Leipzig,* II (1922), 14–16.

Der Ehrlösungsgedanke und seine Deutung. ("Veröffentlichungen des Forschungsinstitus für vergleichende Religionsgeschichte an der Universität Leipzig," No. 8.) Leipzig: J. C. Hinrichs.

1924

Religionswissenschaft: Prolegomena zu ihrer wissenschaftstheoretischen Grundlegung ("Veröffentlichungen des Forschungsinstituts für vergleichende Religionsgeschichte an der Universität Leipzig," No. 10.) Leipzig: J. C. Hinrichs.

1925

Mahayana, besonders im Hinblick auf das Saddharma-Pundarika-Sutra: Eine Untersuchung über die religionsgeschichtliche Bedeutung eines heiligen Textes der Buddhisten. ("Untersuchungen zur Geschichte des Buddhismus und verwandter Gebiete," No. 16.) Munich-Neubiberg: Schloss.

Meister und Jünger: Zwei religionssoziologische Betrachtungen. Tübingen: J. C. B. Mohr.

1926

Das Verstehen: Grundzüge einer Geschichte der hermeneutischen Theorie im 19. Jahrhundert. Vol. I: *Die grossen Systeme.* Tübingen: J. C. B. Mohr (P. Siebeck). This volume became the dissertation for the theological Doctor's degree at the University of Heidelberg in 1930.

Die Typenlehre Trendelenburgs und ihr Einfluss auf Dilthey: Eine philosophie- und geistesgeschichtliche Studie ("Philosophie und Geschichte," No. 11.) Tübingen: J. C. B. Mohr.

1929

Das Verstehen: Grundzüge einer Geschichte der hermeneutischen Theorie im 19. Jahrhundert. Vol. II: *Die theologische Hermeneutik von Schleiermacher bis Hofmann.* Tübingen: J. C. B. Mohr (P. Siebeck).

1931

Einführung in die Religionssoziologie. Tübingen: J. C. B. Mohr (P. Siebeck).

1932

Typen religiöser Anthropologie: Ein Vergleich der Lehre vom Menschen im religionsphilosophischen Denken von Orient und Okzident. ("Philosophie und Geschichte," No. 40.) Tübingen: J. C. B. Mohr (P. Siebeck).

1933

Das Verstehen: Grundzüge einer Geschichte der hermeneutischen Theorie im 19. Jahrhundert. Vol. III: *Das Verstehen in der Historik von Ranke bis zum Positivismus.* Tübingen: J. C. B. Mohr (P. Siebeck).

1934

Das Problem des Todes in der Philosophie unserer Zeit. ("Philosophie und Geschichte," No. 49). Tübingen: J. C. B. Mohr (P. Siebeck).

1942

Johann Gustav Droysen. ("Heimatklänge," Vol. XIX.) Treptow a.d. Rega.

1944

Sociology of Religion. Chicago: University of Chicago Press.

1946

Church, Denomination, and Sect. Evanston: Seabury-Western Theological Seminary.

1947

Sociology of Religion. ("International Library of Sociology and Social Reconstruction.") London: K. Paul, Trench, Trubner.

1951

Types of Religious Experience, Christian and Non-Christian. Chicago: University of Chicago Press.

B. TRANSLATIONS OF BOOKS OF JOACHIM WACH

1951

Religionssoziologie. Translated from the 4th edition by Helmut Schoeck. Tübingen: J. C. B. Mohr (P. Siebeck).

1955

Sociologie de la religion. Translated by M. Lefevre. Paris: Payor.

C. EDITOR AND COEDITOR OF JOURNALS

1935

Editor of *Religion und Geschichte*, No. 1. Stuttgart: Kohlhammer.

1934–38

Coeditor of *Zeitschrift für Missionskunde und Religionswissenschaft*, Vols. XL (1934)–LIV (1938). Berlin.

D. ARTICLES IN SCIENTIFIC JOURNALS

1923

"Bemerkungen zum Problem der 'extremen' Würdigung der Religion," *Zeitschrift für Missionskunde und Religionswissenschaft*, Vol. XXXVIII, 161–83.

"Zur Methodologie der allgemeinen Religionswissenschaft," *ibid.*

1924

"Gedanken über den 'Nur'-Psychologismus," *ibid.*, XXXIX, 209–15.

1925

"Wilhelm Dilthey über 'Das Problem der Religion,'" *ibid.*, XL, 66–81.

"Mahayana, besonders im Hinblick auf das Saddharma-Pundarika," *Zeitschrift für Buddhismus*, VI, 331–48. Also published in *Der Pfad*, III (1925), 153–90.

1926

"Henri de Montherlant," *Preussische Jahrbücher* (Berlin: G. Stilke, CCIX (January), 196–206. Another manuscript reads "August 1927"!

1927

"Idee und Realität in der Religionsgeschichte," *Zeitschrift für Theologie und Kirche* (Tübingen), N. F. VIII, 334–64.

"Max Weber als Religionssoziologe." In *Festschrift für Geheimrat Prof. Gock.*

"Jakob Burckhard und die Religionsgeschichte," *Zeitschrift für Missionskunde und Religionswissenschaft*, XLII, 97–115. Another manuscript lists the following date: 1928/29 and also has different page numbers: 484–97 but the same volume: XLII.

1929

"Und die Religionsgeschichte? Eine Auseinandersetzung mit Paul Althaus," *Zeitschrift für systematische Theologie* (Gütersloh), VI, 484–97.

1930

"Zur Beurteilung Friedrich Schlegels," *Philosophischer Anzeiger*, IV, 13–26.

"Zur Hermeneutik heiliger Schriften," *Theologische Studien und Kritiken* (Stuttgart and Gotha), CII, 280–90.

"Die Geschichtsphilosophie des 19. Jahrhunderts und die Theologie der Geschichte," *Historische Zeitschrift* (Munich), CXLII, 1–15.

"Philosophische Strömungen der Gegenwart in Frankreich," *Neue Jahrbücher für Wissenschaft und Jugenbildung*, VI, 282–85.

1931

"Das religiöse Gefühl," *Vorträge des Instituts für Geschichte der Medizin an der Universität Leipzig* (Leipzig), IV, 9–33.

"Hochschule und Weltanschauung," *Akademische Deutschland* (Berlin), III, 198–204.

1932

"Typen der Anthropologie." In *Die Wissenschaft am Scheidewege von Leben und Geist: Festschrift Ludwig Klages*, pp. 240–48. Leipzig.

1934

"Religiöse Existenz," *Zeitschrift für Missionskunde und Religionswissenschaft*, XL, 193–201.

"Geleitwort," *ibid.*, pp. 1–2 (as coeditor of the journal).

1935

"Sinn und Aufgabe der Religionswissenschaft," *ibid.*, L, 133–47.

"Eine neue katholische Philosophie der Religionsgeschichte," *ibid.*, pp. 375–85.

1936

"Eigenart und Bedeutung der American Episcopal Church," *ibid.*, LI, 373–78.

"Interpretation of Sacred Books," *Journal of Biblical Literature* (New Haven, Conn.), LV, 59–63.

1939

"Religionssoziologie." In S. R. Steinmetz (ed.), *Gesammelte kleine Schriften zur Ethnologie und Soziologie*, pp. 479–94.

1945

"Sociology of Religion." In G. Gurvitch and W. E. Moore (eds.), *Twentieth Century Sociology*, pp. 405–37. New York: Philosophical Library.

1946

"Caspar Schwenkfeld, a Pupil and a Teacher in the School of Christ," *Journal of Religion* (Chicago), XXVII (July), 157 ff.

"The Role of Religion in the Social Philosophy of Alexis de Tocqueville," *Journal of the History of Ideas*, II (January), 74 ff.

"On Understanding." In A. A. Roback (ed.), *The Albert Schweitzer Jubilee Book*, pp. 131–46. Cambridge, Mass.: SCI-Art Publishers.

1947

"The Place of the History of Religions in the Study of Theology," *Journal of Religion* (Chicago), XXVII (July), 157 ff.

1948

"Spiritual Teachings in Islam: A Study," *ibid.*, XXVIII (October), 263 ff.

1949

"Hugo of St. Victor on Virtues and Vices," *Anglican Theological Review*, Vol. XXXI (January).

1950

On Teaching History of Religions. "Pro Regno Pro Sanctuario." Nijkerk: G. F. Callenbach N.V. Uitgever.

"Im Rückblick aus den Vereinigten Staaten." In H. H. Schaeder (ed.), *Carl Heinrich Becker: Ein Gedenkbuch.* Göttingen.

1951

"Christian Propaganda: A Genuine Dilemma," *Advance* (Chicago), Vol. LXIV (December).

1952

"Why We Can't Mind Our Own Business," *ibid.*, Vol. LXV (January).

"Radhakrishnan and the Comparative Study of Religion." In P. A. Schilpp (ed.), *The Philosophy of Sarvepalli Radhakrishnan*, pp. 443–38. New York: Tudor Publishing Co.

1953

"Rudolf Otto und der Begriff des Heiligen." In A. Bergsträsser (ed.), *Deutsche Beiträge*, p. 200–217. Chicago: Henry Regnery Co.

1954

"General Revelation and the Religions of the World," *Journal of Bible and Religion*, XXII (April), 84 ff.

E. ARTICLES IN ENCYCLOPEDIAS

1. *Religion in Geschichte und Gegenwart.* Edited by H. Gunkel and L. Zscharnack. 2d ed. Tübingen: J. C. B. Mohr.
   Vol. I (1927):

"Bruderschaften, I. Bruderschaft, religionsgeschichtlich."
Vol. II (1928):
"Erlöser. I. Religionsgeschichtlich."
"Erlösung. I. Religionsgeschichtlich."
"Erlösung. V. Religionsphilosophisch."
"Erlösungsreligionen."
"Erscheinungsformen der Gottheit."
"Göttergebote."
Vol. III (1929):
"Inkarnation."
"Jüungerschaft."
"Messias. I. Religionsgeschichtlich."
Vol. IV (1930):
"Mittler. I. Religionswissenschaftlich."
"Religionsphilosophie."
"Religionssoziologie."
"Religionswissenschaft."
Vol. V (1931):
"Staat. II, A. Religion und Staat in der ausserchristlichen Welt."
"Stadtkult."
"Stamm und Geschlecht."
"Stand. III. Religionsgeschichtlich."
"Theophanie. I."
"Typenlehre."
"Verstehen."

2. *Handwörterbuch der Soziologie*. Edited by A. Vierkandt. No. 1 (1931), "Religionssoziologie," pp. 479–94.

F. BOOK REVIEWS

1924

Ludwig Klages' *Vom kosmogonischen Eros*, in *Zeitschrift für Missionskunde und Religionswissenschaft* (Berlin), XXXIX, 41–42.

1926

Ruhle's *Sonne und Mond im primitiven Mythus, ibid.*, Vol. XL, 60–61.

1928

Christoph Schrempf's "*Sokrates, seine Persönlichkeit und sein Glaube*," in *Theologische Literaturzeitung*, LIII, 193–95.

Karl Beth's *Religion und Magie*, in *Orientalische Literaturzeitung*, XXXI, 459–63.

1931

Rudolf Otto's *Indiens Gnadenreligionen*, in *Die Christliche Welt* (Gotha), pp. 20–25.

1932

Theodor Litt's *Kant und Herder als Deuter der geistigen Welt*, in *Theologische Literaturzeitung*, LVII, 233–35.

Romano Guardini's *Der Mensch und der Glaube: Versuche über die allgemeine Existenz in Dostojewskijs grossen Romanen*, in *Zeitschrift für Missionskunde und Religionswissenschaft*, XL, 193–201.

1935

Alexandra David-Neel's *Meister und Schüler, ibid.*, L, 357–58.

Alfred Bertholet's *Das Geschlecht der Gottheit, ibid.*, p. 358.

Adolf Erman's *Die Religion der Ägypter, ibid.*, p. 390.

1946

A. K. Coomaraswamy's *Hinduism and Buddhism, Journal of Religion*, XXVI (January), 59 ff.

H. A. Hodges' *Wilhelm Dilthey: An Introduction, ibid.*, pp. 217 ff.

1947

J. A. Archer's *The Sikhs in Relation to Hindus, Moslems, Christians, and Ahmadiyyas: A Study in Comparative Religion, ibid.*, XXVII (January), 62 ff.

J. M. Yinger's *Religion in the Struggle for Power: A Study in the Sociology of Religion, ibid.* (April), 131 ff.

René Guenon's *Introduction to the Study of the Hindu Doctrines, ibid.*, pp. 136 ff.

G. E. Grunebaum's *Medieval Islam: A Study in Cultural Orientation*, ibid. (July), 219 ff.

Réne Guenon's *Man and His Becoming According to the Vedanta, ibid.*, pp. 221 ff.

1948

C. H. Ratschow's *Magie und Religion, ibid.*, XXVIII (October), 286 ff.

B. Malinowski's *Magic, Science, and Religion and Other Essays, ibid.*, p. 288.

V. Ferm's *Religion in the Twentieth Century, ibid.*, pp. 288 ff.

1949

S. de Grazia's *The Political Community: A Study of Anomie, ibid.*, XXIX (April), 157 ff.

1950

E. T. Clark's *The Small Sects in America*, in *Theology To-day*, VII (April), 122 ff.

C. S. Braden's *These Also Believe: A Study of American Cults and Minority Religious Movements, ibid.*

1952

J. H. Fichter's *Southern Parish*, Vol. I: *Dynamics of a City Church*, in *Journal of Religion* (Chicago), XXXII (April), 139 ff.

L. Sherley-Price's *Confucius and Christ: A Christian Estimate of Confucius*, in *Church History*, XXI (June), 179.

R. L. Slater's *Paradox and Nirvana: A Study of Religious Ultimates with Special Reference to Burmese Buddhism*, in *Journal of Religion* (Chicago), XXXII (July), 224 ff.

1953

E. J. Jurji's *The Christian Interpretation of Religion: Christianity in Its Human and Creative Relationships with World Cultures and Faiths*, in *Theology To-day*, X (July), 277 ff.

Posthumous Works

The Comparative Study of Religions, ed. with Intro. by Joseph M. Kitagawa (New York: Columbia University Press, 1958).

Vergleichende Religionsforschung, mit einer Einführung von Joseph Kitagawa (Stuttgart: W. Kohlhammer Verlag, 1962).

El Estudio Comparado de las Religiones, recapilacion e introduccion de Joseph M. Kitagawa (Buenos Aires: Editorial Paidos, 1967).

In Memoriam: Joachim Wach— Teacher and Colleague

Joseph M. Kitagawa

On August 14, 1955, my wife and I arrived at Orselina, Locarno, home of Professor Joachim Wach in Switzerland. We knew he had had a heart attack, but until we arrived we were not aware of how serious it was. The following day we visited him in the hospital. Although he looked weak, and breathing bothered him, he immediately started asking many questions about Chicago and the whereabouts of his students. Because he was not able to write, he also asked me to inform Dean Jerald C. Brauer that he had declined the offer from Marburg University. "It has become clear in my mind," he said, "that my vocation is to develop what I have started at Chicago."

He was not aware of the critical nature of his illness. During the six days we were there, he spoke hopefully about returning to the United States in September, and we discussed many plans for the future. He also enjoyed a brief visit from Dean William Hawley, who was in Switzerland that week. On August 20 he looked much better and stronger. We left Switzerland, hoping and praying for his speedy recovery.

How surprised and distressed we were on August 28 to receive a telegram in England that Professor Wach had died the previous day. We flew back to Switzerland on August 29. That night his sister, Mrs. Heigl-Wach, and I said prayers in the chapel where his body lay. Suddenly, I was filled with memories that many of you share with me.

We can visualize him sitting in his apartment, reading or listening to favorite records. He always kept on his desk a picture of his beloved mother. Every Wednesday he attended the Worship Service at Bond Chapel, and he looked forward to the luncheon with students which followed. Those who studied under him, as I did, will remember him imparting his encyclopedic knowledge with utmost modesty. Indeed, he loved teaching, and he loved his students. He was always a welcome addition to any social gathering, full of fun and interesting stories. He was delightful when he spoke about his comical episodes, such as parking his car in front of Swift Hall and looking for it around Ingleside Avenue; or bumping into the only other car in a huge parking lot. He was a lively participant in parlor games of all kinds. In Swift Hall it was a familiar sight to see him rushing back and forth between his office and the telephone. He laughed heartily, he smiled gently, and he spoke with passion!

An American student who studied under Professor Wach at Leipzig once wrote: "Dr. Wach attempts not to plant a tree but a hedge!"—a not surprising reaction to Professor Wach's great concern with the interrelations of various branches of knowledge in the study of religion. He had a sensitive mind, seeking missing links in a gigantic methodological scheme for the study of various dimensions of religion. He often quoted the words of E. Burnouf, who wrote in 1870:

> This present century [the nineteenth century] will not come to an end without having seen the establishment . . . of a science whose elements are still dispersed, a science which the preceding centuries did not have, which is not even yet defined and which, perhaps for the first time, will be named *science of religion.*

This infant discipline of science of religion captured the imagination of young Joachim Wach. Thus, as early as 1924, he set forth the framework of his study in a book, *Religionswissenschaft.* From 1926 to 1933 his concern with the problems involved in the understanding of different religions led him to produce his three-volume work, *Das Verstehen.* His first major publication in English was

Sociology of Religion, which dealt with the sociological expressions of religious experience.

In 1951 he published another book, *Types of Religious Experience*, with the dedication: "To My Dear Colleagues of the Federated Theological Faculty of the University of Chicago." In this book there are important essays, some of which he intended to elaborate later on.

Professor Wach gave the Barrows Lectures in India in 1952. During the academic year 1954–55 he gave a series of lectures at various American universities at the invitation of the American Council of Learned Societies. In these two lecture series he articulated his methodological and theoretical framework. Before he was taken ill, he had almost completed a manuscript based on these lectures, published posthumously under the title, *The Comparative Study of Religions*. This work reveals his mature judgment based on thirty years of teaching and untiring labor.

Professor Wach possessed an unusual combination of high academic standards and genuine human concern. In dealing with friends and students, he was kind and long-suffering. It was exceedingly difficult for him to "flunk" a student, because he could not stand seeing a student suffer from failure.

While he loved all his students, he had a special place in his heart for those who majored in the history of religions. To him, they constituted the "Sangha," or community of disciples. He was educated in the continental, humanistic and encyclopedic tradition, and he was proud of it in his modest way. But he saw the difficulties of such training in this day, especially in the American setting. Rather, he envisaged a highly developed team of scholars dealing with various aspects of the vast discipline of *Religionswissenschaft*. For himself, he chose to labor in the methodological and theoretical dimensions, leaving the study of particular world religions to his disciples.

In one of his books, *Types of Religious Experience*, he says:

> We have passed the stage of surveys as they are offered in the current text-books and manuals of the history of religions. A great deal of work still remains to be done in purely historical and philological research. Meanwhile, however, the student of the history of religions is pressed for *answers* to the quest for the meaning

of all these expressions of religious experience, and the meaning and nature of all religious experience itself [p. 228]. (My italics.)

Professor Wach was brought up in the Neo-Kantian Protestant tradition. But early in his life he recognized two other systems of interpretation, namely, Roman Catholic and Marxian metaphysics. After he came to the English-speaking world, he encountered the school of emergent evolution, exemplified by Alfred North Whitehead. He had a very high regard for William Temple, another Neo-Kantian and a student of Caird, who also took Whitehead seriously. At the same time, Professor Wach was attracted by the theory of ontological stratification of Nicolai Hartmann, though he did not accept it *in toto.*

In addition to his scholarly concern, he was deeply interested in the "realization of religious truth." Joachim Wach as a humble believer found congeniality with many non-Christians in this respect. Thus, on the one hand, he could honestly say with Hendrik Kraemer: "It has pleased God to reveal himself fully and decisively in Christ; repent, believe, adore." On the other hand, he rejected Kraemer's subsuming of all non-Christian religions under the heading of "human-enfolding."

His life was not an easy one. His separation from his family must have been hard on him, devoted as he was to his mother, sister, and brother, all of whom lived in Europe. Fortunately for us, however, world events persuaded him to settle on this side of the Atlantic. After World War II he enjoyed annual visits with his family in Switzerland. His family was greatly comforted by the fact that he spent his last few months in Switzerland.

In a real sense, however, Professor Wach's place was in Chicago. This is where he lived and worked to establish the discipline of the history of religions as an integral part of the theological curriculum in a university setting. Almost unconsciously, he considered himself a bridge between the theological faculty and other disciplines on the campus. Once when Professor Sidney Mead marveled at his capacity for finding his way around the jungle of the university, Professor Wach said in his characteristically modest way: "There are paths through the wood, you know!" Basically, he was an urbane, cultured cosmopolitan, who lived and breathed the university life.

On August 30 his family and relatives gathered in Lugano for a private funeral service. The presence of his old friend Professor Wilhelm Pauck, formerly of Chicago, comforted the grief of the family. During the service I was asked to speak on behalf of the theological faculty of the University of Chicago and his former students.

The following day his ashes were buried in a quiet cemetery in Orselina, overlooking the deep, blue water of Lake Maggiore. At the family's request, the burial service was conducted jointly by the local Lutheran pastor and a clergyman of the Anglican church, for Professor Wach was raised a Lutheran in Germany and became an active member of the Episcopal church in the United States. Among many flowers given by his friends was a wreath from the Theological Faculty of the University of Chicago. Despite his physical absence, he will remain with us as a source of inspiration to his colleagues and students, a true friend, scholar, teacher, and a humble servant of God. May he rest in peace!

(Address given at the memorial service for Joachim Wach at the University of Chicago, October 5, 1955.)

Index